The Stru
the So

The Struggle Behind the Soundtrack

Inside the Discordant New World of Film Scoring

STEPHAN EICKE

McFarland & Company, Inc., Publishers
Jefferson, North Carolina

ISBN (print) 978-1-4766-7631-9 ∞
ISBN (ebook) 978-1-4766-3700-6

LIBRARY OF CONGRESS AND BRITISH LIBRARY
CATALOGUING DATA ARE AVAILABLE

LIBRARY OF CONGRESS CONTROL NUMBER:2019943404

Front cover image photograph by Madeleine Farley

Printed in the United States of America

*McFarland & Company, Inc., Publishers
Box 611, Jefferson, North Carolina 28640
www.mcfarlandpub.com*

Process as process is neither morally good nor morally bad. We may judge results but not process. The morally bad agent may perform the deed which is good. The morally good agent may perform the deed which is bad.
—Robert Penn Warren

Acknowledgments

My therapist likes to remind me that I achieved two major goals within the past two years: completing this book and getting it published. I would have achieved neither of these goals without the support of dear friends who encouraged me and guided me through the process. I am grateful that several publishers rejected the proposal for this book, since it made it possible to work with my editor Natalie Foreman. She and McFarland have been most supportive. They can pride themselves for giving writers a chance by agreeing to publish books that are somewhat specialized. I would like to thank Gary Dalkin, Matthew Townend and Caz Morley, whose editing skills turned my Denglish sentences into proper English. An especially big thank you goes to two of the most wonderful friends anyone could wish for: Gary Yershon and Matthew Saxton, who guided me through the entire writing process with interest and encouragement, suggesting changes when necessary. If they were irritated by my talking about this project constantly for two years, they had the grace not to show it. This book wouldn't exist without them.

Needless to say, I wish to thank all the people who agreed to be interviewed for the book and those who helped me set up the interviews—the composers, their assistants, managers and agents, who decided that a book was a prestigious project to be involved in. I don't have the space to name them all, but they can be sure of my deep gratitude. This gratitude extends to all my delightful friends and family, even the ones who may not be interested in film music but who knew how important it was for me to complete this book. They helped me in various ways to achieve this goal. I thank you all and send you my love.

Table of Contents

Acknowledgments   vi

Introduction   1

The Sound of Change   3

Sir, You Are Standing on My Toe, Sir   22

Lieutenant Gadget   50

Something Familiar, Something Similar   78

Turn Down the Sound, I Can't Hear the Music   105

Let's Do It Together!   130

The Hans Method   153

Instead of a Fireman   178

Summary   202

Chapter Notes   205

Bibliography   209

Index   211

Introduction

"Fuck art," she said. "I mean really, Michael. Fuck art, okay?
Isn't it funny how we've gone chasing after it all our lives? [...] There's
an interesting proposition for you: what if it doesn't exist?"—Richard
Yates, *Young Hearts Crying*

"I don't think you would call this the Golden Age of film—or television—scoring. There are a lot of forces at work that have made it more difficult
to make scores that are serving the picture as well as they could, and second
of all move the art forward." Mychael Danna sat in his studio in Los Angeles,
a teacup in his hand, an ancient sword nailed to the wall behind him.

> Film music seems to be valued at its lowest point in at least a generation. You
> can tell that just in a simple market force way of budgets. It's common knowl-
> edge that Marvel low-balls. They pay very little for the music, much less than a
> film that is going to gross a $150 million at least in America. A music budget
> for a film like that ten years ago—before the superhero craze—would have
> been a certain amount, and these are maybe half that, or less. Then you take
> the fact that they have a well-documented anti-thematic approach. Film music
> has really lost a great deal of its value. It's a dark time for film music.

Composers working in the media have always complained about their
jobs. In the late '70s, David Raksin (*Forever Amber*, *The Bad and the Beautiful*)
said, "It should be news to no one that many people believe the industry has
been plundered, ruined by incompetence, and left to twist slowly in the wind
by men whose principal interest—whatever they be—do not lie in filmmaking."[1] In the late 1990s, Elmer Bernstein (*The Ten Commandments*, *Far from
Heaven*) said:

> I think it's unfortunate that composers have a very difficult time getting a
> chance to write real film music, good film music. It's not for the lack of tal-
> ent—talent is tremendous out there. There are all sorts of gifted people, but
> they don't get much of a chance to really write good stuff because of the nature
> of the films.[2]

If anything is surprising about Danna's chagrin, it is his honesty. He is, after all, one of the most sought-after and prolific composers working in the film industry. He is not a bitter semi-retiree who hasn't received any offers for the past umpteen years, or someone who has proved incapable of adapting to new musical styles, influences and tastes. Whereas composers in the latter category have always had an ax to grind, the bitterness of busy craftsmen currently working in the Hollywood film industry stunned me. Mychael Danna wasn't the first one to complain. Neither was he the last. Marco Beltrami, equally sought-after and prolific, is just as disillusioned—or so it seemed: "I feel bad for the young composers who are up-and-coming. They have to deal with these problems. I don't know how much longer I will do this anyway. I have other interests as well."

I was intrigued by those who complained bitterly about their working conditions. What exactly were their problems? What was it, apart from temp-tracks and decreasing budgets, that angered these composers so much? I found myself unable to stop thinking about the complaints of prolific composers after listening to them for years on and off the record, composers who have given film aficionados so much joy over the years. Therefore, I set out to investigate their claims. Is it really as bad as they say? Are the complaints merited? How do other composers, sound designers, orchestrators, musicians and music editors view the current film music landscape? How do they see the changes that are supposed to have occurred within the past twenty years with digital editing, the ever advancing technology and the influence of Hans Zimmer's Remote Control Productions that is as powerful a voice in film music as ever?

This book, which is the result of these investigations, was born out of my desire to understand the current landscape in film and film music, how the changing working conditions have affected not only the composers but also their music.

The Sound of Change

We're descended from the indignant, passionate tellers of half-truths who in order to convince others, simultaneously convinced themselves. Over generations success had winnowed us out, and with success came our defect, carved deep in the genes like ruts in a cart track—when it didn't suit us we couldn't agree on what was in front of us.—Ian McEwan, *Enduring Love*

My dear friend Chris and I embarked on a journey from New York City to New Jersey one morning in early October 2013, rode past the large trees with their yellow and red leaves and the houses which stand back from the street, nearly in the woods. After about 45 minutes, we reached a small town, a village really, sleepy, quiet, with only a few shops and two or three restaurants. David Shire lived here, the composer of scores such as *Zodiac*, *The Conversation*—and nearly *Apocalypse Now*, which he had gotten fired from before he could eventually record it.

In time for our appointment, I knocked on the door and a tall, skinny elderly man with sharp blue eyes opened, noticeably distressed. As it turned out, David Shire had just taken his two dogs out for a morning walk and one of them had been hit by a car while crossing the street. I arrived at a bad time. Shire had just moved in a year before and parts of the house still looked unfinished. The corridor was so narrow to all sides that I had to squeeze my way through it, following my host to the right through a sparsely decorated wooden seating area. To the left was a small kitchen, straight through a noble and elegantly furnished piano room, remarkably different from the rest of the house. Shire's wife, actress Didi Conn, was in New Haven to act in a play that day. While Maddy, a giant gray border collie, roamed around our feet, Shire made himself a cereal, anxiously waiting for the call from the vet where he had taken his injured dog. When I called Shire one week later, I learned the dog died soon after I had left.

We began talking in the kitchen and moved into his studio after he had finished his breakfast. I sat down on a couch with pillows so soft that I sank in a couple of inches and didn't even bother trying to get up because I knew it would cost me too much energy. To the right of the sofa was a small shelf with videos from the movies Shire had scored. Placed in the middle of the shelf was the Oscar he had won for the song *It Goes As It Goes*. Towards the end of the room at the right was an upright piano, a fireplace and a modest computer set-up to the left. Maddy lay down in front of the furnace, her fur blending in with the floor, making it hard to distinguish dog from carpet. Shire was glad to do the interview, concentrating on elaborate answers, only jumping up occasionally when the phone rang, hoping it was the vet with good news. He admitted at one point:

> I have gone through a period in the last 15 years of gradually becoming more and more marginalized and going through the various stages of reaction to that. First disbelief, then frustration, anger, depression and then acceptance. There are so many good people coming up and it's nice that some people remember what I did. And that is important. I tended to feel for a while that once you are not active anymore, that's it. And to be honest about it, I never felt that I reached the legendary status that John Williams did.

Shire was modest about his achievements but probably correct in the evaluation of his status. Although he had shown a musical versatility unmatched by most of his peers to this day, he never made it to the A list. He is hardly mentioned in the same sentence as John Williams or Jerry Goldsmith. Yet his achievements include *The Taking of Pelham 1–2–3* where he fused twelve-tone music with funk; *The Conversation* where his bluesy score become one entity with Walter Murch's sound design; *Zodiac*, with its dark, brooding, Charles Ives–inspired impressionism; *Short Circuit* with its mix of orchestral and electronic colors; *Return to Oz* with its inspired, large orchestral themes; *The Hindenburg* with its Richard Straussian late romanticism—and the countless musicals and revues he wrote along with lyricist Richard Maltby.

As the fame and success of the composer is always dependent on the films they work on, it comes as no big surprise that Shire became marginalized. He was unlucky in many respects. None of it was his fault. When the New Hollywood arrived in the late '60s and early '70s, he was asked to score pictures that became some of their directors' biggest flops—indeed, some of the biggest flops of the era. He did *Drive, He Said*, directed by Jack Nicholson, *Steelyard Blues* and *The Fortune*. Even more importantly, he lost important projects: Shire was offered *Rocky* but turned it down because he didn't want to do a boxing movie. John Badham wanted him to score *WarGames* but the producer not only refused but screamed, "David Shire? I would never ask him! I would never go near him! I hate him! Don't ever mention his name again!" When Badham and the producer walked around the studio a few weeks later, he started yelling again, "There is this David Shire! This terrible person!" Badham looked at the producer and explained, "That's not David Shire. That's Dave Grusin."

Return to Oz, despite all its cinematic qualities, was terribly marketed and had a heavy conceptual problem: it was too dark and gruesome for kids. After *Return to Oz*, Shire would only work on feature films occasionally, instead being employed to work on television movies before David Fincher rediscovered him for *Zodiac* in 2007. *Zodiac* didn't lead to a successful comeback in Hollywood. When he eventually found work, it was because of earlier scores of his to which he was asked to pay homage. Shire is still surprised that he received most offers to compose for movies because of his score for *The Conversation*, an unobtrusive piano score, rather than because of *Return to Oz*, "for which I was able to work with one of the best orchestras in the world. But, as I like to say, 'Life is what happens while you make other plans.'"

Plan to Be Spontaneous—Tomorrow

It is not only Shire's connection to big movie flops that made him more or less vanish from the Hollywood scene in the late '80s. Shire still stands for melodically inspired, sometimes jazz-infused soundtracks, for a style that went out of fashion in the '80s where the movie industry preferred instrumental, electronic pop music.

Composers are fragile souls. There are countless biographies in film music which go without a happy ending: Max Steiner's music was out of fashion in the late '50s. He received hardly any work anymore, became blind and increasingly frustrated and bitter about the movie business. In the '70s, disillusioned about the fact the he was not approached for movies anymore, Hugo Friedhofer lived in a small, two-room apartment, suffering from depression and alcoholism. George Bassman, who had scored Sam Peckinpah's *Ride the High Country* and several successful pictures in the '40s, lost his home, became a drug addict and died alone in a hospital. It is difficult to get into the business but ridiculously simple to get out. As always in life, luck plays an important role but, as a composer, you also have to be flexible, adept and diplomatic. As the music world changes, so do the demands of directors and producers. Several composers sustained long careers because they could either adapt or had a strong working-relationship with a successful director. It is worth taking a look at how the sound of film music has changed over the years before focusing on the actual working conditions of the composers in later chapters.

There are two truths in life: "Everything used to be better," and "Everything used to be worse." The most poignant quote on the state of films and their music was given by Elmer Bernstein: "I think that the state of film music is a reflection of the state of commercial motion pictures, which is a reflection of the state of the times."[1]

As society changes, so does the film industry. To keep the engine running, the film industry has to react quickly to these changes—in politics, in taste, in public demand. In the course of its history, Hollywood hasn't showed itself to be particularly good at spontaneity. Instead, it has always tried to hold onto the current system as long as possible. When it did change eventually—from the studio system/Golden Age (roughly from the '30s to the late '50s) to the New Hollywood (from the early '60s to the late '70s) to the Independent Era (from the early '80s to the late '90s) to the current New Studio System—so did film music. The fall of any of these eras resulted from changes in society. These systems in Hollywood eventually collapsed because its producers and directors proved incapable of adapting to new trends. Even the New Hollywood, with its anarchy and auteurism, turned out to be remarkably conservative and was run into the ground through the constant clashing of egos.

Hollywood has always been at least twenty years too late when it comes to music. Sometimes it was even later: Arnold Schönberg developed the twelve-tone technique in the first decade of the 20th century. It took nearly 50 years until this approach was used for a full film score (Leonard Rosenman's *The Cobweb* in 1955). Jazz was already well-established in the music scene when it was used in an underscore (Alex North's *A Streetcar Named Desire* in 1951). By the time Louis and Bebbe Baron wrote the first full electronic score for a U.S. production (*Forbidden Planet* in 1956), European composers had been experimenting with it for years. It would take even longer until the employment of electronics for movie productions became an actual trend in the late '70s. Its conservatism—not only in music—brought Hollywood to its knees several times and will doubtlessly continue to do so. Let's take a brief trip through these different eras and their musical changes.

Full Blast

"The first sound films were mostly musicals," said Miklós Rózsa. "With the exception of the technical novelty, they didn't bring anything new to the screen. They were mainly photographed operettas or musical comedies. The pictures seemed to lose for some time the aesthetics they had achieved in the last years of the silent era. The song hit became the most important element, and everything was built around it and sacrificed to it."[2]

The first sound films—and nearly every production through to the end of the so-called Golden Age—heavily favored light music in the Romantic spirit of composers such as Richard Strauss. For their romantic soap operas and screwball comedies the studios employed composers who had a background in light music, such as Max Steiner, Herbert Stothart, Franz Waxman, or composers who wrote concert works but whose music sounded old-fashioned enough to be deemed appropriate for these films, such as Erich Wolfgang Korngold. Schönberg had already experimented with twelve-tone rows, George Antheil had written his *Ballet Méchanique*, and Edgard Varèse was busy with larger-than-life pieces for mostly percussion instruments in complex rhythms; but the music that came out of the big studio productions in the '30s and '40s could only be described as out of fashion. Said Elmer Bernstein in 1973, "In the Thirties and Forties the writing of symbolic music was very popular—music which immediately tells you where you are, so to speak. [...] These are things which you could not do today because people want more sophisticated ways to create the same effect."[3] In fact, symbolic music didn't tell the viewers anything they weren't already seeing on screen.

Another common phenomenon was that the music in the '30s and '40s sounded mostly similar conceptually. The studios all had their own orchestras, so-called staff orchestras, compiled of session musicians who were called up anytime a new film score had to be recorded. While that was easy to organize, it led to a standard orchestration from the '30s all through the '50s. Compositions not written for the usual size of the staff orchestra were rare. Said Hugo Friedhofer, "All the big studios had big orchestras under contract. And they had to utilize them. So the composer was forced to write more expansively and extensively than he might have liked."[4] The eventual result was that every film opened and ended in a blaze of sound—full blast. This was no time for subtlety.

The first composer to break with that tradition of a standard orchestration for symbolic music in a Romantic vein was Bernard Herrmann, who had the luck of working with enfant terrible Orson Welles. Herrmann's scores, from *Citizen Kane* onward, neither employed a standard orchestration, nor were they strictly symbolic. Instead, Herrmann, strongly influenced by the modern masters of that time, namely Béla Bartók and Charles Ives, illustrated what went on in the heads of the film's characters, liked to use nine harps instead of one when appropriate, and mixed late Romantic influences with impressionism and what would later be classified as minimalism. The new generation of composers would later criticize their predecessors for lack of subtlety. Henry Mancini said, "Your thoughts became molded into thinking that the thirty-five piece studio orchestra was the only means of scoring. Only occasionally would you go beyond that concept, and that was to increase the orchestra, not to decrease it. The general musical concept was one of bigness, lushness."[5]

In the late '40s, several things happened which would give way to a style of scoring that was much less restricted and allowed the composers more freedom. The Second World War had a big influence on the creative industry in the U.S. Especially in California, the European intellectuals who had immigrated from Europe mixed surprisingly well with the stars of the movie industry; Hanns Eisler loved his new "Heimat," Thomas Mann went to have brunch with Johnny Weissmuller, Arnold Schönberg played tennis with Groucho Marx, and Bertold Brecht smoked cigars with Charlie Chaplin. The influence these artists had on each other is not to be underestimated. Even more importantly, the major studios had controlled the programs in the theaters for decades by deliberately keeping out foreign films and discouraging domestic competition.

This worked for quite some time until the U.S. Supreme Court decided on the anti-monopoly ruling in 1948 which heavily affected the eight major studios. Not only were they forbidden to keep out foreign productions, but they also had to sell their own theaters. The court ruling was financially disastrous for the studios. But it turned out to be only the beginning: with the advent of television, profits declined even further. To make up the shortfall, studios had to rent out some of their equipment—ironically mostly to studios for television productions. In 1958, studio orchestras were abandoned. The musicians had demanded to receive re-use fees for the music they had performed whenever a piece of theirs was played on television. The studios didn't want to give in.

As a result of the Supreme Court ruling and the success of television, more and more independent movies were produced which allowed the composers greater freedom. One of the first and most striking examples turned out to be *High Noon*, the influential anti-western by Fred Zinnemann, produced by Stanley Kramer and Carl Foreman. Unusual for the time, Dimitri Tiomkin broke with the Hollywood tradition of movie scoring by delivering a much quieter score which neither began nor ended with a huge blast of sound. It also centered on a theme song, performed by Frankie Laine, which foreshadowed the affection for pop tunes in the following era. The film and its song turned out to be a major success, while increasing numbers of studio productions from the majors landed with a thud.

Repercussions

There were other reasons for the abandonment of the traditional late Romantic style of film scoring in Hollywood. They had more to do with the political situation in the '50s than anything else. The '50s were a difficult decade for the U.S. The Vietnam War started, and Senator McCarthy drove a relentless campaign against communism—spying on citizens, interrogating them, trying to persuade them to betray friends and family members who sympathized with communism, and putting countless people on a blacklist, making it nearly impossible for them to find work and earn a living. Young adults, students, sons and daughters of powerful men who ran the studio system of the Golden Age were furious. Around the same time, rock 'n' roll emerged, the youth culture blossomed, the first teenage magazines were printed and sold, Roger Corman—benefiting from the court ruling in 1948—started to produce and direct independent movies about enraged bikers and dangerous monsters from outer space, and suddenly the Romantic spirit of the '30s and '40s didn't seem appropriate anymore.

Just as important is the fact that aspiring directors now had better chances to watch foreign movies following the Supreme Court ruling. Italian Neo-Realism and later the French Nouvelle Vague turned out to be major influences which swept over in music as well, most prominently with Michel Legrand and Georges Delerue who moved to California in 1967 and 1981 respectively and became sought-after composers in Hollywood.

The generation which blossomed during the '50s was fundamentally different from their parents' generation. A new, angry, sound evolved from composers such as Alex North, Elmer Bernstein, Jerry Fielding, all of whom suffered from McCarthy's blacklist. But they were lucky eventually: they found directors who were as angry as they were and who were the leaders of something new and fresh (Elia Kazan, Sam Peckinpah). In the New Hollywood, more value was placed on the director-as-auteur than on the producer. In the as-of-yet unpublished biography on Jerry Goldsmith, written by his daughter Carrie, the composer remembered his experiences in his early days in the industry: "In those days, a director would come on and shoot the picture and be gone. The producer would do all the pre- and post-production."

Furthermore, these composers were musically not directly influenced by 19th century romantic stranglehold but more advanced, curious about current developments in the musical world, by jazz and the avant-garde. Such young composers had a radically different upbringing and background than the generation before them—they had grown up, after all, during the Depression. Lalo Schifrin came from an oppressive political regime in the Argentina of the '50s. Quincy Jones ran around Chicago with teenage hoodlums ("All I saw were dead bodies, tommy guns and stogies, and piles of money in back rooms. I had my hand nailed to a fence with a switchblade when I was seven. When you're a kid, you want to be what you see, and I wanted to be a gangster till I was 11").[6]

There were also economic factors behind film music's greater restraint in orchestration. There were no studio orchestras anymore. Budgets mostly had to be calculated from project to project. Those projects which used a rather small ensemble or utilized songs proved to be successful. The young, aspiring directors were taken by the music of the Beatles and used their songs or similar ones in their movies. The sound of Hollywood had changed. It became difficult for the older composers to get work. Howard Blake remembers an occurrence during the recording of Herrmann's music for the thriller *Sisters* in 1973, when Blake asked his then-friend, "This is a terrible movie! Why are you doing this?," to which Herrmann replied in tears: "I just want to work."

Upcoming composers were glad about the freedom they could exercise. Leonard Rosenman was able to write twelve-tone music for *The Cobweb*, David Shire could mix tone-rows with funk in *The Taking of Pelham 1-2-3*, Don Ellis came up with a dissonant and aggressive score for *The French Connection*, Lalo Schifrin wrote catchy jazz, with some cues based on the Modes of Limited Transposition by Olivier Messiaen, for *Mission: Impossible.* Jerry Goldsmith recorded Bartók-influenced music for John Huston's *Freud* and the challenging *Planet of the Apes*, Henry Mancini gave the world instrumental pop tunes like *Baby Elephant Walk* that became a chart hit. The New Hollywood showed a musical variety that hadn't existed before. The '60s generally were an artistically inspired and inspiring time. It seemed Hollywood was successful with what it was doing—musically and otherwise. Film music LPs started to come into fashion and sold reasonably well.

However, the era was not without its problems. The concept of the New Hollywood was to give more authority to the director, while the producer was simply supposed to give money and shut up, which was contrary to what had been done in the Golden Age. With the egos of directors running amok, the system had to collapse sooner or later. Francis Ford Coppola, Peter Bogdanovich and William Friedkin, among others, relentlessly neglected the market by not caring about the financial appeal of their projects, and instead making movies which were close to their heart but flopped so disastrously (*Apocalypse Now, One from the Heart, At Long Last Love, Sorcerer*) that few producers were willing to bankroll them.

One of the composers who assessed the failing of the New Hollywood correctly was Dimitri Tiomkin in 1973:

> Hollywood was a wonderful place when I first went there…. It was a bright dream about a beautiful democracy in a world under the shadow of tyranny. I suppose there were fakers and phonies but I can't help thinking there was an innocence which has now vanished. Once Hollywood forgot the dreams and got down to reality, it failed.[7]

And then *Star Wars* happened.

Welcome to the '80s

Steven Spielberg and George Lucas were young directors who were less interested in making social comments in their films but more in entertainment which appealed to everyone. With *Jaws*, studios discovered the value of the so-called wide breaks. Increasingly, theaters would show a single movie which would lure millions of people in. Massive advertising in print and TV made these people go to the theaters immediately instead of relying on word-of-mouth propaganda and reviews. Studios wanted to see profits more quickly. *Jaws*, a huge hit, had proved that there were no limits. Rather quickly, studios reasserted their power. In other words, as director John Milius said, "Steven was the one who ran out to buy the trade papers. He was always talking about grosses."[8]

Another development took place: CAA (Creative Arts Agency) became the largest agency in the movie industry. Many executives left their jobs at the studios to work as agents who then became more and more powerful in Hollywood. Said George Lucas, "Once the corporations bought in, and once the agents, lawyers, and accountants took over, people who read the Wall Street Journal and cared less about the movies than the price of stock, that's when the whole thing died."[9] *Star Wars*, by Lucas, was the natural successor of *Jaws*, which taught everybody in Hollywood the invaluable lesson that both kids and young adults, as well as grown ups, would come back again and again to theaters to watch highly entertaining blockbusters that didn't need to rely on big stars on the screen. These corporations, agents and lawyers, which all wanted to have a piece of the pie, then started to put together package deals for every movie production, which turned out to be cheaper and less bureaucratic. How these creative forces actually spent the money was up to them. From the money of the package deal, the composers could pay for a large orchestra which was more costly than a synthesized score, and have less money in their own pocket as a salary, or choose to invest in a recording with a chamber ensemble, enabling them to keep more money of the package deal.

Although John Williams had written a large symphonic piece for *Star Wars*—a throwback to the Golden Age style of scoring—these kinds of scores didn't become the way to go during the Independent Era. The increasingly electronic sound of pop music had a big influence on film scoring in the '80s and early '90s. It was not only pop music though: Giorgio Moroder, Vangelis and Tangerine Dream were the front runners in instrumental electronic music and therefore also assigned to work on film scores. As rock and pop music became more and more complex with its influences from all sorts of genres—in fact too complex to simply be put underneath a scene—popular musicians were then asked to write film music in the style of their non-film work.

The '80s also led to the democratization of movies due to the quickly blossoming VHS market. Young directors were enabled to pick up cheap camera equipment (another achievement of advancing technology in the '80s) and get their movies out. Video labels were desperate to release movies on VHS and would distribute anything that you could drill two holes in and throw into the VHS player. The independent market flourished. One of the companies that used this development wisely was Miramax, headed by Harvey and Bob Weinstein. The first independent movies they picked up for distribution to show in theaters and later put on VHS were costly flops and nearly bankrupted the company. But both brothers were smart enough to learn from their mistakes.

They started marketing independent movies for the masses, setting up test screenings where a randomly chosen audience could mark on a piece of paper what they liked about the film and what not (including music). The movie was then adjusted to the demands of the test audience and re-cut, mostly without the approval of the director, sometimes including the score which they started tampering with as soon as they could afford commissioning a replacement soundtrack. Eventually, this led to the collapse of the independent market as soon as the Weinsteins had tasted blood and realized that they could make more money with entertaining crowd pleasers rather than challenging arthouse films. Before that, everything seemed possible for young, aspiring directors. For B movies, the scores understandably needed to be produced cheaply. A lot of the younger directors turned to friends and band members to provide a score. Said composer Daniel Licht in 1999:

> I came [to Los Angeles in 1991] when everyone decided that you didn't need a real orchestra anymore, but there were still a few people who you could talk into hiring an orchestra for low-budget films, *Children of the Night* being a perfect example. If they were making that film today, I doubt very much that I could convince anyone to let me hire an orchestra. The budgets have shrunk to meet the availability of cheaper synthesizer scores, and new directors budget even less money for music.[10]

Directors and producers—no matter whether of B-pictures or of costly blockbusters—realized that music could now be produced more cheaply. It was also preferable, as electronic music was still highly popular in the '80s and early '90s. But as popular music changed, so did film music. When Miramax was at the top of its game in the mid- to late '90s and entertaining crowd pleasers dominated the movie scene at least in the U.S., electronic music was largely out of fashion again and studios and distributors went back to employing orchestral scores with the influence of synthetic elements. One of the prime examples is Thomas Newman's *American Beauty* with its minimalism that would go on to inspire not only composers but also studio heads, determining the sound of the era.

Meanwhile, the Weinsteins kept interfering with the music of their productions. This not only led to an increase in soundtrack rejections but also to direct confrontations, the most startling occurrence being the clash between a short tempered Harvey Weinstein and composer Elliot Goldenthal who had scored *Frida* for his partner Julie Taymor, a confrontation that occurred after a less than pleasing test screening. Writes Peter Biskind:

> For reasons best known to himself, Harvey just exploded. He tore up the scores, turned to Taymor and screamed, "You are the most arrogant person I have ever met. This is what my brother told me, and he's right." (Bob had just met Taymor for the first time.) With a parting shot—"Go market the fucking film yourself, I'm selling it to HBO"—and he made as if to go. Then he turned on his heel. Looking at Bart Walker, Taymor's agent, he roared, "Get the fuck outta here." He pointed at Elliot Goldenthal, Taymor's partner, an Oscar-nominated composer who wrote the music for the film, basically for nothing, and continued at the same volume, "I don't like the look on your face. Why don't you defend your wife, so I can beat the shit out of you."[11]

The New Status Quo

The so-called Independent Era eventually merged with the New Studio System in the late '90s. The big players in the field of distribution weren't interested in challenging indie films but rather in easily marketable crowd pleasers. Around the same time, Michael Bay premiered *The Rock* and *Armageddon*, two expensive action films which, much like *Star Wars* earlier, could be enjoyed by both young adults and their parents. So began an era in which Hollywood concentrated on blockbusters for teenagers and young adults, resulting in a flood of superhero movies and countless sequels, pre-quels and remakes (*Fantastic Four, Man of Steel, Captain America, The Avengers, Iron Man, Thor, Spider-Man*). The original hope was that the big studio productions would subsidize the smaller productions. But, very much like the economic trickle-down-effect, this was quickly proven to be non-sense: "'They're not subsidizing everything else,' says Scorsese. 'They are it. That's all. The person who has something to say in a movie has got to make a picture for $50. They're smothering everything.'"[12]

As the film industry changed, so did the music. Says John Ottman,

> Movies became more fast-paced so composers have less time to write a theme that has a beginning, a middle and an end that could actually ever exist in a film with no long moments like in *Dances with Wolves* or *Out of Africa*, where you can actually just let the theme go. Technology created this syndrome where composers were doing five, six movies a year because they could. Because of technology and editing, filmmaking and composing, the time-frame to write a score has shrunk. So the cranking-out attitude became even more prevalent. And then scores become like a product. Today there is really no film I can think of where you can have a long thematic idea that plays out.

The studios adopted the idea of test screenings from the independent distributors. Today, every single blockbuster undergoes at least one, sometimes several, test screening(s) with an audience chosen by the studio before it is released. This had a huge impact on composers as well: when a film was due to be shown in a test screening, rarely was its score already recorded. But showing a film to a test audience without music would be highly irritating. As a result, temp tracks became increasingly popular—pieces of pre-existing music which are put on an early cut of the film. Technically it was now possible to do just that, and it was not only done for the test audience, but also for directors to be able to communicate their musical ideas to the composer, and for editors to get a feeling for the rhythm of a scene. The trouble was— and still is—that when a test audience likes the temp music used for a test screening, the composer will be asked to follow it closely. After all, music is able to alter a scene enormously. And nobody wants to risk putting on new music when a film had scored high on the test sheet. As pop music became less melodic, so did film music.

Another reason for the new, hip sound had already occurred in the late '80s and can be boiled down to one name: Hans Zimmer. The aficionado of electronic music turned out to be at the right place at the right time. He had successfully transported the musical zeitgeist to theater screens by scoring one of the biggest hits of 1988: *Rain Man*. Zimmer became one of Hollywood's most sought-after composers, scoring a string of high profile projects throughout the '90s (and to date), first by delivering completely electronic scores and later by adding symphonic elements to it with the help of orchestrators like Shirley Walker. The fusion of synths and symphony became a fashionable trend as many films scored that way had proven to be highly profitable.

Zimmer quickly became a star. Many of his colleagues were then honored to mimic his style as countless of his cues made it into rough cuts of new projects as temp tracks. Zimmer's music was not necessarily melodic, relying rather on motifs and short themes than on subsequently developed melodies. Zimmer was less influenced by classical pieces but instead took the basic vocabulary of rock music and transplanted it into film music with strings replacing the rhythm guitar, the orchestral percussion being the drummer and the horn section taking over the job of the lead singer. Says Joe Kraemer, composer of *Jack Reacher* and *Mission: Impossible—Rogue Nation*:

> An aesthetic has arisen where it's a combination of sources. From the one end you have Zimmer who came from rock music and synth programming, and from the other end you have Thomas Newman who comes from a legacy family of "legit" Hollywood composers. The harmonic sounds Zimmer is choosing are dictated by traditional rock music skills—it's mostly in D minor. On the other side you have Thomas Newman who created music that hypnotized you and put you in a sort of state. The thing that's really clever about the music

and very interesting is that it works with anything. If you put that music over a scene where people are sad, it feels sad. If you put it over a scene where people are angry, it works with the anger. It's emotionally ambiguous. I think that's why editors fell in love with it and used it in pretty much everything for ten years as temp music. That created this whole aesthetic of, "Let's not have music actually say anything." So the thought of a theme with a tune that's clearly major or clearly minor really started becoming anathema to the trends in filmmaking.

Another important aspect is that the music of Zimmer and Newman is generally very well suited to work as temp music because it's easy to cut as opposed to a cue which constantly changes meters or has a strong melody where the editor can't simply take out a few bars to make the music fit to the edit as a temp.

The Complaints Continue

Composers have always complained about contemporary developments in their field. They sense their era giving way to another, presaging less work for them. All the same, the number of composers working in the industry today who seem dissatisfied with the status quo is large.

"In America right now, the studio system very much feels like the music industry felt before Nirvana showed up," continues Kraemer.

In the late '80s and early '90s, before *Nevermind* came out, before *Smells Like Teen Spirit* came out. Music had reached a point where it all felt packaged. It was metal, it was packaged by bands, it was product. Everything was over-produced, the image was overdone. There was too much focus on the image and production value and not necessarily on the writing. Kurt Cobain leveled all that. It's not stagnant, but we are ready for that new different thing, not only in terms of the screenplays and in terms of the movies that are getting made but also in terms of the way scores are being conceived.

Even though Daniel Pemberton is one of the most promising newcomers in the industry, he is challenged by the current working conditions and the effects they have on the music:

I have been doing these big studio movies lately and they are a nightmare because they re-cut it every day. You are writing something that is working really well to picture and literally when I finish it, I send it over because they wanted it within four hours and then they go, "Oh yeah, we changed that section." That happens every day. So you end up having to work out how to keep up with that and make something interesting. That's a difficulty with most modern movies. If you are writing orchestral music it's a nightmare when they re-cut the picture all the time. I think that's why most modern film music is much simpler because it's much easier to edit.

Composers complaints are understandable from one angle: Most of the composers working today grew up in the '60s or '70s, when film music was at its most daring during New Hollywood. Nearly all of them experienced the phenomenon of *Star Wars* in 1977 when they were kids or young adults, became fans of the film and were all mesmerized by its large, symphonic, melodic music. Composers who favor symphonic, melodic film music now hardly seem to fit in the industry.

Edwin Wendler makes the dilemma clear:

> I usually tell people that all this music that my generation has grown to love— all the John Williamses, all the James Horners, all the Elmer Bernsteins, all the Maurice Jarres, all the Jerry Goldsmiths, even going earlier to Bernard Herrmann, Max Steiner and Korngold—there seems to be no place in this industry for. I was definitely hopeful. It was the spark that made me go, "I want to do this kind of music." The symphonic language that was used was something that was very inspirational at a young age.

In a way, the studio productions of today are a continuation of the crowd pleaser productions of the late '70s and early '80s such as *Jaws*, *Star Wars*, and *Superman* in that they are marketed as a cinematic "amusement park" to teenagers and young adults. They don't necessarily pay homage to the symphonic music of theoe days, though. "I want to write something that's in that style of Spielberg and his composer of choice John Williams, and Robert Zemeckis and Alan Silvestri," muses Wendler. "But when I do that and it's put up against the picture, it always gets rejected, at least in the cases that I've worked on. They realize, it's okay to make visual references to that genre, but for some reason if you put music of that style up against it, it dates it immediately in their mind."

Audiences have changed, and so has the music they listen to in their pastime. What was hip in the '80s can feel pathetically out of date today. The ambition of these studios is not primarily paying homage to a certain era but giving the audience something they can relate to. Also, complex orchestral writing is not perceived as cool. As we live in a time where everything is about the image, publicity, sex-appeal and marketing, a musician like John Williams is the opposite of a posterboy for this generation. It is not the craft of writing which is admired but the glamour of a Trent Reznor, a rock musician in a leather jacket, a star who is very well suited to drive in some additional marketing power as opposed to the writing of modulations, shifting the tonal center, changing meter and tempo and coming up with a challenging counterpoint. Joe Kraemer concludes:

> Even if a director asks for [complex orchestral writing], there aren't a lot of guys out there who can do it, certainly not young guys who are currently at the forefront of studio hiring lists. Another aspect is that the film business

seems to reject anybody who wants to be in it. Look at so many film com-posers who don't want to be film composers, who want to be rock stars. Or they studied something else and only ended up doing film music by a series of flukes. The people who actually studied it and who actually want to become film composers are marginalized as too desperate. The film music business has a long history of people doing it because they had no other choice or by acci-dent.

When hiring musicians who are cool and hip but not classically trained composers, their orchestral musical language is less complex than the lan-guage of John Williams or Jerry Goldsmith. But daring concepts have always been the exception. Bernard Herrmann had to fight hard, as did Miklós Rózsa. With the vast pool of different musical styles today, much more diverse film music can be created than before. Mica Levi wrote an avant-garde score for *Under the Skin* by mixing orchestral and electronic elements; Gary Yer-shon created an impressionistic, at times harshly dissonant score for Mike Leigh's *Mr. Turner*, earning him an Oscar nomination; Ennio Morricone proved to be still a fresh voice when twisting his own Western scores and adding new elements in an unusual orchestration with the heavy use of bas-soons in *The Hateful Eight*, earning him an Oscar; Gustavo Santaolalla brought on introvert folk music for *Brokeback Mountain*, earning him an Oscar; Ryuichi Sakamoto and Alva Noto created a unique soundscape for *The Revenant*, gathering a Golden Globe nomination; Michael Giacchino found ways to incorporate jazz and, unusually, a harpsichord in *Doctor Strange*; Cliff Martinez pulled all stops when delivering a cheeky electronic score for *The Neon Demon* and poking fun at the seemingly glossy fashion industry musically.

Conceptually interesting and daring film music is still being written. We think it not being the case and complain about the supposed lack of daring concepts only because we live in the here and now. When looking back, we tend only to remember the art which survived. If art survived, it did because it was good, because it delivered something unusual. Thus we forgot about the vast output of mediocre works. Living in the here and now, we are much more exposed to the mediocre works of our own time than those of the past. Our impression of today's art is therefore diminished. How one will look at today's film music in a few years or decades remains to be seen.

The film industry is going to change—and maybe we are at the beginning of a new era already, with movies like *Sicario* and *Arrival*, or even *Interstellar*, offering both entertainment and complexity which also affects their scores. As Henry Mancini said in 1973, the Golden Age of Hollywood consisted of a system where everything was "geared to abundance." Hollywood is facing a similar situation now. Now, more money than ever is being spent on blockbusters, which rely more often than before on the success on the Chinese market. If a movie fails domestically, directors no longer need to panic immediately because they can still hope for a success in China.

Where Have All the Melodies Gone?

Complained film music agent Richard Kraft (as far back as 1991), "Scores are so chintzy now. You used to get five or six good themes in a picture. Now, if you get one, you're grateful."[13] Comments John Ottman:

> It's an art to create a score that's thematic in a modern movie. It can be done. When the difficulty of it is exposed, especially to the new generation of composers, the baby is thrown out with the bathwater. They feel to go thematic is to be cheesy, to go thematic is to feel dated. Therefore, let's throw everything out with the bathwater and let's do something completely, utterly non-thematic that has no sense of story whatsoever. There is a way to be relevant, to write a modern relevant score on today's films that is thematic. It just takes a lot of work, a lot of forethought, it takes a lot of effort and it is just not easy. If you got four or five movies to stand up and you did it in that sort of "It's just another job" attitude and just cranked it out, then there's less attention paid to how can we raise the bar in this film and do a thematic score. It can be done.

Ottman experienced how hard this can be when scoring *X-Men: Days of Future Past*, his return to the franchise after he had already scored the second entry in the series in 2003. For *X-Men 2*, he had come up with a strong main theme which recurs throughout the score. It was only logical to him to include it in *Days of the Future Past* as well. Unexpectedly, he ran into problems with the executives. While some producers at Fox agreed to utilize the theme, others did not, resulting in a fierce battle between the opposing parties. In the end, the theme did prevail because there were enough people in positions of power who encouraged Ottman to reuse it. To take on the battle for the theme was a risk even for an established composer like John Ottman, and even he could only persuade the producers to a certain degree.

What had happened between *X-Men 2* and its sequel from 2014 was the *Batman* franchise by Christopher Nolan, which had set a new standard for composers and producers of how to score an action film. This standard, as employed by Hans Zimmer and James Newton Howard, was to rely on soundscapes and motifs, avoiding a multitude of themes and tunes. The influence on the industry was immense. Says Matthew Margeson:

> Let's say there is a film that comes out that has very little melody but just more the sense of wallpaper music. That movie grosses $800 million. Joe Smith, an upcoming director, is like, "I want to make something that's like that." So it could come down to a more bureaucratic, financial decision, too.

There is certainly a lot more of, "We just want a mood. We just want the action music to be strictly rhythmical." There are composers that are hired to just get the job done and rip the temp. Hopefully the trend will change.

Both fashion and personal experience can influence a composer's work. As James Newton Howard put it, when explaining in 1999 why he had moved away from the employment of strong melodies in various variations:

As I look back on some of my older stuff, [the theme] comes back a little too often for my taste—I just find that some of it is too melodic, too thematic, too much of the time. [...] It's about the recitative—like music being too thematic in nature—too melodic and melody-driven, which is a form that has become boring to me. I think that I am only lately getting away from that or becoming able to write freely. I think that it's really all about counterpoint—more counterpoint and less melody. Just dig into the texture of the music rather than the melody or the theme.[14]

Joe Kraemer shares his take on the lack of melody and the emotional subtlety in today's film music:

Music is a language. It's a vocabulary. If one looks at writing a score as a way of telling a story in a musical language, one can tell a story with very simple words, like "He got up. He went to the door. He opened the door." Or one could tell the story with flowery language, like "Every morning, Ernest got out of bed, stumbled to the door, brushing sleep from his eyes," very descriptive language rather than just getting the point across. The language of film music used to be more literate. What you had was a situation where somebody couldn't really make a film that was acceptable on its own terms until they reached a certain degree of success because they had to have a certain amount of money in order to do it and you couldn't raise that amount of money privately.

Spielberg as a young kid learning to make movies on Super 8 with other kids from the neighborhood, pretending to be soldiers in Iwo Jima. It was such a massive leap that you had to accept that as the reality of the film. To help with that he would use scores from war films. Spielberg became very comfortable with the idea of music giving size and scope to the film. In the '80s what started to emerge was an ability to make films that could be taken at face value for little money. What you had was a film like *El Mariachi* or *Sex, Lies and Videotape* where the film could come out and could be released.

There was no chance that Spielberg's war film with the kids on the streets was going to be released as a film. In order for it to be released it had to have a music soundtrack that was cleared. That meant the filmmaker had to find somebody on their own who could do the score, usually for no money. Who do they end up finding? They end up finding the keyboard player in the band that plays in their town or lives down the hall from them in film school, not a trained musician with an orchestra. That composer writes the score and they realize, "Oh, if I hold this D minor chord for four minutes, it really is moody and deep."

I don't mean to be harsh but they are dealing with a much simpler level of understanding of orchestral music and film music and what can support a film. So the filmmaker grows up with that and their voice relies on that simpler kind of music. They are not comfortable with music making a big front statement the way Spielberg was, making a silent film where the music was telling the story. The tail end of that generation is Tim Burton and Bob Zemeckis. Soderbergh is the next generation. And then the music video guys like Fincher and Michael Bay who come from a rock music place. They make their films like music videos and score them with bands.

Kraemer himself hopes, as history repeats itself, that he and other old-fashioned composers such as Edwin Wendler, might very well have a chance to make a career as an A-lister:

As far as my own work goes, by the nature of the fact that the projects I worked on were sort of retro, I have become a last man standing of an era. You could analyze that Hollywood has driven miles away from what I want to do or what I am most successful at doing. My hope is that I am so far behind the times that I will end up being a trendsetter again. *Star Wars*, for example, was so old-fashioned, it was new again.

I really love thematic composing and thematic writing and I love orchestral scores and I love music that is definitely emotional and that has come in and out of favor in Hollywood. It really fell out in the '60s with *The Graduate* and *Easy Rider*. If you look at John Williams' work up until *Star Wars*, it was much less cut from a traditional cloth with the exception of *Jaws*. *Jaws* was the first step towards a fully orchestral classic sound. From then out it was much more exploring that Korngold and Steiner world of orchestration mixed with his jazz sensibility in terms of his arranging. What do I want to do? I want to do that kind of thing. I want to write complex and yet accessible sophisticated scores but that when little kids hear them, they understand the music.

With more films like *Arrival*, which was not a studio production, this could lead to a change which seems to be at our doorstep already. And if it does lead to a change, it will also lead to a change in the working environment for film composers.

The internet and smart-phones are partly responsible for the change in the film industry. Movies and TV programs can now be watched on a smart-phone on the daily commute. We, being accustomed to the quick fix, being used to have everything available when we need it, have lost patience as a society. Will it give rise to more challenging productions and more value on "special experiences," as history repeats itself frequently? This has happened before: the Golden Age didn't only collapse because of the Supreme Court ruling but also because the times were a changin'. It is probably best to close the first chapter and start the subsequent elaborations with a comment by film music historian Tony Thomas who sarcastically observed,

In the light of knowledge about the circumstances and conditions under which film composers work, we have every reason to be grateful that any good scores have been written. The film composers of the most intelligence and the most integrity often pay a price for their excellence—less fame than their more flashy colleagues and lessening opportunity in a business that has become more and more commercial.[15]

Will the current studio system be able to survive much longer? Will the independent studios and auteurs take over again as history repeats itself? Will the working conditions for composers in the film industry improve? No one can predict the future. Let's talk about the present instead.

Sir, You Are Standing
on My Toe, Sir

"We could begin by something quite simple," said Albinus, "a stained window coming to life, animated heraldry, a little saint or two." "I'm afraid it's no good," said the [producer]. "We can't risk fancy pictures."—Vladimir Nabokov, *Laughter in the Dark*

I stood amidst passionate *Doctor Who* fans and felt increasingly uncomfortable. The occasion was a concert of *Doctor Who* music, composed by Murray Gold and conducted by Ben Foster. Whoever thought that television music doesn't sell was proven wrong that afternoon in the Wembley Arena in London in 2015. What a spectacle! The Tardis; mummies and Daleks occasionally moving through the flabbergasted, excited audience, Peter Capaldi—the Doctor of that time—silently watching the events unfold in the front row to the left; amplified electric guitars, etc., etc. Since I have never been a *Doctor Who* fan and had only watched one episode to prepare myself for things to come, I was not sure what to make of it. Everybody else was thrilled, though. A friend of mine, who played guitar in the orchestra and was Murray Gold's longtime assistant, had graciously offered me a ticket. Since I could envision nothing more thrilling than driving out to the north of London on a gray Sunday afternoon to attend a two-hour show of music from a TV series I never watch with people whose fascination for the subject escapes me completely, and to eat a hot dog at the venue for $9, I accepted only too happily. In a way, it was also my preparation.

A few days later I was due to meet Murray Gold at the Royal Albert Hall to talk to him about his career. Gold has been active in television for years. He scored all episodes of *Doctor Who* since its revival in 2005 until 2017. He also contributed to *The Musketeers* and the documentary series *Life Story*. I met with him during rehearsals for a concert of his music for this nature documentary. Royal Albert Hall, Wembley Arena—surely, here was a composer who had made it by concentrating on television. Starting his career in London, he had long since moved to New York and reportedly owned some property in Los Angeles as well. He had admirers, and even stalkers all over the world. He could fill the most prestigious concert halls in the UK with his music. He certainly didn't have to worry about a lack of employment for the next few years. Picture yourself a contented composer and you see Murray Gold. Or so I thought.

I was a bit early for our interview which was scheduled for the break in the *Life Story* rehearsal. Gold welcomed me and offered me a seat next to his. David Attenborough was still rehearsing his lines on the stage, concentrated and self-critical. A few minutes later, a break was due. Gold and I retreated to his dressing room, and it didn't take long before the face of success changed. Immediately, I took a liking to him: he was nervous, slightly anxious, and rather pessimistic about life. Here was a man who was strangely detached from the success he had achieved, who didn't care too much about his status but who fought the daily struggles of life and didn't try to mask it. If anything, he seemed a bit weary of being constantly approached by fans, of continued exposure to the pressure the job brings with itself. And he was only too happy to admit it as I was only too happy to hear it. In fact, Bob Woodward and Carl Bernstein couldn't have been more glad to meet Deep Throat than I was to listen to Murray Gold who detailed his adventures with the U.S. channel NBC which set out to produce a show called *Crossbones* in 2014:

> I went to California. I arrived there and somebody said, "Walter Parks wants to see you." [...] It was for their first TV project called *Crossbones*, a pirate show. We had a great time. I really liked him. [...] He said, "I love your music, it's always got so much mischief in it, not like these very Germanic composers," and then he mentioned somebody and said, "It's fine but there is never any sense of humor." I thought this is great.

Although Parks and Gold proved to be an instant match, the music production turned out to be less harmonious. The show was filmed in Puerto Rico while the post-production took place in New York City where Gold was based. After waiting for months for an episode of the show to arrive, he finally rang up NBC to inquire of the show's status:

> The clock was ticking. It started to get towards springtime and then we got word that they were going to close down post-production on this date in May and we still hadn't had any finished episodes. So I rung up whoever I could and said, "I am doing this show called *Life Story* in the UK and we are recording in June. There is going to be four hours of music in this six-part show." They said, "We are trying to speed things up." I said, "It's not a matter of whether you are trying to speed things up, I am just telling you that I'm not going to be on that show anymore." And they said, "Please don't tell us that, we have gone through so much."

Eventually, the first episode out of nine did arrive for Gold to score who immediately began writing and mocking-up the music. When he received the first episode, he had only five weeks left for his job on nine episodes of the show in total. After sending the music for episode one, he was in for another excruciating wait, since NBC kindly informed him that they had to discuss the episode's music with the first layer of executives. Gold nodded his approval and inquired further:

> "Okay, what happens after that?" "They'll come back with notes." "And then we go on to episode 2." "No, then we send it to the second layer of executives." "Does the first layer of executives make any difference? Can we not just send it to the second layer?" "No, we have to comply with the process here." "Well, you haven't got time to do that. Can you not see that?" "Even if we have two weeks left, we have to do it this way." "In that case you are going to have to do with a different composer because this is lunacy." I had to leave the show. I don't even know what happened to that show. I don't even know if it was on.

It was indeed on but was canceled after its first season, which had received its musical score by Mateo Messina. Messina was approached to score the series a few days after Gold had waved goodbye. Since studios don't move the time of a show's first airing if they can prevent it, Messina had even less time than his predecessor. Messina's challenge: writing approximately 300 minutes of rousing swashbuckler music for nine episodes within 34 days. Things moved quickly after he had been offered the job, as the composer remembers:

> I sent them the music at night and it all went very quickly. I got a call the next morning, saying, "Everybody likes what you put forward." I got another phone call on that day or the next day. It was quite weird because the director was in Ireland, the writer was in New Zealand, the production team was in Puerto Rico. They then said, "We have a deadline in 34 days. We have nine episodes that need action and adventure musically. We want it to be orchestral." "Okay, let me see."

As it turned out, it proved impossible to write thematic orchestral music as well as record and mix within a month. With time pressing and with the approval of the show's producers, the composer turned to orchestral samples. After he had already composed the score for the first two episodes while sitting in a studio in Seattle, Messina spotted most of the remaining episodes with the director, who was still in Ireland at that time. In spite of all his work and notwithstanding the looming deadline, Messina was uncertain that he would keep the job: "The very first episode was absolutely critical. If I hadn't passed the test with the director and the network I would have gotten the boot. I think when I turned in a solid theme that they liked and four ideas, I was safe."

To be able to finish his job in time, Messina surrounded himself with three orchestrators, an assistant who also acted as the score coordinator, programmers, engineers, and a music editor who provided a second opinion on the musical output. The pressure was on, and the producers made sure that Messina met their standards by giving feedback constantly throughout the remaining four weeks: "I always got notes for certain cues when I missed the tone that they wanted or when something had to be changed because of the special effects. I couldn't see all the effects. A lot of the pirate battles were still in front of a green screen." However, the feedback was surprisingly limited since the network was well aware of the fact that their composer "was up against it."

To the producers' credit, they abstained from their customary layer-by-layer-process but gave feedback all at once, since Messina had made it clear from the beginning that he would need the feedback within twelve hours after sending a cue for approval. Messina's three orchestrators proved necessary: each could only orchestrate one cue a day, while their employer would usually write three cues a day, if not more. Luckily for Messina, he was only sent a handful of temp tracks to serve as a guide, which he didn't have to copy note for note. He was thus able to write more freely and therefore more quickly.

Crossbones is an extreme example of the power structure in the film and television industry, but not the only one. In fact, one wouldn't have to look very hard to find similar cases where the composer was not only subjected to an especially tight deadline but also to a flood of notes from different layers of producers. Composers have always had to fight battles (creatively, financially and time-wise) with directors and producers. Said David Raksin in the late '70s:

> It should be news to no one that many people believe the industry has been plundered, ruined by incompetence, and left to twist slowly in the wind by men whose principal interests—whatever they be—do not lie in filmmaking. The disastrous unemployment resulting from this circumstance has become worse as film companies have made more and more pictures abroad. American composers find it difficult to believe that the use of foreign composers is not related to the fact that they work for less money. As to the remaining available jobs, they are further curtailed by the relegation of the film sound track to the humiliating status of an adjunct to the recording industry.[1]

There are countless stories from composers of what they see as the ruthlessness of studios they have had to deal with. This is not surprising, given that producers like to focus on the financial aspects of music production whereas composers prefer to concentrate on its creative aspects. This being the case, composers can fall into traps and damage both their financial and creative situation. This isn't new.

Happy Captives

One of the great advantages composers had in the Hollywood studio era was limited contact with producers. This seems ironic considering the fact that at that time it was the producers who really were in charge of the films while the director was the hired hand who left after the shoot, leaving his employer in charge of post-production. Composers usually reported back to the head of the music department, most of whom were composers first and foremost rather than businessmen simply keeping an eye on music budgets. People like Alfred Newman (at 20th Century–Fox) and John Green (Metro-Goldwyn-Mayer) understood the struggles of their colleagues and more often than not came to their defense when their music was subject to criticism. More than half of the film composers in the '40s were employees with studio contracts. Such composers could always be lent out to individual productions at other studios, often for considerable amounts of money.

Some composers consciously decided against signing a contract. Erich Wolfgang Korngold went on the record in 1940, saying: "So far, I have successfully resisted the temptations of an all-year contract because, in my opinion, that would force me into factory-like mass production."[2] It was a fear that was very much grounded in reality since heads of music departments would assign their composers to given films, regardless of how busy these composers already were. Declining the job was not an option, leading the composer and orchestrator Herbert Spencer to describe his peers and himself as "slaves": "We signed the usual seven-year-contract. It sounded big, but every year they could either pick it up or not. Those things are things of the past; you were really slaves. But I loved it because I could learn a lot about pictures."[3] Or, in the words of Miklós Rózsa: "We were captives, but for the most part happy and well-paid captives."[4]

Composers at that time had a lot on their plate. They were usually given four to six weeks to score a movie. While the copyright to their music belonged to the studio (much like today in most instances), they received a weekly paycheck—regardless of how much they worked. A composer waiting for a new project to arrive would receive his $300 a week anyway—the amount of money that was paid in the '40s at Metro-Goldwyn-Mayer—without writing a note for the studio. Max Steiner, on the other hand, received an annual paycheck when under contract at Warner Bros. for seven years which paid him the then handsome amount of $100,000. When his employer loaned him out to other studios, he could earn some extra money while most of his fee would be forwarded to Warner Bros. If the studio didn't agree to their composers leaving for a few weeks to work on a film for another studio, the composer had to decline or use a "front"—writing the music but giving the credit to a colleague.

A different yet in some respects similar case was the production *Up in Arms* which was supposed to be scored by Ray Heindorf, as explained by film music historian John Morgan. When Heindorf got in trouble, Max Steiner rushed to help and wrote nearly the whole underscore. But since the film was produced by MGM and Steiner was under contract at Warner Bros. at that time, he couldn't take screen credit. Cases like this still happen today, as demonstrated by *Pirates of the Caribbean*, which Hans Zimmer was approached to do. As it happened, Zimmer was working on *The Last Samurai* and couldn't take credit for the Johnny Depp vehicle, thus recommending his Remote Control colleague Klaus Badelt and other helping hands while Zimmer provided the main theme (as already heard in *Gladiator* and *Drop Zone*) and some additional cues.

When having to deal with several movies at once, it sometimes became necessary to spend the night in the studio. Composers often had to work around the clock to get the work finished in time, not only on cheaply and quickly produced B movies. Looking back on his career, Alfred Newman rather regretted the amount of time he had spent at 20th Century–Fox as a composer and head of the music department: "I sometimes think I was much overworked and perhaps a bit too timid to stand up for my rights. I've worked Christmas; I've worked the Fourth of July—in fact, I've worked when two of my children were being born and I should have been there in case anything went wrong."[5]

As demanding as the schedules were when working under the studio system, most composers who had learned their craft under these circumstances would later look back in fondness at the good old times when every department was on one studio lot and the craftspeople could learn from each other directly. Henry Mancini started working for Universal in the early '50s:

> I had the great fortune to spend a six-year-period, from 1952 to 1958, at Universal, and it was like an apprenticeship. It was six years of training in which I was required to do just about everything a film composer comes across in the course of his craft—arranging, adapting, orchestrating, using stock material, working fast, working against time and slim budgets, and generally functioning. It prepared me to face just about any assignment that would come up in the years ahead. Sad to say, that kind of training is almost impossible to get in the industry today.[6]

Moreover, since the orchestras were under contract at the studios as well, and therefore paid by the studio, the composer received his weekly, monthly or even annual paycheck as a writer's fee instead of having to worry about how much money he could afford to spend on an orchestral recording by paying for it out of his own pocket. According to music editor June Edgerton: "The whole world had a different spirit then. Everyone was in there to really do their jobs. Now everyone gripes if they have to do a little bit extra or something. But then you thought nothing of it. [...] There was much more spirit than I find now."[7] Now, composers sometimes do have to ask for a little extra.

Pinball

In the late 1960s, financial misfires such as *Cleopatra* and *Doctor Dolittle* played their parts in the collapse of the studio system. Producers were blamed for budgetary mismanagement and the status of directors changed accordingly. Composers began to be answerable to directors rather than producers, often without communicating with other departments as had been the case during the Studio Age. They were paid a writer's fee and worked their way through a project. A niche was created for composers' agents since composers were now booked on a project-by-project basis. With the decline of the New Hollywood era in the late '70s to early '80s, this model changed again. As mentioned, producers came back into power: directors like Peter Bogdanovich and Francis Ford Coppola had demonstrated, in the producer's view, that they could not be trusted with complete control. (Directors like Bogdanovich and Coppola were later lectured by Howard Hawks who reminded them: "The studio system worked because we couldn't be excessive, we couldn't just do what we wanted to do."[8])

Therefore producers became important again for composers as well. Even distributors like Miramax demanded to have a say in the process, at the time of the final cut at the very least. Thus composers were forced to report to several parties—directors, producers, distributors at the same time. Finding a common denominator that satisfies all parties is the ultimate challenge for any film composer.

Although Matthew Margeson wasn't active back in the '80s, and can therefore bathe in the golden light of nostalgia only from second-hand experience, he bemoans the fact that he is now dependent on multiple parties and a test audience:

> That's one of my big hangups about Hollywood these days. A lot of the time there is no single vision by the production itself. There is a director and maybe a film editor and maybe two producers and a financier and a test screening audience. It becomes filmmaking by committee, and I do believe that some of the art and the vision is lost when that happens. The editor or a visual effects supervisor can all help to get the job done but the vision has to remain a singular entity because otherwise there are too many cooks in the kitchen.

Creative input is not only unavoidable but often desirable. Klaus Badelt admits as much:

I really appreciate getting opinions—but I am insecure. There is no such thing as a bad idea. I learned from the biggest directors who listen the most. It's actually mostly the younger directors who listen the least to others. Maybe that's also because of insecurity and they think they need to prove themselves. I don't need to prove myself.

On the other hand, being exposed to a multitude of conflicting opinions soon creates a dilemma for composers. They not only see their creative vision diluted but are unsure about whose voice to follow. Carter Burwell explains:

Everything is done by committee. But I don't want to be working in that area. If I knew that that's what the film was going to be I would not work on that film. I can't work that way, honestly. It's inevitable in that situation that it will end up with people saying, "Here is something that always works. Let's just do that." There are many factors that push people in that direction in any part of this industry. It just makes your job easier if you go with the thing which you know works. It makes for uninteresting films, though.

The reason for the resurgence of the producers' role in the American film industry has an economic foundation. This is not surprising considering the amount of money a heavily-advertised blockbuster costs nowadays (from $200 million up to $400 million in the case of *Avatar*). These films have to be financed first, and few studios are willing to carry the financial burden and the associated risks alone. Instead, co-productions with other studios are made, sometimes with financing corporations which have little experience in the film world. Editor and sound designer Walter Murch reflects on this significant change that has occurred in the American landscape in the past 15 to 20 years:

What has happened in the last twenty years or so, because of the way films are financed, there are sometimes 15 or 16, sometimes 20 producers on a film because each of them has put in some money or was the person to be the conduit for money to come into the film. They almost always want to be heard and to have their opinions felt about the film as the various drafts are written, as the casting is done, as it's being shot, as it's being edited. It's a large number of voices to try to balance.

Rachel Portman laments the fact that she is now exposed to the opinions and feedback from more producers than she was twenty years ago:

If you are doing a film for HBO or a film like *A Dog's Purpose* there are producers coming in. There are many voices. They are wonderful people in that music supervisors try to get the comments from everyone and unify them to have one voice. They then tell you the comments. But you do get comments from many different places. For someone starting out who hasn't got that much experience in handling situations such as this I should think it would be horrendous now. If you don't have the experience you think, "I think I can find a thread through here." You have to think creatively in a different head-space about how to accommodate so many different styles.

However, independent productions can be just as difficult for a composer when it comes to dealing with a multitude of different opinions. It is, after all, much more difficult for an independently-produced film to break even, receive a few award nominations, or indeed just get noticed. Although there are fewer voices to be dealt with, they can just be as interfering, as Carter Burwell notes:

> I have worked on several of [Focus Features'] films and I and the directors I worked with found them just as intrusive in the process as any studio executives. [...] What you could say is that the larger the budget the more people are going to get involved and have opinions because everyone wants to make back the money that they had spent, which means they have to sell more tickets and make people go and see the movie. They are generally less interested in something that challenges the audience or makes the audience uncomfortable.

Preparation of Alternatives

Especially on a franchise helmed by different directors throughout the years, composers have to appease not only its directors and producers but increasingly often the marketing department as well. This is particularly true if the franchise has a fan base already. For example, the head of marketing might demand a more frequent use of the product's signature theme. But it can also go the other way around, because of personal preferences that have nothing to do with the franchise per se.

An example par excellence is Christopher McQuarrie's film *Mission: Impossible—Rogue Nation* from 2015. Joe Kraemer had incorporated Lalo Schifrin's well-known main theme for the '60s show in his new score, much to the liking of the film's star and producer, Tom Cruise. As it turned out though, the head of the marketing department at Paramount had an intense dislike for Schifrin's tune and wanted it removed from the film. Only because of Tom Cruise's insistence did the marketing head finally relent—but not without a small victory on his side: for the film's first trailer, Joe Kraemer wrote a piece based on Schifrin's famous melody and had it recorded at AIR Studios in London, accumulating a cost of $100,000 for the trailer music alone. To Kraemer's big surprise, only 20 seconds of his rather expensive arrangement were featured in the trailer—the rest consisted of a pop song and some purely electronic underscore.

The marketing department is heavily involved with setting up test screenings to make sure that the product will satisfy the market it was aimed at. The fallout from these can affect the composer if not directly, at least indirectly. As Carter Burwell explains when talking about test screenings:

> It's right around the time that the composer starts working on a film that they are typically testing the film. They edited the film, hired the composer, started doing previews and tested it. My indirect involvement is that the director, the producer or the studio will come to me and say, "The audience doesn't like this character." Or they will say, "The audiences don't like this character. They don't find her to be warm and we want her to be warm." Or, "The audience doesn't find this relationship is working." Or, "They don't understand this aspect of the story." I do get reports like that and it's one of the roles of the composer to pay respect to that because music is usually the last thing that happens with a film. Music is called upon to solve whatever problem the film has.

In a case like this, where not only the director but powerful executives need to be satisfied, it will take some effort on the composer's part to steer through a music production and deliver the goods. Alan Silvestri remembers spotting a film, initially with a director and later with three producers: four times in total with people who all turned out to be in disagreement with each other in terms of the placement, structure and style of the music. "At some point one has to take care of one's self, if you will," says Silvestri with a smile; he was able to solve the dilemma by spending a substantial amount of time on diplomacy. This involved setting up a conference call with all four interested parties to agree on a common approach. However, this was not possible.

Silvestri started writing and had his cues approved by the director. The composer recalls receiving a communication from the studio, informing him that there was "a problem" with one cue. The suggestion was made to sort it out with the director—much to the bafflement of Silvestri, since the director had already approved the cue and was indeed satisfied with the work his composer had come up with. It was the studio executive who "hated" this particular cue and wanted it removed—surgically, as quickly as possible. The studio executive was able to communicate his wishes and Silvestri set to work. His approach to solving the problem was simple: since the executive and the director disagreed vehemently and couldn't reach a compromise, Silvestri wrote a new cue based on what the executive had explained to him. "What are you going to do? I did both. This is not my battle, I am not going to be in the middle of a disagreement between the director and the studio executive," explains the composer who gave both of them what they had asked for, letting them figure out their problems with each other.

In extreme cases, preparing a few versions of one especially controversial cue is not enough. Marco Beltrami remembers,

> We had a film where the director and two studios were involved. Actually, it wasn't two studios but a studio and a production, but the production was

almost like a studio. They had very different ideas about what the movie was supposed to be. I knew I couldn't please both of them because they would never come to the studio at the same time. So, if I could get them in the room together we could say, "Let's talk about what you like and what you don't like." But they wouldn't come in the room at the same time.

Beltrami then decided it was easier to write two completely different scores which he set out and did. Not only that, but the composer recorded his two scores for one movie in two different studios with different musicians. The choice which cues to go for was up to the producers and the director, a decision-making process Beltrami didn't want to be involved in: "It was less work than going back and forth. It is easier to write a cue twice than it is to do it 14 times."

Being the servant of two masters can take its toll on the body and mind. It is not only the fact that a composer has to be able to work 15 hours—or even more—a day to be able to meet a deadline. There is also a lot of psychological stress involved. Such are the mental and physical demands of this high-intensity job, composers often fall ill with colds or flu after the job is finished until the stress finally ebbs away, and their adrenaline level slowly decreases. This is exacerbated by the fact that composers are more often than not insecure and highly sensitive creatures. Marco Beltrami admits as much when saying, "You have to have a big ego to take on the job, but you are also constantly insecure in order to search for new ideas. You can't really rest on, 'This is the way this has to be scored,' because then you are not growing. It's a constant battle between that."

Even more, the sustained stress to which composers are subjected can lead to long-term health problems. Beltrami continues:

> Most composers are anxious people to begin with. Everybody I know except a couple have pretty bad insomnia. Sitting at your desk for long hours at a time is not good for your body. Staring at screens doesn't make for the most healthy career, either. Somehow your body keeps you healthy while you have the stress but sometimes when the stress lets off you have a tendency to get sick.

Mychael Danna can certainly empathize with this, although practicing yoga has helped him overcome the pressure he faces daily:

> Stress is simply your reaction to events. It's not something that is imposed on you. […] I probably was wired to be an anxious person myself but through decades of pressure and stress I have managed to find philosophical ways to deal with it and be able to feel okay with it much of the time. On my worst, most nasty projects I used to read a series of books about the Vietnam War and books like *Behind the Lines*. I would read these terrifying tales and think, "My life is pretty good. Being a composer is actually not that bad." That helped me for a while. I do have a spiritual readings and things that do really help me in that way. I have been doing yoga for 30 years. Those things really do help.

In the best possible case, the director is powerful enough to act as a go-between for the producers and the composer by collecting notes from the former and deciding what to forward to the latter. When the director is not just a hired hand, staring into the loaded gun of the producer, this works reasonably well for the composer since a clearly hierarchical power structure has been established. This was the experience of Abel Korzeniowski who worked with Madonna on *W.E.* and Tom Ford on *A Single Man* and *Nocturnal Animals*. According to Korzeniowski, Madonna did everything to protect her work from the hands of producer Harvey Weinstein who had demanded certain changes which would have undermined the film's female perspective. Although Korzeniowki did receive feedback from the producer and listened politely, he ultimately served Madonna's vision which made for a straight-forward working process. In other cases, it can be producers who pull all the strings and whom the composer is ultimately working for. In most cases it doesn't take too long to figure this out.

A Bag of Money

Ultimately, it is the producers who negotiate the composer's payment. More often than not, composers working in films now receive a package deal instead of a weekly, monthly or total writer's fee. From their film's entire budget, the producers estimate a certain percentage for music. They negotiate with the composer's agent. The agency has its own interest in getting as much money for their client as possible. This can be tricky when a composer is offered a package deal, since at the negotiating stage there are still many unknowns involved. Abel Korzeniowski explains,

> A package deal is an unfair practice for a composer because agents usually negotiate the deal before a composer really knows how much score there is, even before the spotting session. No one knows how large the orchestra will be, how much score and how many sessions are needed. Oftentimes you may not yet know whether it can be a union project or if it has to be non-union. Then you would have to go to another country to record the score. It's a big unknown. [...] It's like saying, "Okay, you have this amount of money, but we won't tell you how much music you need to record."

Package deals have been in place since the 1980s and they have become more and more popular. It makes the job of any studio easier, after all. Bigger studios used to have a music department (and most of them still do) with the heads of the departments and their accountants taking care of budgeting and micro-managing the music production. It is an arduous process since the list of necessities that have to be paid for in the course of the music making and recording process is a long and fluctuating one. It is not only the composer's writing fee but also the orchestration, the copying, the music preparation in total, the cost of the recording studio, the recording itself, the various musicians, the mixing, mastering, and sometimes even the accommodations of the composer and his team when recording overseas. For the studios it is easier to decide on an amount of money for the composer and let him figure out how much to spend on which necessities.

The package deals, though, have steadily decreased since they first came into place in the '80s. When studios decided to pursue this practice, the studio's music department had a long history of paying for music production and therefore knew what amount was feasible to offer to the composer. One after the other, these experts retired and made way for a new generation of accountants who didn't have any experience in budgeting film scores. Music budgets shrank steadily. Composers now have to work with what they are given. That might not be a satisfying amount, considering the various parts of, and forces in, the music production process which have to be paid for with the package deal. Edwin Wendler summarizes,

> Package deals also include the money for mixing and mastering. It means I as the producer give you, the composer, our entire music budget with the exception of maybe songs that we are going to license. Everything that has to do with the instrumental underscore you have to take care of. "See you later!" That's how it goes. The composer then gets to keep whatever is left after paying for the music production costs. Depending on how ambitious the composer is he gets to keep a sizable portion of it or nothing at all.

Directors don't usually have much to say in these matters, but they can have an influence on how much money their composer will eventually receive. Since the music budget makes up a certain percentage of the total budget, a director can make a case for enhancing or reducing the proposed budget. This happened on a blockbuster production from 2015 whose title cannot be mentioned here. The director negotiated with his producers to reduce the music budget of this $150 million movie from $1.8 million to $1.5 million in order to liberate money for other elements of the film, such as special effects. Needless to say, composers will never learn about such behind-the-scenes negotiations.

While most of the big players at the studios are capable of acting as accountants when it comes to the music production process, it is a headache they can very well do without. They prefer to leave all necessary calculations to the composers and their team. Studios were inspired to do just that by smaller independent companies who relied on offering their composers package deals for years before their bigger classmates started this maneuver. "I even worked with package deals on a big studio film like *The Finest Hours,*" explains Carter Burwell.

That surprised me because it was produced by a big studio. They are perfectly capable of hiring musicians and a studio themselves. I guess they just decided that this is a financial model they want to follow. It's been true for ten years. It's been common in the independent film world for as long as I have been there because there is no studio that knows anything about hiring musicians or working with a musician's union. They just don't have that knowledge.

This is not unexpected, considering the fact that oftentimes independent studios are put together for the purpose of releasing one film before dissolving again, leaving little room for the filmmakers to acquire an in-depth knowledge of music production processes and budgeting. Before package deals were a common procedure in the industry, composers had good reasons to agree to them, sometimes even offering them to studios in the first place. A composer could negotiate a package deal of $1 million, decide to record the music in a cost-efficient venue overseas, save money by replacing live musicians with some samples and electronic elements and thereby keep a substantial amount of the package for themselves without ever telling the studio how much the actual music production cost. This started to backfire quickly, though, as soon as the studios learned about these cheap tricks. Consequently, studios started to lower the amount for package deals since they were—rightly—convinced that their composer could record the music for less money. But while budgets have shrunk, demands haven't.

As Abel Korzeniowski indicated above, the problems start with the unknown factors involved when negotiating a package deal. A composer is therefore well-advised to limit the unknowns early on and budget strictly and carefully. Korzeniowski continues, "Part of success here in Hollywood is preparing for the recording session. It doesn't only mean budgeting, it also means scheduling enough time for different things, anticipating overtime and giving yourself room for mistakes. You have to work in a very specific order."

Budgeting as efficiently as possible is a challenging task since many aspects of the music production process remain unknown until shortly before the actual recording. This involves the money that has to be put aside for music preparation since the calculation a responsible company offers depends on the size of the orchestra and the complexity of the music. Composers are unlikely to know any such details when they agree to join the production. Nor will they be certain of them during the process of creating demos for the producers and director. Possible re-arrangements and re-orchestrations will have to be made, sometimes shortly before recording, making it necessary to spend more money on the music preparation than originally envisioned.

An experienced composer might expect extensive changes to occur late in the process and be able to calculate how much these are likely to cost. For these reasons, it is in the best interest of composers to do the budgeting themselves instead of relying on accountants, as Marco Beltrami explains:

I try to be on top of it myself, to know what's going on. I'll send out the budgets from everybody. You get budgets from all the different departments that are involved, the orchestration and music preparation, the copying. You estimate that. I always try to pad it a little bit in case it goes over. You have to figure out that type of stuff. Sometimes schedules get pushed. Just figuring that out isn't that hard. When schedules get pushed, when they are making edits, when things change, when you have to re-orchestrate your music, then it gets tricky. I always try to get some help from my agents. They are pretty good at that. I then try to work through that.

It is also worth noting that composers as creative forces are not necessarily keen on accounting. Not only do they have to have experience in the industry to estimate how much money to put aside, but they also have to be good with numbers in general to avoid any miscalculations, let alone the fact that doing the budgeting themselves eats up a lot of the time they need to write and deliver the music on time. Matthew Margeson admits,

I dislike package deals. For the sole reason that now there is a percentage of my brain that is not just thinking about music. I have to double click on a Microsoft Excel file, I have to do phone calls and a lot of hiring and negotiating. There is a lot of energy wasted on more administrative things instead of just writing the music and having someone else worrying about all of that. I think it's a bad thing if it limits your creativity.

Carter Burwell agrees:

What makes a package deal difficult is that I have a tremendous amount of logistical work to do. As I am writing the music I also have to figure out how many musicians we need and how many sessions with these different musicians. I have to ask myself, "Do I really need an oboe player for that session?" I am trying to save money by scheduling it. In a studio they would have someone with a spread sheet who does that all day long, but in a package deal I have to do that myself. I have to figure out how to book the musicians most efficiently, and how many sessions we need. You are going to travel sometimes. Sometimes I have to pay for my engineer to get to London. It's very time consuming when I'd rather be writing music. The bigger the project is the more time consuming it is. If there is 90 minutes of music it is going to be three times as time-consuming to plan as it is with 30 minutes of music.

Nasty surprises can occur when producers and directors keep demanding changes to the music, come up with new ideas for the orchestration, or make a new arrangement necessary if the cut changes, as it does frequently these days. Decisions like these can quickly spiral out of control by messing up the composer's calculations and budgeting. In the end, music preparation and recording might cost more than originally planned, requiring the composer to spend money intended to be kept as part of the writing fee. More often than not, changes that come up during the music production process have already been included in the contract made between studio and composer as the basis of the package deal, making it impossible for a composer to argue for an increase in the music budget. It is therefore the composer who carries the risk if something unexpected happens that wasn't agreed upon or indicated.

That doesn't mean that renegotiation is impossible. Depending on the contract in place, the skills of the composer's agent as a negotiator, and the changes that a film score has to undergo during the music production process, the studio can in special circumstances allow for an increase in the package deal after the contract is signed. The most obvious reason for a successful renegotiation is if the whole concept of the score changes by becoming a symphonic venture instead of a chamber music recording. If the music production has to be moved to a different location—because of scheduling conflicts, for example—the studio would cover the additional costs, including flights and accommodations for the composer and any crew that needs to be at the recording. If the composer, however, miscalculated the cost of the actual recording, negotiating for more money is a hopeless undertaking, as Marco Beltrami explains:

> Renegotiating can be tough. The times where it works is if the film they are asking you to do has something that wasn't originally there. Let's say, for instance, they have gone back in and done re-shoots, so your workload has changed significantly. Then the contract is different. But if it is a case of you saying, "I totally misjudged and misfigured it, can I get some more money," that usually doesn't fly.

If a renegotiation is out of the question, composers often have to fight with themselves about how much money to spend on the music recording instead of fighting with the music department as was the case before package deals came into place. Working with a package deal can result in a clash between the composer's creative vision on the one hand and the need to stay solvent on the other. Joe Kraemer describes such a clash:

> I did one film with a package deal and I barely broke even, let alone made any money with it. I think it changes the criterion behind which you make certain decisions that you shouldn't have to do. Let's say you have a take and you are recording, you are paying for everything yourself. You have to get × amount of music done and you are so worried about your own budget that you are sacrificing the time to make the movie better. In a sense you are punished for wanting to make the movie better. When you divorce the fee from all that stuff it's better for the movie as an artistic venture. Is it better for the movie as a business venture or a commercial venture? I don't know. But it's nothing that a composer should have to deal with. [...] You don't want to be in a situation where the composer is happy with the take but the director is saying, "Do another take," and the composer is saying, "Dude, that's my money you are

spending." I would do whatever I can to figure out how to protect the film as much as myself.

It is worth noting that budgets not only can increase during the music production process, but also decrease during the composing process. The latter situation may cause the composer severe financial problems, if they have agreed to the score's concept and, regardless of the changing financial situation, are expected to realize it. One composer who experienced this dilemma was Brian Tyler when he was scoring *The Expendables*. According to James Fitzpatrick, contractor for the City of Prague Philharmonic, Tyler had scheduled six recording sessions in Prague for his score. Only two days before the scheduled recording, the composer had to call up Fitzpatrick and reduce the sessions from six to four because his music budget had been cut. The same amount of music still had to be recorded, but in much less time than originally anticipated.

Executing a contract can often take weeks or even months and is often due to the involved bureaucracy. Understandably, composers are hesitant to wait for the finished contract to arrive before they start composing since it eats up a lot of their precious time and reduces the amount of time they have in which to compose the score. In that case, they have to rely on the deal memo, or the oral agreement that they made with the film studio or the responsible music department.

Everything for Nothing

Before composers receive anything for their work, though—be it a package deal or a hot meal—they have to sign a contract. More often than not, they are expected to work for hire. So-called "work for hire" agreements are signed between the composers and the responsible studio. A composer working for hire gives all the rights in his music to the production company which can then exploit the music in whatever way it chooses. However, the composer by law is entitled to a writer's share which makes up 50 percent of the publishing pie (the other 50 percent of the pie, the actual publishing, goes to the production company via performing rights organizations [PROs] such as ASCAP and BMI). Depending on the success of the film and the exploitation of the music, the writer's share can be worth more than the actual payment to the composer in the form of royalties.

For production companies, it is important to own the publishing rights to the music in order to have the freedom they need to market and distribute the film. A film can only be distributed if its music rights are cleared. According to Edwin Wendler,

The employer, meaning the production company, has the rights to the music and can do with it whatever he or she wants. Sometimes it comes with sync and master agreements, sometimes it doesn't. That in general is the structure of how contracts are being done now.

To ensure that composers receive royalties they are well advised to check the cue sheet that will go to the respective PRO. Otherwise they run the risk of not receiving any royalties. Marco Beltrami remembers:

The music supervisor put his name on the cue sheet instead of mine. First of all, they said they don't have the money for the movie. I then paid for the recording and said, "If the movie does well, let's make the agreement that you pay me back on that." It was an important movie for me and I really wanted it to be successful. The music supervisor agreed to that and later said he had never said that in the first place. Then I was wondering why I never saw any royalties from the project. Then I checked and he had put his name on the cue sheet. He was fired and sued by the company. I don't know what he is doing now. Those things happen now and again, I guess.

Composers working in the U.S. film industry rarely own 100 percent of the publishing rights in their scores. However, composers working on small-budget movies can negotiate for a percentage of those rights as compensation for the possibly nonexistent fee. In the past few years such opportunities have decreased in number, as Edwin Wendler confirms:

It used to be the case that for low-budget and independent movies the composer would either keep all of the publishing [income] or a sizeable portion like 50 percent. That seems to be less and less the case now. Even on small indie movies where the upfront payment is relatively small, the composer then also loses a big chunk or even all of the publishing.

Occasionally a composer writes a film score for next to nothing in exchange for enhanced publishing rights. Since music budgets have decreased steadily in the past few years (except on blockbusters featuring superheroes and animated animals) composers can face the uncomfortable situation of being offered a minimal music budget which might allow for the recording of a chamber ensemble, leaving nothing for the composers themselves. Such projects are not necessarily undesirable. Composers who are usually hired for the big blockbusters of their day might want to seek some diversity and engage in the music production of a smaller film that triggers their imagination. Although these films can't pay the composer the money he is used to earning when working on blockbusters, there are compromises for both sides, though, which can make a collaboration possible.

Danny Elfman went on record to confess: "I would say that I own the rights to maybe 5 percent of what I've written. Every year, I try to do at least one $1 film. On those films, I do own the publishing. Obviously, if they're only paying me a dollar I gotta get something."[9] Similarly, Hans Zimmer agreed to score Werner Herzog's *Invincible* for $1. And so it goes: if the music budget is especially low, the composer tries to retain all the rights to the music—meaning 100 percent of the publishing income instead of only the writer's share as is usual in the industry.

The income the composer generates then comes from royalties through the usual sources and—depending on how successful the movie is and how successfully the music can be exploited—the composer can make a substantial amount of money in the long run to make the job worth it financially after all. To get to that point can be difficult, though, since smaller production companies which dissolve after their (independent) movie has been produced often have little knowledge of publishing and are insecure about setting up the contract with the composer accordingly, as Edwin Wendler explains:

> That leads to very strange scenarios where the producer's attorney convinces the producer that they must keep at least a portion if not all of the publishing but the producer doesn't even know what that means. They don't even know what publishing is, they don't know what performance rights organizations are. In some cases when it comes to writing the cue sheet, the composer is then faced with the challenge of, "How do I fill out the cue sheet if the producer doesn't even have a music publishing company?" The composer then has to help the producer set up a publishing company and get it registered.

Even if the composer was successful in negotiating with the production company to retain the publishing, it doesn't automatically mean that he or she will be successful in exploiting the music and therefore generate money with it. How much money can be made if the composer owns the publishing rights depends on the size and success of the film and how talented the composer is at advertising their music. Negotiating to keep the publishing rights is the first step, but it doesn't end there, as Abel Korzeniowski explains:

> If a deal is too small, we usually try to keep the publishing. Sometimes we even keep the master rights to the recordings. It's one way of doing it. This is all assuming that you can actually make money on licensing later, which may work. It may not work. You may end up with just the ownership of your music. It doesn't necessarily mean it will become popular for licensing. Nonetheless, it's important to understand the potential value of your music if your producers tell you that they have very little money but that they are also not willing to let you keep the publishing. It's not right. The value that they would acquire is theoretically much larger than what they pay for. Eventually it diminishes the value of what we do. You just have to understand that if they don't hire a composer, they will license music. That way, they end up paying more than if they had hired a composer to record new music.

And that is damaging to the whole industry.

When composers own the full publishing as well as the master rights the royalties they receive can be substantial. Moreover, they can be multiplied by, for example, selling the score to libraries for use in commercials, trailers and so on. But in order to maximize their income from such sources, composers need to spend time and effort on marketing their work. It is much easier to sell music for a successful franchise than it is to place music for financial and critical flops in commercials or trailers. This way, composers are very much like gamblers when they agree to write music for a film in exchange for the full publishing rights. They have no way of knowing how successful the film is going to be. Therefore they have no idea how much money their music will make eventually. Not even an established composer like Carter Burwell is comfortable making such a prediction:

> There is a pattern. The pattern is that I have no idea whether the film is going to be successful. I have no clue. When I watched the playback of *No Country for Old Men* for the first time from beginning to end in a while—and I had seen the film a hundred times already—I said to Joel [Coen] sarcastically, "Well that's a real crowd pleaser. Every character we cared about is dead. The only character who is still alive is the bad guy." It was a complete surprise to me that this movie was successful. It is of course a wonderfully made film—but I have worked on a lot of wonderfully made films that didn't do well at the box office.

John Ottman complains: "The crazy thing about that is, why should the composer be the one person who is taking the gamble on that movie by doing it for nothing upfront and hoping the movie makes a lot of money whereas every one else is being paid?"

On Cutting Edge

Naturally, composers can only keep the publishing rights if they haven't already been sold to a third party. One such particularly big player in the market is Cutting Edge Group. Cutting Edge finances film score recordings in exchange for master rights and publishing. It is not an uncontroversial company among composers, with some musicians calling it the "vile devil" (John Ottman) at the worst, or some saying "I have heard complaints from other composers about them" (Marco Beltrami) at the most favorable. Its bad reputation among composers can be boiled down to two reasons: they pride themselves in working not for composers but instead for producers and directors—and the interests of producers/directors are not necessarily in line with the interests of composers. The second reason is that when Cutting Edge first entered the market the company showed little understanding of the sensitivities within the creative industries, as composer-agent Darrell Alexander of

Cool Music Ltd. puts it: "They rather brazenly went in and changed the business because they had lots of money. They didn't do it slowly, they did it with great force and everybody was taken aback by their style. It's not a property business, it's an artistic business."

Indeed, composers have had a hard time trusting the company. Mychael Danna worked with Cutting Edge on two films that were directed by his long-term friend and collaborator Atom Egoyan (*The Devil's Knot* and *Remember*), and neither were exactly happy experiences:

> They are business people. They are not artists. Motion pictures and television clearly are a combination of art and business. It's always been that and it always will be. That's understood, and that's actually a healthy thing. When the balance goes way out of whack you have a situation where the decisions regarding the music are all about money now. They are all money decisions. There is no question that this has negatively impacted the effectiveness and quality of music in media.

Cutting Edge's CEO, Philip Moross, has a rather colorful history as a businessman. Before he co-founded Cutting Edge, he trained as an auditor and then served as chairman of a real estate development business which specialized in the refurbishment and development of luxury residential projects in London before it started undertaking works on large-scale hotels and leisure projects in Switzerland. Moross then entered the clothing business which saw him swapping client endorsements (by the likes of Jason Statham and Denise Van Outen) to retailers. In return, he received catalog space for his own company that manufactured clothes in India.

Cutting Edge is a hedge fund company, financed by several big firms which have nothing to do with film music per se and have only marginally to do with the creative industries as a whole. In 2008, Cutting Edge raised a $15 million fund, "backed by [...] Aberdeen Asset Management,"[10] an investment giant "serving institutional investors such as insurance companies, pension funds, treasuries, banks, sovereign wealth funds, family offices and foundations."[11] Cutting Edge also raised $13 million in 2008 from Bramdean Asset Management, an investment company which entrusted $21 million of clients' money to Bernie Madoff, a fatal decision that its manager Nicola Horlick blamed on the "systemic failure of the regulatory and securities markets regime in the U.S."[12] Furthermore, Cutting Edge was able to raise £2 million from Octopus Investments, which focuses mainly on technology, energy management and gym chains.

In 2012, Cutting Edge received a substantial investment from Wood Creek Capital Management after they had been in discussions with ICE Capital which counts Museum Masters Intl. as one of their clients, a company which handles the estates of Andy Warhol, Keith Haring and Pablo Picasso.[13] The talks with ICE Capital about funding amounted to nothing, but two years later, one of ICE Capital's co-founders and managing directors, Darren Blumenthal, entered Cutting Edge's business directly by starting to work as a director and as the managing partner in Cutting Edge's asset management division, Conduct.[14] Conduct is Cutting Edge Group's own "value-oriented private equity investor. It deploys capital on behalf of its investors, which include world-class pension funds, hedge funds, and other institutional and individual investors."[15]

Conduct is only one of 21 subsidiaries of Cutting Edge Group, two of which (Resonant Music General Partners and Resonant Music (1) Limited Partnership) are located in everyone's favorite holiday resort, the Cayman Islands, as stated in the company's accounts made up to June 30, 2016. Resonant Music (1) Limited Partnership is a music publisher that published—among others—Lorne Balfe's *Ironclad*, Christian Henson's *Black Death*, and Alex Heffes' *The First Grader*. Resonant Music (1) Limited Partnership (with a fair value of £7.4 million on June 30, 2016[16]) was co-structured and raised by Sturges J. Karban, the chief executive officer and board member of none other than MIJC, the Marijuana International Corporation,[17] a cannabis distribution and compliance company situated in California. Karban worked for Cutting Edge Music Services as director and also structured 3AM Music Limited, 4AM Music Limited as well as 5AM Music Limited and Starr Score Holdings, LLC—all of which are now subsidiaries of Cutting Edge Group.

Starr Score Holdings, LLC holds the phonographic copyrights to scores such as John Ottman's *Non-Stop*, Carter Burwell's *Carol* and Marco Beltrami's *The November Man*. Although Marco Beltrami is right that he never dealt with Cutting Edge directly, his music is owned by a subsidiary of the company—it's all rather "murky," as Darrell Alexander puts it. Also, Beltrami's score for *The Woman in Black* is owned by none other than Resonant Music, as is Alexandre Desplat's *The King's Speech*. 3AM Music Limited owns £3 million worth in music copyrights (as of June 30, 2015) and is not only related to Cutting Edge—which consists of Cutting Edge Music (Holding) Limited, Cutting Edge Music Services LLC, Cutting Edge Music Services Limited and Clearscore Music Limited—but also to Octopus Investments (which invested in the company) which charged the management fees, the monitoring fees, part of the consultancy fees and the legal fees and is therefore a debtor of 3AM Music Limited.[18]

Cutting Edge was also lucky enough to team up with Wood Creek Capital Management in 2013 to buy the renowned film music label Varèse Sarabande. As was reported at the time of the acquisition, Cutting Edge was now managing a combined $100 million of third party funds.[19]

Mychael Danna explains why composers have had a hard time trusting Cutting Edge with their music: "If I administer the publishing then I know what's going on. If it's someone else I have less trust. Let's assume they cease to exist in two years. They will then sell that company to someone else. You look at that situation and decide, 'It's not worth it.'" The same fear is shared by Darrell Alexander who explains,

> The worry is that the rights have been controlled by Cutting Edge at that moment—but give it a few more years and they will be controlled by another massive giant. I am sure they will want to sell them to Universal or BMG and they will get lost in the millions and millions of copyrights out there. The administration of copyrights is all over the place. We work in publishing all the time and we see from all these publishers what a mess all this is, what an absolute mess publishing is.

It was exactly this that made Philip Moross go into the film music business. As he elaborates, "You have the master recording industry, you have the publishing industry and you have two forms of copyright. There is a lot of leakage where revenue goes into different pots which is unaccounted. It is a black box." Cutting Edge's goal is to track what the company is entitled to without any such leakage mentioned before. Based on a number of different assumptions, the company identifies what it is entitled to and collects the appropriate royalties through PROs (royalty collecting societies) or other administrators. Part of this money is then forwarded to composers—since they own the writer's share in their works—while the remainder stays at Cutting Edge (the publisher). "My main motivation," emphasizes Moross, "is to ensure that those who are entitled to revenues see the revenues: the composers, the publishers and the producers—if there are any on the record."

This is only one of the business procedures that keep the company's employees busy. Usually, a producer contacts Cutting Edge to act as music supervisor and/or financier. If there are insufficient funds with which to hire a composer, Cutting Edge will invest in the production in exchange for the publishing and master rights to the film's score. In such a case, the deal with the production company is already struck before the composer gets involved. In other cases (when the company is not involved as financier and/or supervisor), Cutting Edge buys the publishing rights from composers after they complete the film. Cutting Edge then exploits the music by putting it in its library and trying to sell tracks to other companies for trailers or commercials.

Having made its first big splash in the first years of the 2010s by investing around $100 million in, for example, buying the established soundtrack label Varèse Sarabande, it started to pursue more and more composers to get them to sell their publishing. It also started acting as music supervisors on projects, which saw it working much more closely with film studios in the post-production process. John Ottman blames Cutting Edge for diminishing fees and package deals in the industry. Cutting Edge is now managing music production for Joel Silver with whom Ottman has enjoyed a close working-relationship. However, "they handle everything: they negotiate the deals with the composers, they budget the scores. But it is in their interest to pay the composer as little as possible and to spend as little as possible on the score because it's a money maker for them. My fees for Joel Silver films used to be three times what they were when Cutting Edge came in."

Mychael Danna had the same experience when working on *The Devil's Knot* and *Remember*, as he explains:

> Suddenly they will take the music budget, and what's left over is one quarter of what it started with. There will be $20,000 to do a score. Those films are generally impossible to work on in my experience. I worked on two films for the director I have worked with all my life, Atom Egoyan. Believe me, I was extremely unhappy. If it wasn't Atom Egoyan I would not have done those films. I have had that experience. There is nothing that I have seen that makes me want to repeat that experience.

The amount of money Cutting Edge gives for music budgets depends, of course, on the film. It would be in Cutting Edge's interest, though, to finance film scores properly for their library usage. For a budget of $10,000, clients can hardly expect to receive a high-end product in the form of an elegant film score that can be placed successfully in expensive commercials or trailers. But when composers work on low-budget films, Cutting Edge's investment can be dizzyingly small, as Darrell Alexander confirms: "They give $20–40,000. It's nothing. You are talking about very little money here." It would be too easy, though, to blame this development on Cutting Edge alone. Producers also bear some responsibility. Instead of topping up their existing music budgets with Cutting Edge's funds, production companies and producers simply cut the music budget to spend on other requirements.

Previously, Cutting Edge also had to face the fact that not all the money it gave to producers for the music was used solely for that purpose. For example, production companies redirected the investment to their special effects department. At least this was the case before Cutting Edge got wind of that strategy and changed their contracts, as Moross makes clear:

> In large cases we will pay the composer directly to make sure the money goes to the composer directly. We did have earlier on in our time that people would take six figures from us and spent ten percent of that on the composer. You then turn around and say, "Okay, we are not doing that," because the quality is compromised. You can't pay someone $10,000 and get the value of $100,000. It doesn't work like that. That was four or five years ago. We learned that that was happening on smaller films.

As mentioned, if it turns out that a production company is not able to hire a composer to write new music since the budget is too low, Cutting Edge offers to act as a music supervisor. It encourages the production company to license already existing pieces from its library, which includes between 400 and 450 scores (as of August 2017). Oftentimes composers don't have the time or connections to place their music in a library or an advertisement to generate income with it. As established above, composers and their teams are so busy acquiring new work, writing, orchestrating, mocking-up, conducting and recording, they have precious little time left to serve as their own publishers. Placing that work in the hands of a company which specializes in doing exactly that can have its very own benefits. For Cutting Edge, selling pre-existing music is a risk-free business. After all, it has the time and resources to turn the music it owns into pure gold by placing it in trailers or commercials. Even if a film flops, Cutting Edge will make its investment back, although it will take longer than with successful films.

By owning the publishing and the master rights, Cutting Edge is entitled to do with the music whatever it pleases. This doesn't necessarily please the composer, let alone the director, as music editor Gerard McCann recounts:

> I have one particular film in mind. Years later the director said to me, "They were using my music in a commercial." It was music that was well received. I said, "Well, it's not your music." "What do you mean?" "You spent all the music money on the set, so you did a deal with the devil. You got your composer, the orchestra and the music for your film and that's the end of the story. It is now owned by them. They can do with that what they want."

In order to do with the music what Cutting Edge wants, it helps to be able to re-mix it. McCann continues:

> If they pay for a score, they will determine things like stemming and mixing because it's their entity. They don't want a tutti recording. They get stems and then they can do with it what they want. They can put short clips in their music library, 40 or 60 second clips, which are designed like most libraries to work with advertisements. They can say, "This cue would work much better with an electronic beat," so they are taking the film score but are adding their own hip-hop beat because they can get all the elements and strip them out to do something new. That's where the value of that music is to them. They get library music at a reasonable rate that somebody else promotes, which is the film company. It's library music that has a higher commercial value. It won't sell for more, it is done for library rates, but it will get more exposure and attention. So it will get more use and they will get more money. That's what they like. They like the idea of having a film score and then the tune is on 20 different commercials over the next six months. They thought it through.

It is a business practice Cutting Edge is reasonably proud of, with Moross saying: "Recently we were using the music for *Sicario* by putting in some electronic effects and layering it. Music from some of these films has been on five or six trailers this year already, meaning these were five or six scores layered atop of each other. We do that. The composer gets a fee." Moross insists on respecting the composer's wishes by abstaining from re-recording and re-mixing if the composer openly (and loudly) opposes such practices. The persuasive argument that is used with composers when trying to get their music recorded in stems in order to re-mix and use it in commercials or even other feature films later on is that the cash flows into the composer's bank account without the composer having to do any extra work for it. As Moross puts it,

> In our catalog we have a significant proportion of the best composers in the world. We have a number of scores by Rachel Portman. If you want a Rachel Portman score just use our music and act to it. Rachel Portman is not going to mind because she is going to earn from the usage. The director shouldn't mind because he wants a Rachel Portman score.

As it turns out, Rachel Portman does mind. When confronted with Cutting Edge's business practices (the company owns her music to *Their Finest* and *Belle*), Portman is surprised:

> Cutting Edge are using what used to be the composer's publisher's share for the recording. It's a very sad development. I think music is undervalued when you think about what music adds and how important it is. The fact that it's become quite acceptable and normal to not keep any publishing at all or only very little is sad. Cutting Edge owns the publishing of *Their Finest*. They are making money out of it. Really, it's the kind of thing that would have been shocking ten years ago but gradually composers are beginning to accept worse and worse deals. It's totally changed.

In Portman's case, the music is not as easily usable for commercials and the like since the composer insists on recording the sections of the orchestra together as opposed to stemming—which might be the reason why she has never seen a check from Cutting Edge in the first place: "I don't think any of my cues that they own has been used in a commercial. [...] I don't think I ever had one check from them. That's bizarre. It's pretty interesting. Where would that income stream come from? Do I get a check from them? [...] I will ask Darrell [Alexander, agent] about it."

Rachel Portman is not alone with her impression that the revenue composers receive for the use of their music in secondary sources amounts to next to nothing. Darrell Alexander confirms his client's suspicions:

> Yes, [Rachel] would get the royalties from PRS. You have to understand: in ten, fifteen years of quite a few Cutting Edge deals I don't think I have ever seen one reuse of any bit of music from my clients. I think that sums it up. They confidently claim to successfully place music on the secondary market— and I am sure they have, but I have never seen any, certainly not on a commercial. [...] The trailer and library market is saturated.

According to Mychael Danna:

> If what Cutting Edge said was true then people would be lining up to work on films that have Cutting Edge involved. That is absolutely not the case. If what Cutting Edge says was true, composers would be talking to each other, saying, "Hey, you should get on a Cutting Edge film because I just got a check for $100,000 for a commercial that they sold." I haven't heard that talk. If I did, then I would change my tune, but I just don't see it.

Cutting Edge's job is further complicated by the fact that musicians in Los Angeles, New York and London are unionized. They receive residuals when music they have recorded is used in a commercial. For Cutting Edge, this proves to be a major issue, as Philip Moross admits: "The majority of the time you can't use the music because the advertising agency doesn't have the budget to pay the musicians and the licensee." For this reason alone, Cutting Edge prefers to record with ensembles that are not unionized. Moross emphasizes this is not a blanket rule—if a composer insists on union musicians, they will be provided. In that case, Moross's chances of seeing revenues from secondary usage are understandably slimmer.

Cutting Edge can make a substantial amount of money with master rights and 100 percent publishing rights, but these are not always available if they are owned by a big studio. In this case, Cutting Edge's agenda is to make composers give up at least a part of their writer's share. That way, Cutting Edge can expand its business and generate income with secondary usage of the composers' works. Philip Moross admits as much:

> There is one big composer in America right now. We want to buy his writer's share because he has already sold the publishing. We want to buy 50 percent of his writer's share. The reason is he doesn't own any publishing, the studio does. […] We have the ability to exploit it. We can say, "We will give it to Jay-Z to place it in one of his songs."

Until Cutting Edge came along, the writer's share was sacrosanct in the industry. It has always been a source of further income for composers, a sort of retirement fund. It is not illegal to sell it, but to do so is frowned upon.

Alexander's fear is that Cutting Edge is collecting copyrights in order to sell them for a profit further down the line. This would be every composer's nightmare. As Mychael Danna pointed out, he already has a hard time entrusting a large hedge fund company with his music. Philip Moross has a different take on his company's financial value and overall possibilities:

> One of the financial people who looked after the evaluation for us discovered that in his data bank there were three or four different catalogs that did similar things to what we do—but we collect up to two-and-a-half to three times more than the others, just because of our registration process and our ability to keep a very detailed approach to it. It's very efficient. That's for the composer. It's about understanding

that our world is not only about creative competence but about understanding how you can maximize the value by being diligent.

As part of their diligence, Cutting Edge acquired Varèse Sarabande in 2013. It was founded in 1978 and quickly built its reputation as the leading film music label. Says Philip Moross: "It's a very good tool for us with composers because we can put soundtracks out that others might not. It's not an expensive business for us to run and it makes good money for us. We want to expand and grow that business as long as we can. We like it. It's a full integration."

A substantial number of scores that Cutting Edge have financed therefore have made their way to CDs issued by Varèse Sarabande (*Their Finest* and *Belle* by Rachel Portman among them). As if to confirm Darrell Alexander's fear of Cutting Edge selling off assets for profit, in early 2018, Varèse Sarabande was sold to Concord Music with which Cutting Edge also managed to sign a multi-year distribution and services agreement. Concord now covers Cutting Edge's existing catalog of soundtracks. This new partnerships works nicely for Moross. However, he still has problems winning the trust of composers and their agents. Mychael Danna says: "If you talk to agents, they roll their eyes. If there is a film that is a Cutting Edge film, my agent will say, 'It's a Cutting Edge film. Next!' They write them off." Darrell Alexander supports this: "Sometimes I told producers, 'We don't want to work with Cutting Edge on this.'" It wasn't worth his while.

Lieutenant Gadget

A fire: what is remarkable about that? If a fire goes out, you strike a match and start another one. That is how I used to think. Yet in the olden days people worshipped fire. They thought twice before letting a flame die, a flame-god.—J.M. Coetzee, *Disgrace*

Before the door even opened I was greeted with a Spanish name and how great it was that I was finally here. Then the wooden door swung open. Aggie Murch looked slightly baffled to see me standing there, a pale young man in a red blazer who looked neither Spanish nor especially comfortable in the warmth of the London spring. After her realization that I was not the cleaning lady after all, I timidly informed Walter Murch's wife that I had an appointment with her husband. Obviously, she was not aware of any meeting that was supposed to take place in their cozy little flat in the north of the Big Smoke, but she nevertheless kindly invited me inside to inquire if I really did have an appointment or if I was simply a film nerd who had decided to stalk her loved one on this sunny day in early 2017.

As it turned out, my story was backed up by Walter Murch himself who appeared from the back room in a thick brown leather jacket. We shook hands, we wandered into the upstairs room, we sat down at a wooden table. Walter Murch poured me a glass of tap water. We could begin. With Walter Murch, it is best to jump directly into deep conversations on the subject of art—any art, really—in order to avoid awkward silences and gaps between thoughts and sentences. Small talk is best avoided.

Indeed, what a fascinating man to talk and—more importantly—listen to. He had agreed to be interviewed by me and now here we sat at his wooden table. Alas, the man who has been responsible for the sound and silence of well-known motion pictures couldn't get any peace, as silence proved to be impossibly hard to come by. Shortly after we began, the cleaning lady arrived, albeit a little late, and ventured into the upstairs room to hoover the floor. Murch decided to venture outside on the small terrace to resume our interview there. Two minutes later, a neighbor started working with an electric hedge trimmer. We were surrounded by noise. Was it okay for Walter Murch?

He found it hard to concentrate, fell into silence, looked at the floor, deep in thought. Finally, he suggested we walk into the park nearby to be, ironically, undisturbed by the noise of the neighborhood. We took our drinks and went. The sun was shining brightly, it was way too warm for me in a light turtle-neck sweater and blazer, and I was wondering how it felt for Walter Murch in his turtle-neck and leather jacket. We sat down on a bench, and were quickly surrounded by airplane noise and screaming children. Murch smiled and waved at the latter to calm them down. We talked about silence.

But we also talked about technology. Murch, who has always moved with the times, was one of the first editors to embrace digital editing and to make full use of it. He is technologically well versed without succumbing to the temptation of overusing digital technology. This sets him apart from many in the film industry. Ironically, we human beings have the tendency to misuse and abuse the newest technologies by not accepting any boundaries, regardless of the consequences for our species and professions. Take digital editing, a wonderful development that has enabled editors to work more quickly and with more freedom by being able to change scenes and shots with the press of a button. It has also enabled producers and directors to have their films changed right up to the day of the print master, increasing pressure on their composers who more often than not now have to change their music constantly during post-production.

Mock-ups are another example of the easy abuse of technology: composers can now present their individual cues to the director and producer before the actual recording. It is a great security for them since there are likely to be fewer surprises for their employers at the orchestral recording. But is that really the case? Instead of taking the mock-ups as a rough guide for the director to understand the themes and melodies, composers take great pains in elaborately crafting these demos by making them sound as natural—and live—as possible. This not only eats up an excessive amount of their time, but also runs the risk of the director getting used to the mock-up itself.

How come we are not able to make the best use of the technology we have developed? Are we so immature? Walter Murch pondered this thought, smiled, and answered slowly:

> There is always a danger with any new technology. The zoom lens is invented and when people start using it, people go crazy with it. Suddenly there are zooms all the time and eventually it settles down. Now the zoom lens is used all the time but you are rarely aware that it is a zoom lens. It takes time to metabolize a new technology into a mature use of it. I don't know where we are on the ladder of that particular technology. The danger is that it gets over-

used and gets used in inappropriate ways when it is introduced because people get excited about it. That's understandable. That's just human nature.

What is a mature use? Mobile phones have been around for ages but we use them more often than ever—and we are not even talking about all the apps that have been invented for us to doodle around with. Is it a mature use to still force your employees to be constantly on call even on your holiday? As hopeful as it sounds that we mature into new technology, I found it hard to see any evidence of this. We simply get accustomed to that technology. Digital editing is still used to change the film right up until the day of the print master when everything should be in order and ready for distribution. Is that mature?

Walter Murch looked into the green landscape, his thick glasses reflecting the sun. "Eventually with maturity it settles down, but the situation with digital technology is that it hasn't really settled down," he conceded.

It has been a churning force in our lives for the last 20 years since the mid–1990s and maybe a little bit earlier in sound. On every film we work on now there is an agonizing couple of weeks before shooting starts where we have to design the workflow for whatever the new technology is that we are using. We have to try to use it in the best way and not get caught in unexpected traps and make it efficient and artistically as transparent as possible. Every two years the universe is reinvented in a sense and we have to compensate for this reinvention. Eventually it may settle down but the nature of software is that it's not limited by physical hardware. So it may never settle down.

It is the job of inventors and scientists to push the boundaries, to never be satisfied with the status quo but to always keep thinking about new possibilities that may seem ludicrous at the moment. Composers can work much faster than before by using MIDI and sequencers instead of pen and paper. They can mock-up their music, send it to the director and make adjustments to the final recording even after the actual recording. They can do that because their music has been subjected to striping. They can play around with sample libraries, which get better and better, closer and closer to the actual sound of a live orchestra instead of sounding like an electronic imitation in a tin can.

The developments in technology composers have had to keep up with are not to be underestimated: the Synclavier, Casio keyboard with sequencers, programs like ProTools, Logic and Cubase, sample libraries, analogue and digital synthesizers…. Doubtless, technology has affected their work process and the actual sound of their work. It has influenced the whole industry because everybody can now produce music that sounds good, regardless of the quality of the composition. It has increased competition and decreased budgets.

Traditional composers who have been active in the business for decades moan about this state of affairs, while young composers welcome the flood of new technology and possibilities. The digitization has had its effects on their everyday life and, ultimately, their careers. They have to use the technological tools out there—and the most recent ones at that. A substantial amount of time is spent keeping up with current developments in the field of technology because no one can afford to continue using outdated tools. According to Alan Silvestri:

> There may be some people out there who have resisted the wave of advancement in technology. I know from myself it is as much a part of my daily life and study as the study of music, keeping up and keeping current with the movements in technology. I came from the day where you would go and have one meeting with the director. You would see the film and never see the film again and the next time you saw the director you'd be on the recording stage, spending a fortune. Every cue was something new for the director. That is for the most part completely gone now.

Give Me a Sound

Composition technology as an invention has brought advantages that no composer who works in the industry, or considering a career in it, would want to miss. Since all the necessary software and the obligatory MIDI keyboard fit easily into a travel bag, it has enabled composers to be less dependent on an actual workplace. Samples and electronic instruments have also expanded the color palette that is available to composers who can use effects and sounds never available before. These have become part of the musical language and opened up possibilities for new, interesting compositions that would have been impossible years before. This, of course, has influenced every composer's writing, as Alan Silvestri explains:

> The color palette, if I could call it that, that is now available to the film composer, has increased exponentially, so the tools and the materials have expanded far beyond acoustic-only instruments. That I think is bound to have a profound change on every composer's writing. It's still the same composer and it's still the same mechanisms that the music moves through and is developed in but with the addition of all of these new ways of making sound. I would have to say very definitely it has affected my music-making and my music.

New and possibly inventive ideas can be heard, music from people who wouldn't have stood a chance before the advent of digital technology, whether these people have undergone a traditional education in composition or not. Before sample libraries came up, keyboards could already mimic the sound of various instruments in the orchestra. Sample libraries took it to a whole different level. Since the late '90s, these libraries have sprung from earth like daffodils in springtime. They offer the users the chance to hear the whole orchestra, or single instruments from it, on their computer.

For this purpose, software developers recorded orchestras and individual players and built libraries from these sounds. Composers can connect their keyboard to the computer via MIDI, hit a key and hear that note played not by a keyboard sound but by a flute or a violin section. These individual libraries are interconnected with a sequencing program like Cubase, Logic, ProTools or Digital Performer and an interface like Kontakt or PLAY so that the composition in the sequencing program—put there by the composers by playing their keyboard which the computer then translates into actual musical notes via the MIDI interface—can be performed with the sounds of the sample library. These libraries are not only available for classical instruments but have enjoyed great success with ethnic instruments, voices, various percussion instruments, and sound effects as well as so-called atmospheric soundspheres.

As, over the years, more and more such libraries have been released, the market has expanded, offering products with very specific sound profiles. There is, for example, the big brass Hollywood sound with more reverb to it than a different library which was recorded with another set-up and which therefore sounds different, more intimate in this case. And so on. The selection is now utterly endless. When young composers are looking for their first sample library to buy, they are confronted with the tough challenge of making a decision since the amount of products is so vast.

The variety of sample libraries has very much benefited every composer and the whole industry since each library has its own specific sound, preventing all composers from sounding alike when delivering a piece played by samples. This is especially important since samples are widely used in film music, not only for demos or the so-called mock-ups but even for a final score if the producers don't have the money to pay for a live ensemble.

There are favorites when it comes to sample libraries. Certain patches surface in the works of widely different composers. Resorting to patches has caused grief for the rather traditional composers who prefer to conceptualize their scores away from the computer, such as Joe Kraemer, who bemoans the new simplicity and its temptations while composing:

> A big problem in contemporary film composing is that the production value has exceeded the literacy of the composers. A cue can just be a sustained note with a drumbeat. [...] The painting and dragging and dropping of loops and holding one button on a synth patch is not composing. I am not saying it's not a valid result but it also only works once. It's like Rusty Oilcan, which was the sound file on *Distorted Reality*, one of the first CD-Rom based samples. It was

everywhere. Every TV movie, every episode of *Law and Order*, when you wanted to show that some psychopath was nearby, you used Rusty Oilcan. It was a bowed sound. Producers should care. Why should they care? For the same reason they should care that their movie is unique and not the same garbage that everybody else is doing, that they argue about dialogue being fresh.

Some libraries indeed feature these patches for the sole reason of making the composer's job easier. Christian Henson, co-founder of Spitfire, admitted as much: "My favorite is *Sable Ensembles*. Composers pretend to write every individual line but we are all up against the clock. It's all about two hands. [...] There is a patch on it, flautando, a very specific set of instructions I gave the band. [...] That's my writing patch. I write every piece of orchestral music from that patch. I absolutely love it."[1]

How much the music can change and get manipulated in the mix to express the individual sound and style of the composer depends not necessarily on the person in front of the screen—the composer or orchestrator—but rather on the producer and director who have to approve the product sent to them by their employee, and also on the possibilities of the individual library and the state of the art. Composers manipulating their electronic scores or mock-ups. The aim is to produce music that sounds different from everybody else's.

The ideal way of working is to not rely on the standard default setting. However, composers often tend to use the factory default setting when working with a sample library for a simple reason: lack of time. To be able to manipulate such electronic sounds, the composer needs an expertise and experience that is not to be underestimated, demanding time and concentrated labor that composers working on studio productions (or especially TV shows) often do not have. As Gerard McCann observes:

> What sample libraries tend to do is make a lot of things sound the same across the board because people tend to learn to use them in the same ways. Most of the time they will be running a sample in mezzo-forte because most composers don't have the time to get inside the *Vienna Strings* and start really nuancing every little angle to it. It tends to be a little middle of the road.

The dilemma of sameness in sound when working with sample libraries is not one that applies to the live ensemble. After all, the sound of a score recorded with live musicians depends heavily on the individual musicians who get to perform the music: their interpretation, the small imperfections of human playing, the breathing and the pauses, the conducting. Samples don't have their own life: unlike real musicians, they will always sound the same when not processed and manipulated.

More than a few composers resort to creating their own sounds and libraries. One of them is Rob Simonsen:

> For me, creating your own sounds is very satisfying and very rewarding. I do that a lot. I also have friends who have interesting set-ups with modular set-ups or interesting guitar effects pedal set-ups that run through different sound sources to create ambiences. On almost every project I have done I am making things just for that project. I really try not to use stock sounds and effects because everybody can buy that. It can be fun.

Composers, especially when working for television shows, often do not have the time to build and develop their own sounds, thus ending up with generic templates.

In Proper Range

Sample libraries also have had a huge influence on the sound of live recordings, even if these libraries were used just for the mock-up. When delivering mock-ups to the director for approval, composers will usually use techniques and ranges that sound good with samples, running the risk of the sample library dictating the sound of the final recording. This has become much rarer than used to be the case because sample libraries have become more convincing. Almost all sampled orchestral techniques sound satisfying these days. There are still some effects, however, which composers are careful to avoid, such as fast runs or arpeggios for strings. Their fake sound could prevent the director from approving the mock-up. If, therefore, the composer doesn't write any fast string runs or arpeggios, the final recording won't have any either. Says Richard Bellis:

> We have to do a mock-up in order for the cue to be accepted. That means that the mock-ups have to be excellent, they have to sound really good. We have to do them with samples. Samples don't sound good in every register on every instrument. So we start writing the cues around the ranges in which the samples sound best. Then we take this and give it to the orchestrator and the orchestra. We are robbing ourselves of ranges in which the orchestral instruments sound great.

With the development of technology and especially sample libraries and sequencers, it has become possible to present a mock-up to the employer that sounds close to the possible final orchestral recording, leaving little room for the imagination or surprises. Although Jeff Rona—who has developed sample libraries himself—disagrees with the assertion that there are certain techniques which sound awful even today when played by a sample, he gives an example of a sample dictating the sound of the final recording by naming Klaus Badelt's and Hans Zimmer's well-known score for the epic *Pirates of the Caribbean* which was recorded and fused with samples in 2003 when libraries were less elaborate than they are now:

There is a level of instant gratification in playing a really nice sample. It just feels good and you might get a little fixated with a narrower thing. Take for example *Pirates of the Caribbean*. It's all staccato. That might have been very different if that had been written ten years later when there is more access to different articulations—staccato, legato, marcato, the in-between articulations that the older samples didn't use to have. That's a good example of the sound of samples dictating an entire score if you will, or at least a very specific theme. Composers will gravitate to certain things that sound good with samples. I agree that this will have an effect on some of the musical choices you make.

Despite the continuously improving quality of sample libraries, they do still have their limits, especially when it comes to a highly elaborate experimental score that will eventually be performed live. In that case, the composer can run into trouble soon, as happened to Atli Örvarsson who came up with an experimental concept for the independent film *A Single Shot* which premiered in 2013.

The trouble for the composer was that the sample libraries and sequencers could in most cases not convincingly mock-up the techniques he had envisioned to be performed on live instruments during the final recording: Örvarsson opted for diving into the world of the music of the 20th century (quasi-Penderecki) which he had studied in college to abstain from going the "easy, boring" way. He re-familiarized himself with some techniques of that period and wrote the music from scratch, without using any of the programs available. As a result, Örvarsson had to describe his ideas to the director:

This time I had to tell him, "You have to trust me. What's going to happen is the strings are going to rise up for 15 seconds and then this happens…" I had to describe it to the director in words. Some of that I was successfully able to mock-up with samples but it's incredibly hard to make a sound even close to realistic. The director was very supportive and said he trusts me. It was a grand experiment.

However, this was largely possible because the film in question was an independent production where the director didn't have a dozen producers breathing down his neck. The music might have turned out to be completely different had the project been a big-budget studio production. Even if he had decided to use the available libraries for string effects, the composer would have had to study the library closely and examine what effects are possible and how they can be manipulated before starting to actually write the music and how to approach the composition best according to the available sounds. Writing with pen and paper was the easiest and quickest way to proceed.

Copy and Paste

Loops have become a favorite in today's film music landscape. They are short—often purely electronic—snippets that can be repeated endlessly within a musical piece. It's quick and easy to do when working with sequencers and can, if done well, provide the composition with a hip modernism that pays tribute to the pop music of its time.

Next to piano scroll notation, all sequencing programs nowadays offer a traditional music notation page as well, which still is of undeniable importance to composers working with sequencers, as Jeff Rona elaborates: "I use Logic and it has scoring notation in it. I use it every day because I might improvise an idea and I can't remember what I just did but I want to change things."

When working with the so-called piano scroll notation, composers use an assortment of colored bars which indicate (a) the instruments the composer has been writing for, (b) the duration of a note written for that instrument and (c) the dynamic of that note. With sequencing programs, composers can write not only the music for the traditional instruments but also add a sound effect or loop to their composition. Since these effects are easy to implement and delete, it is a simple matter to find out which loop, effect or rhythm works best for the particular composition that is already on the screen.

These effects become colored bars of their own and, like all bars, can be copied, taken out or moved from one section to another. To add more detail into piano scroll notation, most composers nowadays work with an expression pedal and a modulation wheel which indicates the intensity of the note being played, whereas the expression pedal is responsible for the overall volume. Thanks to these tools, the composer and orchestrator can see how a note is meant to be played—if the expression pedal goes up, it leaves no doubt that the note in question is meant to be played in a crescendo, for example. "You can see that when you look at a score page," says Rob Simonsen,

> but with the piano scroll notation you can select all of the regions for everything that's going on and look at it at the same time, which I do sometimes. It's a very quick way of getting the whole thing. You have multiple pages of score in view and you get the whole thing right there. You can make adjustments. Grab a thing and modulate it if you want. There are quick and dirty tricks. Are they short cuts? Sure, but the job requires that you can use short cuts and use them effectively.

These short cuts have been heavily criticized by composers who started working in the industry by composing with paper and pen—the traditional way. In the late '90s Joel McNeely said,

The way things seem to be happening now is troublesome. A lot of people who are composing now never pick up a pencil—they sit at a keyboard and noodle around, play some things in, and then hand that off to an orchestrator who will extract a sketch from that, and they'll extract a score from that. [...]²

These short cuts, as described by Simonsen, by cutting and pasting certain sequences have enabled composers to churn out music more quickly by looping notes and working with repetitive structures to get the job done in time. This has affected the quality of the music itself, according to Nan Schwartz:

It's cutting and pasting. It's a combination of the composer's lack of skill and imagination to think of anything else and them being under a lot of time pressure. If they get eight bars that they like, they just keep looping it. "Oh, now I have 32 bars, now I have 64 bars." They get a lot done in that time. That becomes the paradigm that people become used to hearing.

Since the single parts for instruments in the piano scroll notation can be moved around quickly, it has enabled composers to write variations on their themes or motifs in no time at all. After all, the music for the string section can be played by a woodwind section as well by simply choosing different samples. Composers can change the key of the composition with just a few clicks, delete or mute selected instruments or add an additional instrument by playing the corresponding part on the keyboard. All this takes much less time than it would when working with pen and paper, and there are clear advantages to it. This copy-and-pasting has also enabled the composers to spend much less time on the individual composition by just repeating structures to be able to move on to another piece, given the pressure they experience in their everyday job.

Copy and pasting is also tempting for a completely different reason, as Gerard McCann says:

Economically sometimes the budget isn't there to record 45 minutes of orchestral score but the composer wants to write for the orchestra. So you start temping with the score before the recording. You say, "Actually, 4M2 [act 4, music cue number 2] is a good basis for 8M4 [act 8, music cue number 4]. So we take that but we need to cut the eight bars out." That is fine. But it needs a different beginning and a different end and possibly a different solo instrument over the top. So you break down your recording sessions so that you are not recording those 40 bars again but you do record the first eight bars which overlaps and you do record the back eight bars that overlaps so you have got a new beginning and a new end but you are bolting in the meat of the sandwich from the one time you recorded it. The demo will sound different. It happens to contain 20 of the middle 40 bars from this cue, but it's a different piece of music, a different piece of music that is basically a variation of an old, already existing piece where the middle part remains the same, made possible by simple cutting and pasting in the sequencer.

Therefore, the composer doesn't come up with a new piece of music per se but takes the middle part and glues it together with a new beginning and a new end. On the day of the recording, the middle part doesn't have to get recorded again. Instead, the composer will record the new beginning and the new end and leave it to the music editor and/or the mixing engineer to create the new piece of music out of the three separate parts (beginning, middle, end). That way, only one minute of the new piece needs to be recorded instead of the whole three minutes. With this trade off, the composer saves time and money, money that he can spend on more rehearsals or on more live recordings that the budget may not otherwise have allowed for.

The composer might not be required to resort to copying and pasting by the editor, director or producer. The dilemma of simple copying and pasting can start much earlier when the composer delivers the first mock-up, carefully assembled to sound like a live orchestra to enable the director to get an impression of how the final recorded piece would sound. Directors are very impatient by nature and can't wait to fool around with the one mock-up they have. According to Gerard McCann:

> Every editor and director either with or without the music editor are immediately starting to temp with the score demos in other places. They will say, "Oh, that works really well. She comes out of the bathroom, let's take the piece and chuck it down here." Sometimes the editor and the director will say to the composer, "We love 1M2 which works really well in several scenes. We will get our music editor to cut it so that it fits. We know it's just one demo so you would make it different but 90 percent of the material works," because there is no material for them to use. They are not going to wait for you to write all this material and see where it goes. They know where it's going. They tell you where it's going. The composer will then say to me, "Can you edit that? They like the old piece for this scene as well. Can you make it work better editorially?" I will cut and paste and repeat it.

This way, the music editor becomes the de-composer who takes the mock-up that the director has fallen in love with and makes it fit with other scenes the employer wants to have this piece featured in. The choices the music editors have at hand are endless. They can shorten the piece, change the dynamics and articulations, extend it by copying and pasting a rhythm or a long pedal note performed by the (electronic) strings, and thereby take the mock-up apart. Composers have little choice when it comes to these decisions by the director or producer. In a way, it even plays into their hands since the particular mock-up—which was designed for an altogether different scene—has already been approved by the employer. Instead of coming up with a new piece for a different scene, the composers leave the task to the music editor and spend time on other cues. If composers envisaged using the theme of one particular mock-up in different scenes anyway, they can go through the process of writing a film score much more quickly. The side effect is that the film ends up with a mono-thematic score which is very poor in variations and basically a copy-and-paste-job.

Since sequencers also offer the option of having the scene from the movie the composers are working on implemented on the same page or screen as the piano scroll notation, it enables them to react to the picture more closely by hitting every moment musically and emphasizing a hit on screen with a musical hit as well. The music can become static and mechanical. When working with sequencers and a piano scroll notation, the person operating the computer can indeed become locked to the screen, therefore failing to see the overall structure of the scene they are working on. Complains Nan Schwartz, "Most people don't have the skill to sit down at the piano. That's why the music is so dumb, because they are just reacting to what is going on on the screen. There is no continuity, no connection."

For this exact reason, Gabriel Yared chooses to work differently:

> I cannot imagine working and composing watching the picture. It is impossible for me. Once you know a film you know a scene and you start composing with the memory of the scene, not with the scene in front of you on the computer. [...] Composing with the memory of the images is much more inspirational than composing with the image in front of you. Your music not only becomes mechanical but it cannot be elaborated because you are accompanying the images and have no time for reflection, thought, research and questioning which are all necessary phases for every artistic creation. Then you do proper music and you confront it to the images. It's nothing to synchronize it. Synchronizing is the least thing in film music to me. To me, the most important thing is to marry with the spirit of the scene, not with the shot by shot.

When working the way Yared does though, the composers miss out on the instant gratification they can have when working with a sequencer, with experimenting with different sounds their libraries and programs have to offer. Says Rob Simonsen:

> When working with pen and paper, nothing is instant. It's amazing to be able to explore all these different options instantly. It is very powerful and I do think sometimes you have a happy accident when you move a region to a different patch and it's like, "Oh, I wouldn't have thought of having that line played on the flutes." Accidents like that happen when you are just doodling around in your laboratory. You might mix a couple of chemicals by accident that you didn't intend to but the potion it creates is great. If it is an inspiring library it can open up different ideas.

You Can Do It If You Believe in Yourself / Technology

Aspiring composers don't necessarily need to know how to write notes. Thanks to sample libraries and sequencers everybody can now deliver a product that at least sounds good—regardless of the quality of the actual musical content. The only requirement: telling a story musically that matches the images when working on a film. With the advent of affordable sample libraries and other composition software, every person who can afford it, can buy it and start making music in their bedroom, regardless of their musical background. Says Lorne Balfe:

> Technology, Garage Band and computers have opened the window of opportunity far greater than it has ever been to allow people to have one hit wonders, which weren't always there because you needed to buy equipment. Thirty years ago, studio equipment cost the price of a house. Now you can write a film score on a laptop, so the cost is far cheaper. But the fact is, everybody seems to be a film composer nowadays because everybody is able to have the same equipment and work in their bedroom.

Art (or craft) has always been connected to the technology of its time: the pigments that were used to create cave paintings that have survived for millennia, the computer processors that type novels or nonfiction books about film music. Technology has empowered people with original ideas to actually do something with their ideas by putting them into the computer and making them audible or visible. Already in the 1990s, Elmer Bernstein said: "At the risk of sounding arrogant, I will have to say that film scoring has descended to a lot of gadgetry, in our time. For most people, there are too many gadgets and not enough music."[3]

The empowering of everybody to compose music through technology can become a problem if the uneducated music producers feel compelled to venture out of their field to, for instance, write for a live orchestra instead of concentrating on electronic music with which they may have already succeeded. The fact that everybody is now able to produce music and therefore demonstrate that they can produce music that at least sounds good—regardless of its substance or content—leads to another problem that has influenced the film music landscape since the advent of composition technology.

So Many People, So Little Time

Not only has technology been partly responsible for shrinking budgets, it has also led to a shrinking of the amount of time that composers (or anyone else in the film industry) have at their disposal. After all, composition technology has made it (seemingly) quicker to deliver a film score. It is now sometimes expected of the composers to make their ideas audible in a hair-raising amount of time, as Jeff Rona admits:

> The technology has made it faster to shoot, faster to edit, faster to post-produce, faster to do color timing. The technology is there at virtually every point in production, so everyone is working more efficiently—the cinematographer, the editor, the sound designers, the composers. The cost of a movie goes up the longer it takes to finish because most everybody's day is being paid by the week, except for the composer of course, and so they want to finish up as fast as they possibly can.

While this development is only natural, it comes with a problem because it affects a part of the creative process that has nothing to do with technology per se: inspiration. "The technology has made it so that we have less time to develop good ideas," continues Rona:

> Every time I go to the movies I always remind myself that every note I am hearing was approved by somebody other than the composer and was done under terrible conditions. Every film score is done under terrible conditions. The budgets are tight, the schedules are tight and we just have to do the best we can with the time we have. It's never enough. Almost.

With sequencers it is now possible to change the music constantly and send mock-ups back and forth to get them approved. Before the advent of digital technology the composers would sit at their piano and play their ideas to the director. When satisfied, the director would then hear the final score for the first time when it was being performed by the orchestra. In the time in between, the composer had time to write the music with pencil and paper and be undisturbed by comments from the director or the studio about the music since they either couldn't read the notes or simply didn't bother.

Now, producers and directors get a pretty good idea about how the final score will sound months before the recording by having the composers send them mock-ups of individual cues which will then be approved or rejected. In the latter case, comments will be attached and the composer has to oblige any requests. They may have to re-orchestrate, re-sample and re-send—often several times before they get a cue approved. And even if a mock-up is approved, the film will still change and the composers will then have to adapt the music again accordingly by shortening it or lengthening it, depending on the needs of the scenes. Since this often happens shortly before the scheduled live recording is supposed to take place, this not only increases the pressure for the composer but also for the orchestrator.

And so it has happened that everything must now be done quicker and be rewarded with the seductive instant gratification.

The Job It Is a-Changin'

Orchestrators have found themselves in a whole new situation following this requirement to send the mock-ups for approval long before the actual recording. It has changed the order of events. Before the advent of digital technology, the composer would write sketches and then hand them over to the orchestrator to be transformed into actual music that could get played by musicians. Usually, composers could use just one orchestrator for a whole score since the picture was locked and the orchestrator would receive the individual sketches one after the other while the composing process was still going on, therefore having more time to devote to the orchestration.

Within the past two decades, the amount of time that orchestrators have to reach the point where they are satisfied with their work has decreased. It has forced them to work with colleagues instead of on their own (which in turn decreased their fee). When having to deliver mock-ups, it is the composers and their assistants who devote themselves to the orchestration process by deciding which instruments to employ and which articulations and dynamics to use—for the simple reason that the mock-up has to sound as organic as possible to get approved. When approved, it is only too understandable that the orchestration is not allowed to steer away from the arrangement in the mock-up—otherwise the recorded music would sound different from the demo. After all, the approval was given for the mock-up, its sound and orchestration, and nobody wants any surprises after they have already given their approval.

The orchestrator's job is now more than ever simply to clean up the mock-up by transcribing it and oftentimes thinning it out, as Nan Schwartz illustrates with the example of orchestrating for Alexandre Desplat:

> Alexandre sends his mock-ups and they are orchestrated. They are just orchestrated in a way that's never going to work in a real orchestra because there are so many notes and chords. Everyone forgets that when you write a five part string chord on a sampler, every time you add a voice you add another eighteen violins. It sounds really big. But when you get to the real orchestra you are just dividing the orchestra. If you have a six voice chord instead of having eighteen voices on each note you are going to have six voice chords, three violins on each note. That's not going to sound good.

And so the role of the orchestrator has changed, their working method, the amount of time they have at their disposal, and their actual fee. Schwartz summarizes it:

> Gone are the days when you get a print-out from the composer that consists of just a melody and very simple things because demos are a necessity for everyone now and you have to turn in a demo and get it approved before you can

go ahead. Everyone is doing these mock-ups and then the mock-up has to be close to the final product in terms of the orchestra so that the director has an idea. Then the uneducated composer falls in love with his sound and doesn't want his orchestrator to improve it or do anything different. Plus, they don't want to trick the director because the director has already signed off on a certain sound. If you start messing around, it doesn't sound like your demo. I would say it's sort of a mixed blessing. In a way it was better maybe when we got less information from the composer. We had more freedom to make it good. Now we are locked into their midi print-out. If they have written it for the horns, then you better put it in the horns.

Orchestrators have to faithfully reproduce the mock-ups they were given by the composer. Now, composers are not necessarily experienced orchestrators, and may not, in fact, know much about orchestration at all, especially if they come from a nonclassical background but enabled to write orchestral film music by modern technology. John Ottman:

When you are doing a mock-up with all this MIDI technology, you have to present it, so you have to write out all the parts except you have someone to do the mock-ups for you. I do all the mock-ups myself. So the orchestrator's only job is to faithfully reproduce what I did in the mock-up. There is nothing left to the imagination. In the heyday, the orchestrator would actually embellish the piece with musical ideas, bells and whistles. I think today a lot of orchestrators don't have to do that because it's all done. The orchestrator has a big job in accurately trying to reproduce it for the orchestra.

The orchestrator has become nothing more than a copyist in many respects. The changing role of the orchestrator has naturally had an impact on their perspective and outlook. While starting out as an orchestrator used to be a step on a career path (see Hugo Friedhofer, David Raksin, Shirley Walker or Angela Morley) or at least it enabled orchestrators to live comfortably off their earnings, this path now seems closed, blocked by a wall long and high.

When orchestrators had more creative freedom in their work, more value was placed on it and they were often recommended by composers to score their own gigs since composers and heads of the music departments were well aware of the orchestrator's impeccable knowledge of the orchestra. The employment of modern composers like Mario Castelnuovo-Tesesco as orchestrators give them an engagement of some kind while purposefully keeping them from crafting expressionistic music for the studio's films notwithstanding. With orchestrators downgraded to copyists, their status has crumbled.

The musical knowledge of orchestrators seems not to be of any value anymore, as Nan Schwartz' husband Conrad Pope has experienced himself.

Back in the day everyone knew that the orchestrator really knew his stuff. They were great musicians. They were geniuses. Now people don't really value that. They might say, "Well, he is an orchestrator, but he doesn't have his own ideas." It's a trap and Conrad has fallen into that. He is a brilliant composer and he has had a hard time getting quality films to score because people think of him as an orchestrator.

The current situation has been further degraded by both increased pressure and the need to collaborate. Before the advent of digital technology composers were usually content to work with one or two orchestrators at the most, whereas the numbers look different now. For James Newton Howard's rush job of scoring *King Kong* in 2005—after Howard Shore had been let go—no fewer than eleven orchestrators are credited officially. Even for a film production with a modest budget compared to the massive blockbusters, less than three orchestrators seems to be a rarity, with Alexandre Desplat working with three orchestrators on *The Light Between Oceans* (as well as crediting himself as an orchestrator, bringing the total to four), and James Newton Howard working with five orchestrators on *Water for Elephants* in 2011. Jon Brion and Geoff Zanelli employed a total of ten orchestrators for *Christopher Robin* in 2018. It has become harder to earn a living as an orchestrator and some key tasks of their job have been taken over by the composers themselves regardless of their actual knowledge.

How the individual composer thinks about orchestration naturally depends on their knowledge and experience, and, to a substantial degree, even on the digital tools at hand, as Rob Simonsen admits:

> I will often work out a theme on the piano and figure out what it is. I'll build a template which will serve as my sound palette. If it's all electronic, it's all electronic. If it's all orchestral, it's all orchestral, and so on. But even within that different sample libraries have different characteristics. Some string libraries have a more chamber sound, some have a huge sound, some are edgier, some are smoother. I think about the casting. That's how I think about instrumentation and orchestration. It's all about casting. You have got to cast the right players and then you have to capture it in the right place in the right way. Everything is casting because all those things will have an effect on what you will end up getting.

As mentioned previously, it is not so much that in this case the sound of the sample library dictates the sound of the score but that the sound of the score Simonsen wants to achieve makes him decide on the sample library he uses—which the orchestrator then has to listen to carefully to transcribe it for the orchestra in order to achieve the same sound in the live recording. Similarly, the transcription of the samples can consist of taking generic patches the composer put in to save time and adapt them by working on the details and make them work with the other parts of the piece.

Rob Simonsen explains:

Sometimes I'll just use one string patch for everything and then my orchestrators will explode the strings. I get the score back and make corrections or adjustments as needed, but that's pretty much the typical layout. [...] It's often something that's generated by a sample library. Lately it's been long sustains with mutes and then spiccato, staccato and pizzicato. With programming between all of those I can get everything I need. I would say that these articulations are pretty much stock and I don't spend an incredible amount of time on the mock-up. Sometimes there are things that require it but usually I know what I am going for. If it's a gestural sample from something I'll put it in there and in the orchestration we'll figure out our own way of doing something like that.

Since earning a living as an orchestrator has become increasingly difficult, orchestrators have become more timid in order to keep their jobs. This includes not making the composers aware of mistakes they made or advising them against having a 30-bar ostinato played by the orchestra instead of just being played by a sample or modified, explains Nan Schwartz: "As an orchestrator you pretty much keep your mouth shut. You never tell the composer anything. You just try to realize his music and the orchestra."

The Devil Is in the Detail

It might be a beginner's mistake to think that for a mock-up it is good enough to put something together in a sequencer that conveys the idea of the composition but is lacking in detail—the hope being that one will be able to work on the details later after the cue has been approved. Alan Silvestri explains

The potential danger is that because you are writing for a mock-up there can be this tendency to not deliver the level of detail in the piece you might had you been sitting there with pencil and paper. The voice going on in one's head says, "Okay, that shows what the idea is there," but you are not really going there and taking a hard look at the orchestration. You may have an oboe solo playing four bars that will show the idea, but had you been writing this on paper you may have had the oboe and the flute playing together, you may have done this or that with the string background where instead of just string pads delivering the harmony under a woodwind solo, had you been doing it on paper. You may have had more inner moving parts in the string part but this will be good enough to get the idea across. Then of course you are looking at the time ticking away. You are under so much pressure to get through the project. Do you really ever go back there and revisit that material?

The short answer is no, since there are many more cues to get through. There will be cues being sent back and forth, with or without approval, with or without the changes that will have to be made if the director isn't satisfied or if the picture keeps changing. As George Fenton puts it:

Very often you do a mock-up because you want to know if you are going in the right direction. And you haven't really gone in that direction. You have just said, "I am going to do something like this." You then stop working on the detail of the composition. This is the absolute killer: you might submit something that you don't think is finished that everybody says they love. If it's exactly what they want, why should you develop it further? Something psychologically makes you think, "Maybe I have done it. Maybe that's it." Deep down you know if you hadn't played it to them, and hadn't had to mock it up in the first place, you would have taken it much further. You would have asked yourself different questions, you might have gone another way before you had really honed your work. There's a double traffic.

Very few composers can get away with sending a rough idea as a test demo to see whether the director likes it or not. Whether or not they do depends on the imagination of the director. With sample libraries having become more and more realistic in terms of emulating the sound of live musicians, there is no incentive for directors to acquire the skill of interpreting rough demos. Music editor Gerard McCann explains it this way:

Somebody will send something to me where all they have done is a sketch and it's fairly rough. With the samples you know what it's about but it's flat, it hasn't got any nuance. It's not sculptured around the scene because the scene is constantly changing. In a sense they are saying, "Do you like this material? If you like it then we will fit the suit with it. Or do you like this material? Then we will fit your suit with this material. But we won't spend the time fitting the suit five times." So they present musical material that's fabric. You need to look at the fabric and imagine how it will look when it fits you. The big "but" is that it becomes clear that most people can't. The composers will put the fabric against the picture. I will do a quick mix of it as best I can given that it's all in one piece, at least so it's presentable. It's not shaped yet. It just somehow works. It's a sketch. Let's see what they think. It doesn't go down well because the label falls off, the label that says, "This is just a rough idea. What do you think?"

In other words, the directors who are used to getting detailed mock-ups fail to see the bigger picture and fail to realize that what they are getting is by no means the final product but instead just a theme that is supposed to convey a certain atmosphere or describe one of the characters in the film. They therefore blame the demo and in turn the composer if the demo doesn't work in the picture. But why should it, since it is only a sketch? Admits Lorne Balfe:

I look at my mock-up as trying to get it as realistic as possible. What you hear is how the performance is going to be. I witnessed it when the mock-ups haven't been good and the composer ended up losing the job. Directors now have become more accustomed to hearing exactly how it's going to sound but without the real musicians. It's a difficult task but I really do think nowadays it's not just the directors. It's the studios. You have test screenings. You can't go and record music just for test screenings, unfortunately. There can be no error or doubt in the mock-up. You have to be as realistic as possible so that there is no shock when you come to the recording.

If the cue, purposefully or not, is lacking in detail, these details can't ever be added once the cue has been approved—*because* it has been approved. What sounds like an exaggeration turns out to be anything but, since it is worth keeping in mind that the director and the studio heads will live and work with the mock-up right up until the live recording and therefore they will get used to the mock-up and its sound. If they are not consciously aware of the details of the changes when it comes to the live recording, they will be at least subconsciously able to tell that something is different—and therefore wrong.

There is a particular reason why directors mostly insist on receiving precise, detailed mock-ups they will then get used to. When composers were still writing with a pen on paper, directors would only fully hear what they were getting when the score was finally being recorded. Nowadays, directors are able to minimize the dangers of not getting what they want by constantly receiving mock-ups from the composer whenever a new piece is finished. The process of micro-managing has made it much easier for the employers to make sure they get as close to their envisioned goal as possible.

Because films, thanks to digital editing, *can* be cut according to music now, films *are* cut according to music now. Because films, thanks to digital editing, *can* be changed right up until the release, they *are* changed right up until the release. Before the advent of digital editing equipment, sequencers and sample libraries, only with strenuous effort was it possible to watch a scene with the composer's unfinished, pre-recorded demo. With the technology at hand, it has become as easy as peeling a banana—and because it is possible, it is being done.

The composers will send their elaborate mock-up to the director. The quality of the mock-up is tested by putting it under the scene it is supposed to accompany. That way, directors don't have to imagine what a rough sketch would sound like when recorded with the orchestra, or whether it would then work with the scenes. They don't have to rely on their imagination but rather on the quality of the mock-up to convince them that the music works and that the composer is therefore the right choice for the project.

The demand for elaborate mock-ups—delivered piece by piece—not only makes imagining how the final score would sound unnecessary but also allows the director and the studio more control over the film at hand, as McCann explains:

> Producers won't accept demos anymore, something that you can't use but which shows what your intentions are. They will insist on skilled, detailed mock-ups. They have to hear what they are getting. They have to have total confidence in what the music is before they record any of it because they can't

risk—in their view—waiting until three weeks before the final mix before they start hearing what the music is. It scares the shit out of them.

It Doesn't Take Getting Used To

Working with mock-ups has created another conundrum which should cement the composer as someone as committed to bad luck as a death row convict. With directors receiving mock-ups early on and listening to them over a substantial period of time, be it weeks or months, they easily get used to the sound of the mock-up, as imperfect as it may be—since with time one can get used to practically anything. It can happen that the much superior final recording, played by breathing and sweating human beings, gets rejected in favor of the demo—or that at least certain parts of the demo get used in the film along with the final recording. According to Gerard McCann:

> You record it, expecting people to be very happy because the content is already established. But then the people say, "We like the demo. We will go with that." You might have played something quickly on a hissy, upright piano in the studio which then stays in the film. Because it's security. It works. They got used to hearing it for months. It becomes linked with the picture. Then they are trying to break that lock. That's very difficult for some filmmakers to deal with. They know with the temp they can't resolve that unless they are going to license the temp. But with demos they can. They own the demos. There's many a time a lesser version of something has been used in a film for that reason. Curiously enough I have more freedom temping a score than most composers have writing it.

Not being able to satisfy the employer with the final recording is a familiar experience for composers working in the industry, as Lorne Balfe admits:

> There will be something that they get attached to that is slightly synthetic and less pure about the real performance. Sometimes when the real musicians perform it, it changes the whole feel and suddenly you have got this vibrancy and all the emotion that wasn't in the demo. Suddenly it's a different piece of music. It can happen a lot of times. It's not just the instrumentation. I had it where somebody had listened to something as an MP3 and they got used to it. It was put into the edit. When it was fully mixed, it sounded totally different and they preferred the MP3 because there is something about the frequency that they liked.

This happens much more often with music that has a strong rhythmic quality to it as opposed to more romantic, lush compositions which need the performance of human beings to bring out the heart of the piece. It is not only the sound that directors get used to but the rhythmic precision that samples provide. Edwin Wendler says:

The requirements have changed. It is because of the use of samples that you play a mock-up to a director and the producers and they get used to the precision that sometimes comes with quantizing MIDI notes. When they hear the real thing played by an orchestra, they expect the same kind of precision that adds just a little bit of the human touch but not too much because it would draw too much attention to itself.

The same kind of precision that electronic music can provide is expected from the human beings who will eventually record the final score—a quality that no human being can ever provide since no musician is a machine, since every musician has their own style of playing, since every musician is subjected to little fluffs and hiccups, since every musician cannot be expected to start or end a phrase in the exact same split-second as their colleagues. The energy therefore is a different one, and the energy of a live orchestra is automatically inferior to any sample-based ostinato or rhythm that is dead-on every time it is played and that allows for no inconsistencies which are so very much part of human nature.

It is of little surprise that most composers who have had their live recordings rejected in favor of the mock-up have had them rejected if they were particularly rhythmic pieces or at least less influenced by the symphonic tradition of the Western world, as George Fenton remembers:

> It happened to me several times with tracks where I brought players in to play, a real drummer or a real rhythm section to replace what I had done. Something about the lack of proper drumming on your part they found more appealing or got used to. [...] I sent them my original demo and I sent them the mix of the band playing the same thing. They said, "The demo sounds better." Then you just have to say that the reason for that is in certain cases with musicians the music is not so much for an orchestra because it's a language that's very specific. But with a rhythm section the language isn't so specific. They bring themselves to the music. That's why you have them because they are great at what they do.

With the increasing popularity of electronic music in the '80s, directors and studio heads inadvertently got used to the precision this music could offer and, since pop music has always had a big influence on film music, requested their film score pay tribute to it. The process of abstaining from recording strongly rhythmic music with an orchestra naturally accelerated the more composers obliged and fell victim to having their final recording rejected in favor of the precise mock-up.

It has, in fact, accelerated to a degree where the quality of having human beings performing a piece of music can now easily be dismissed and looked down upon because it has become rare to have a rhythmic piece of score performed solely by an orchestra used in a film. This became painfully obvious to music editor Gerard McCann who, without asking for this information, was informed by a director:

"Whatever music he or she writes, whatever we end up with, I don't want to hear sweaty guys playing their instruments." In other words: "I don't want to have music that sounds like human beings are making it." He liked the sound that the samples bring but don't have the human element. He found it distracting in his mind the notion of other humans involved with what's happening on the screen. Anything that would be written that had some humanity to it, a lyrical clarinet line for example, would have gotten rejected. It never got to that point. But it is an interesting point of view because you go, "That's the antithesis of how I feel." That's a red flag early on. He didn't say it flippantly. It was a warning.

Though samples are superior to live musicians when it comes to the precision required in rhythmic cues, such samples still have clear limitations when it comes to thematic or even lush pieces whose quality they are not able to represent fairly. One glaring example of that phenomenon is Alan Silvestri's score for *The Mummy Returns* for which the composer, ironically, hadn't prepared any mock-ups but instead resorted to playing demos on the piano to director Stephen Sommers. Three weeks before the recording, which was to take place in England with 100 players and a choir of 60 singers, Sommers turned up in Silvestri's studio to listen to some thematic ideas the composer had come up with at that point.

Silvestri hadn't done any actual demos and the director therefore had to imagine what the theme would sound like when played by an orchestra. Also, Silvestri's imperfect skills in piano playing proved to be an obstacle. Therefore, the initial ideas turned out to be a disaster. Sommers didn't like anything his composer played for him. After spending some time trying to find out what Sommer's problem with the material was, Silvestri was then left alone when the director boarded the next plane home. Silvestri set out to write and orchestrate the score without ever seeing Sommers again before the actual recording.

Naturally, it was an anxiety-inducing process for the composer who didn't have any mock-ups approved (because there were no mock-ups) and whose ideas had fallen on deaf ears. With the quickly decreasing trust of the director, Silvestri eventually raised the baton in Watford, England, a few weeks later to record the first cue with orchestra and choir assembled in the studio. After the six-minute opening cue for the movie had been recorded, the doors to the recording stage burst open and in came Stephen Sommers himself, running up to the podium much to the panic of the conductor and composer. Sommers had this to say: "That is so you! I am so glad I didn't hear any of this before now because I would have made bad decisions based on material that never could have sounded like this had it been done in a mock-up."

Concludes Silvestri: "I think it's my most glaring example of a situation where if [the mock-up] is meant to be played by the orchestra it will be simulated to a greater or less degree but it will not have that remaining twenty percent of thrill and aliveness that you only get from that live orchestra in the room."

With mock-ups trying to convey rather traditional symphonic pieces, the director can instead be in for quite a negative surprise which in turn could reflect badly on the composer and decide their future on a project. John Ottman remembers the stunned look on the director's face when the score for *The Cable Guy* was finally recorded live: "The director couldn't believe how big the music sounded with an orchestra. The music sounded quite small with my mock-ups which had a lot of reverb back in the day. We recorded the music and it suddenly had so much volume in this room."

The Young Film Composer's Guide to the Orchestra

Since film music needs to react to the picture, it is a rare occurrence for any composer/conductor to guide the orchestra freely in the live recording. Instead, the musicians and the conductor will have microphones in their ears, dictating the speed of the scene and music. Before the advent of digital technology, the music could be synchronized with the picture during the recording with punches and streamers. It was an effective yet elaborate process to make sure the musical hit would be bang on the money.

For this process, a hole was punched into the actual frame where the musical hit was supposed to occur. Streamers would then move toward this punch, preparing the conductor for said punch. Reference-punches could then indicate whether the conductor was going too fast or too slow, making him aware of the necessity to speed up or slowdown in order to meet the punch in the indicated frame. While the conductor would see the frames, the musicians wouldn't, therefore being untroubled by any reference and free to play the music without any technical devices and indications such as a click track. If the conductor is not at 20 seconds in bar eight as planned, he would then need to speed up in order to meet the streamer in the next bar. That way, conducting with punches and streamers can become a math problem for the conductor, albeit a solvable one if the conductor is experienced enough.

This changed with the advent of digital technology when a way was found to guarantee synchronicity of film and music in a more effective and precise way—and without having a possible math problem to deal with, making it easier for the conductors to conduct the music by simply following the click in their ears without having to calculate anything. Click tracks became the way to go. Suddenly, musicians were subjected to headphones through which a metronomic click is fed through, indicating the frames per beat (as opposed to beats per minute). The click track is more precise than punches and streamers and has the welcome quality of not demanding a highly skilled conductor who would know when and how to speed up or slowdown in order to meet the next punch. Instead, the click track is more mechanical and unforgiving. With a composer who is an inadequate conductor, the chances of recording a cue in one go, "cold" so to speak, are slimmer using punches and streamers as they allow the conductor, and therefore the musicians, to make more hiccups and mistakes than a click track which is more rigid.

The click track poses quite a challenge when recording traditional music with an ebb and flow that doesn't have a rigid tempo but rather plays with accelerandi and ritardandi since it is laborious to make the click work according to the free-flowing piece of music with lots of changes in tempo and meters. It is, therefore, much easier to use the click for a more rhythmic piece in order to have the musicians be "bang on the money" with the first take. Says Gerard McCann:

> When the click is straight, when the tempo is consistent, the quickest way to get the music recording is for the orchestra to hear the click. If you take something that's much more fluent it's best for them not to hear the click. It's best for them to be conducted by someone who has the streamers. But sometimes, once you have done it two or three times with a click, you can have a go with doing it wild. It might not fit the picture exactly but it might not matter too much sometimes if it's something lyrical, especially if it's an orchestra that plays together all the time. They will lock in together.

However, the producers might not necessarily be keen on having to pay money for more session time when rehearsing a few times with a click before recording the free-flowing version without a click. An example concerning Gabriel Yared illustrates the dilemma of having to make rather traditional, free-flowing pieces of music work with a click track, as put by McCann:

> He writes freely. But then you still have to come along and build a click track to his free moving piece in order for you to record it. The freedom is there, the musical shape is there but you have to transcribe it into a programmed system. You can't say to the musicians, "Listen to this and just play along with it." That doesn't work. You have to build the ebb and flow at least into a streamer and click track. […] The music has to get handcuffed back in order to record it with the orchestra. Somebody then has to reinterpret it up again.

The click track has become the way to go in film music, though not necessarily to the great enjoyment of composers and musicians. Even composers who grew up with technology and all its advantages strive to be able to record at least one score with punches and streamers for the benefits this system offers, Rob Simonsen reveals:

> One of the things I struggle with is how to get rubato performances using the click. Someday I want to do a project with just punches and streamers. I

haven't done it yet. What happens a lot of times is I'll make something without a click and you have to implement a click so that the players can replicate that performance exactly. Is it as good as when they are just playing free under the conductor speeding them up and slowing them down with punches and streamers? No. I think punches and streamers is the most advantageous in terms of getting a very humane performance.

Nan Schwartz agrees. She asked to record her score for the film *Stella* without a click track:

I hired a music editor and said, "I am going to do a lot of free timing. I need streamers." That was a big deal. They hadn't done any streamers in a while. Everything they did was to click track. I said, "How do people write this thing with any emotion if there is a click track running?" "Well, they don't." That was the answer.

A session musician, who wishes to remain anonymous, commented:

I find it quite interesting that they don't try more often to just have the conductor with a click track. Assuming that all the musicians can hear one another and they are in the same room and not stemming, would it not be sensible if just the conductor had a click track? Then we would play with one another in a rhythmic way. Because some people play right bang on the click, some people are behind it. It doesn't make for such a unified approach.

Using click track is so much and then you have the ridiculous thing when you have a solo and they say, "Just for the last couple of bars ignore the click. It'll still be there but ignore it." "Oh God, do I really have to do that?" It is not easy when the thing is clicking in your ear to try and mold a phrase and play flexibly not with the click but get back with the click by bar 70. It's a little bit tricky actually to produce the right musical effect. So we just live with it. I think we'd all prefer to do something without a click.

The reason for a rather mechanical performance lies not simply in the click itself but partly in the fact that, when playing with headphones, the hearing is slightly impaired. McCann explains:

When they are listening to the click they are hearing with one ear. When hearing with one ear your sense of balance within the orchestra, the sense of intonation even, your sense of physiological balance is different because you are hearing your instrument louder than the others. When you take the headphones off, everybody has got two ears.

But then again, the requirements for session musicians have changed radically over the last few years.

Although the musicians in Los Angeles, guarded by their union, earn more money per recording gig than musicians in other countries, they get to play much less than they used to since London and Eastern Europe have become more and more popular among producers, even if the quality of certain venues in countries such as Czechoslovakia, Poland, Hungary or Macedonia sometimes leaves a lot to be desired, making it necessary for the financiers to have certain cues and sections re-recorded in other, more prestigious places such as London.

With musicians getting less work in Los Angeles, they naturally get to play less, which can have detrimental consequences on the quality of the recording, as Nan Schwartz admits:

> It has an effect on the recording when you are not playing every day. If they are not home practicing and are not on a session, they get less and less practice. London has taken over Los Angeles in its reputation when it comes to the quality of the performance. Most film music is not challenging either. It definitely has been dumbed down.

In turn, the requirements for musicians have changed since the style and general aesthetics of the music required for studio productions have changed over the decades. Most of the scores recorded today are musically not very challenging, according to one musician:

> We did a video game about a month ago. I am glad I don't do that all the time. It is churning out like being in a factory. It is not very satisfying musically, at all. It's not interesting. [...] I have been lucky actually, considering there are fewer really good composers than there were. I don't think there is much doubt about that. I have had the fortune of working for composers who write really well.

The issue of having to worry about getting work was unthinkable during the studio system since orchestras were under contract and used regularly— not only for the final recording but also for rehearsals or simply for testing ideas the composer had: "In the old days, at MGM," said Herbert Spencer,

> if it didn't fit [syncing the music with the picture], they'd do it over again. Look, when you have the orchestra under salary, you could work on Sunday. We'd do anything over again that wasn't right, because we were getting paid anyhow. We'd do it until we got it right. We didn't hurry through the recording at all.[4]

The situation nowadays looks very different. Edwin Wendler elaborates:

> At the height of scoring there were numerous scoring stages in Los Angeles which had multiple sessions every week, sometimes two sessions for two different projects in a single day. Musicians had to routinely cancel gigs because they had committed to something else. That luxury doesn't exist anymore. Partly because of technology, partly because a lot of the business has moved to London and other places. The demands have changed in terms of where their skills need to be.

The musicians who want to get into session work need to be good networkers first and foremost and be able to sell themselves effectively. As hard as it is to get into session work, it's easier to get out—for the same reason that composers can now get fired easily and replaced in a split second: the competition has become enormous, also increasing friction between the session musicians themselves. In today's climate, they're mostly unwilling to stand up for each other. A woodwind player remembers:

> There was one musician I defended because this particular musician played out of tune on a particular project. I said to the fixer, "I don't think it was that musician's fault. I think it was somebody else." I was then told that there have been two other complaints from other composers about that musician playing out of tune. That was the end of that musician after playing for 15 years. I said, "If it is me, I'd like to know." It's the law of the jungle. It's very ruthless. Nobody speaks up. It was probably better if I hadn't said anything because by saying something you end up being a troublemaker and you may end up out on the street yourself. I do much less work for my fixer now than I used to because I said too many things or asked too many questions.

If a musician is accused of playing out of tune or of making any other mistake that costs additional time and therefore money, it could very well be the beginning of the end of their career. Our woodwind player continues: "It's very easy to get out. All you have to do is argue with the fixer, really. You may never see him again. We are at their mercy. It's quite often a no-win situation. Sometimes people only have to play out of tune once or twice and they may never be seen again." To make matters worse, the musicians most often do not know who the people in charge are. It can be any of the people in the recording booth, the fixer or the director. A composer isn't the only person who can get a musician fired by voicing an opinion, or for playing unsatisfactorily.

Something Familiar,
Something Similar

Why should you only get what you think you want, or be limited by what you can simply plan on? Life's never like that, and if you're smart you'll decide it's better the way it is.—Richard Ford, *Independence Day*

David Lynch was sitting in the garden. Smoking a cigarette, drinking black coffee, with his hair combed stylishly backwards and his slightly worn-out black coat, looking exactly like the cultural icon that he has become within the past few decades, his teeth yellow and black from years of chain-smoking. To his right his wife, Emily Stofle, was sitting, a tall brunette beauty and aspiring actress he employed for *Inland Empire*. Few directors have consistently used film music in the way Lynch has, with both scores and songs not only providing a mood but, more importantly, being an integral part of the storytelling of the movie and giving clues to solve the mysteries his movies present.

Here is a man who thinks carefully about the role of music when he develops his projects, about the conception and the meaning of it. To achieve that, he works closely with his composer Angelo Badalamenti from the start, sometimes playing early sketches and demos while shooting, and fusing music and sound design by toying with orchestral recordings and later de-familiarizing them electronically, making it impossible to distinguish music from sound effects. He is, in short, a fascinating subject for an interview about film music.

The year was 2010 and Lynch had just been awarded the Kaiserring in Goslar, Germany, a prestigious prize for his achievements in the field of art. After the ceremony in the small town with its old half-timber houses, he enjoyed a break that was due to be interrupted by our interview. Gentle and calm, with smiling, warm eyes, he offered me a seat opposite his. At one point during our talk we were interrupted by Werner Spies, the art historian who had given a speech for and about Lynch during the ceremony shortly before. Spies not only asked for autographs on a dozen books, but also started talking about his family for an extended period of time.

But where to start the interview with a man who has done everything a director could possibly do with music in his films? The first question therefore was an obvious one—and obviously difficult to answer in its all-encompassing nature. Slightly intimidated and clumsy, I started off by wondering aloud what he wants to achieve with the employment of music in his films generally. Lynch sucked on his cigarette, took a sip of the pitch black coffee and replied slowly: "Every element is a Ten. So music is a Ten. But music isn't a Ten and others are a Seven. Every element has to be as close and as true to the idea as possible." To be able to achieve that, the director is reliant on his composer, a composer he not only trusts to the fullest extent but who also shares his sentiment and can fulfill the vision of the director—a true bond where the duo not only works for a common goal but where both people are really one artist.

David Lynch was lucky to find such a Siamese sibling in Angelo Badalamenti who he met prior to shooting *Blue Velvet*. To be able to make music a Ten, both artists need to understand each other without words if necessary, the composer being the musical mind of the director, the director being the visual mind of the composer. "Music fulfills beautiful functions," Lynch explained.

Many times, music is mood and music is emotion. Angelo Badalamenti is a master at bringing emotion out of music, so powerful his music is emotionally. I guess I did use temp tracks for sure, but a lot of times, the temp tracks end up being the final tracks for these sequences. With Angelo, I have a way of working with him where I talk and he plays. He plays my words. If my words are no good, his music is no good. So I change my words. His music becomes real good if I say good words.

It is no surprise then that Lynch lovingly calls Badalamenti his "long lost brother," a description that requires no explanation considering the closeness of their working process.

A few weeks later, I called up Angelo Badalamenti at his home in New Jersey. Fortunately, I hadn't watch *The Sopranos* before, otherwise I certainly wouldn't have dared to call up an Italo-American in New Jersey, let alone ask him any questions of any nature. It doesn't help that he played Luigi Castigliani, a Mafioso, in David Lynch's *Mulholland Drive*. "Stephan, I am drinking an espresso," he said on the phone. "And you know what happens when Luigi Castigliani spills his espresso. We don't want that to happen."

But, as it turns out, Badalamenti hasn't burned down my flat following our conversation. On the contrary, although the composer was busy writing music for *Stalingrad*, he kindly elaborated on his way of working with his long lost brother by detailing their process:

> It is a very fortunate thing to have someone you have this unbelievable relationship with where all you have to do is look at each other and without opening your mouth you know each other's feelings and you get along and you have respect for each other. He is very gifted. When he hears something and he knows that it's right, he also sees pictures. I know he sees pictures because I see him looking out into space, being mesmerized, and I know he is keying in some certain scenes he will shoot. The music sometimes gives him ideas for scenes to shoot.
>
> The working process has been that David would sit next to me at a keyboard and talk to me very slowly, very softly in my right ear because he sits to the right of me. He paints a verbal picture that would suggest a mood. He plants ideas in my head. It radiates back to my fingers. His words go through my head and my fingers go down to the keyboard and I start improvising. I keep playing and playing based on what he says, and even as I am playing he will now paint me some more pictures. I will be on something for five or eight minutes and now he wants me to go somewhere else and break the mood a little. Now he starts painting other kinds of pictures. I can sit down for five or eight minutes and at the same time we record every note I play. Sometimes if I don't capture what he envisions right away, he will come up with a new set of words. It's one hell of a beautiful way to collaborate. What's better than that? How do you beat that?

Their spiritual bond resulted in a rather fascinating episode as remembered by Badalamenti when talking about his *Dark Spanish Symphony*, composed for the Palme d'Or winner *Wild at Heart*:

> I had a small office across the street from Carnegie Hall. All I had in that office was an old Fender Rhodes. I still have it here in my house in New Jersey. David would love to take it from me and put it into a museum but I am not letting him have it. David came running in and said, "Angelo, you write something, a Spanish thing for this movie, *Wild at Heart*. Play me something Spanish." I sat down and in no time at all I wrote the whole melody of the *Dark Spanish Symphony*.
>
> David was stunned. "Angelo, you are not going to believe what I am going to tell you!" "What?" "I heard this music in my ears—what you just played, the whole piece—while I was riding in the train coming up to your office." "What?" "Angelo, I am not lying to you! What you just played, I heard in my head on the train!" He was dead serious. Dead serious! I am not one to deny that. It can be very perceptive, spiritual, I don't know. Very psychic. But he swears he had heard what I played.

Angelo Badalamenti was right in saying that the relationship he has as a composer with Lynch as the director is very fortunate—and it is also very rare. The advantage Badalamenti has is that David Lynch is an independent filmmaker, and is thus not reliant on a dozen producers who not only tell him what to do but who also demand reports on why he does what he does. This also affects the music. While Badalamenti is the servant of Lynch and Lynch only, the composers for American studio productions are the servants of several people.

Being inspired by temp tracks is a possible way to steer your ship safely into the harbor: pieces of pre-existing music which were put on the rough cut of a film during the editing to give both the producers and the composer an impression of what the final score is supposed to sound like so as not to take any risks. There are several other reasons for the employment of temp tracks which make working in the way Angelo Badalamenti and David Lynch do nearly impossible. Here, the director doesn't sit to the right of the composer, formulating what he envisions the music to sound like and sometimes even shooting the picture according to the music; instead the director delivers the rough cut of a film to the composer with music already on it—not in the form of words like Lynch does, but in the form of music which the composer is expected to draw inspiration from. Temp tracks are not necessarily the favorite subject of discussion for composers.

Digital Editing

Temp tracks is a misleading term in a way. Musical pieces that are being put on a rough cut even during the editing process are "temporary" in the sense only that they are not supposed to make their way into the final film. However, these "temporary tracks" don't represent a "temporary concept" because the concept of the actual film score is very much dictated by the style of the pieces chosen for the rough cut—mostly by the music editor, sometimes by the director, sometimes by the picture editor, sometimes by all three parties depending on the individual film.

The influence of temp tracks can also in some cases be heard clearly in the final score, making it a near-rip off of the pieces used during editing and the test screenings. Moreover, it frequently happens that cues which were originally put on a film as temp-music end up in the final version of the movie for various reasons (see David Lynch's approach described above). In such an instance, the music editor, who chose those temp tracks in the first place, then needs to clear the licenses for the pieces and the studio needs to pay royalties. This can be quite costly depending on the piece. However, no payments are due if the temps stay on the rough cut internally only.

A director suggesting music to a composer, to demonstrate how the music is supposed to sound, is not a new idea. John Guillermin, for example, had Jerry Goldsmith listen attentively to *Also sprach Zarathustra* when suggesting a musical concept for his film *The Blue Max* in 1966. Billy Wilder asked Franz Waxman to draw inspiration from Franz Liszt for the score of *Sunset Boulevard* in 1950. There are few film directors who, even before digital editing caught on, haven't made their composers listen to certain pieces to establish a common language. Orson Welles had a piece of George Antheil's put over the opening credits of *The Lady from Shanghai* as a reference.

The advantage that composers had before digital editing was that the rough cut of the film was put together on a flatbed Moviola where the so-called temp tracks were not glued to a scene. The director and the composer listened to the suggested music on a vinyl player, but each had a comparatively open mind when watching the first cut of the movie without having pre-existing music blasting from the speakers at the same time. Digital editing made it possible not only to cut movies quicker, but also to put musical pieces beneath scenes effortlessly. When digital editing caught on in the early '90s, editors could cut scenes to the rhythm of a certain composition. It wasn't the final composition that would later be heard in theaters, though, because the composer in most cases hadn't even been hired yet.

Digital editing had severe consequences for composers. Before the new technology was widely used for U.S. blockbusters, composers used to receive a "locked cut," meaning the final version of the film minus the score, which obviously still had to be written. Composers could be sure (with the usual exceptions to the rule) that the cut of the film was not to be changed, that the scenes they had to work with would still have the same length when the movie would later be shown in theaters, meaning that adaptations and changes to the score were unlikely to be required. This changed abruptly with the advent of digital editing, as explained by Richard Bellis: "The reason that there was a locked picture is because the negative had to be cut at some point and you didn't want to do that more than once if you could avoid it. Things do not get locked anymore."

Nowadays there are at least three versions of a film: the assembly, which the editor does according to the script, the director's cut, which by any union is a right of the director, and eventually the studio's cut. In case of a disastrous test screening, another cut will be made.

From then on, not only was it possible to place music beneath the scenes and cut the film according to the rhythm of the music, it also became ridiculously simple to change scenes around the clock.

The increased pressure due to digital editing has indeed become enormous for composers, as detailed by a composer who worked on a high profile blockbuster in 2016, complaining,

> They are changing it quite a lot every day. There are bits where I do something that I'm really proud of and cannot wait until somebody hears it and then going to the cinema and finding out, "Nah, that's not in it." Two days ago I

played a piece of music to them that I had written for this movie ages ago. Twenty different ideas had gone in there and now we came back to it. And I find myself dancing in my flat when I am really on to something. That's always a good sign. I was doing that yesterday, so I have a good feeling that this piece will turn up in the movie.

The resentment of composers toward digital editing is therefore understandable. "When you constantly have to re-write cues according to new cuts of a scene, facets of your concepts fall away," says John Ottman.

Your general idea that you wrote is still probably going to be fine but it's going to be hacked up. So you are going to have to alter what you have written. It's a pain in the ass thing of constantly having to conform what you have written to the new picture. I always make a judgment call. If I deem that the music is going to be editable in ProTools later, I am not going to change the cue and I am going to record the original version. I always remind people on the scoring stage, "I know the scene has changed, I know this is the old scene but we are going to edit the music." So I make this judgment call or I'll give the mock-up to my music editor and say, "Can you cut this to make this work?" I am not going to change it. I am going to move on to another scene because it's too laborious to constantly conform your cues to a new cut. Often, most of the alterations in the cut consist basically of tightening.

In some cases, "tightening" is not enough though, as Ottman experienced when he had to record a cue for *X-Men: Apocalypse* on the day of the print master because of new changes to the newly edited scene, the day of the print master being the day the film can't be changed anymore because it is due to go into distribution. Eric Styles, an independent director, visited his friend John Debney when recording the score for *Cats & Dogs* in 2001. Suddenly, Debney was asked to come up with an additional piece because a new scene had been added to the final cut. According to Styles, the usually calm and reflective Debney was fuming.

Needless to say, it causes additional stress for the composer to alter the music for a scene and record the music accordingly on the day when the final print is to be delivered to the distributors. Says Matthew Margeson,

We have become exposed to mathematical problems all the time. It happens every day, and the goal of that point becomes a different part of our brain. How can I now mangle a piece of music and still have the melody intact? Sometimes it makes things a lot more difficult and sometimes in retrospect you say, "It's actually better that we are able to breathe a little bit in a certain section in a film, or maybe speed up something." It's not always the worst thing in the world but it doesn't always make a scene better.

Ending up with a hard drive packed with dozens of versions of only one cue has become a recurring anecdote in every film composer's life—although a rather painful one. Trevor Jones recalls this:

I have a sense of abandoning a project—you get the last cut and you have bandaged the wounds and tried to make the cue work. I just turned up and started again. There was one cue in *Notting Hill* which we had 64 versions of. When working on films as a composer, there is a certain degree of massacre and there is no doubt about it. It is not something one enters into lightly.

The opportunities that are presented by digital editing are tempting. After all, editors don't have to rewind but can change a scene as often as they like. This has had consequences in all areas of life and in all jobs—some good, some bad. What is art about if not reflecting, musing and questioning? Even a composer as technologically savvy as Klaus Badelt reminds us of the dangers when giving an example of an artist he admires:

> Henri-Cartier Bresson was a French photographer who was one of the founders of Magnum Photography. If you look at his pictures of people, you find that he was at the right space at the right time. He had the right moment and he waited for that moment. If you wait too long, it's gone. There is a risk and a thrill connected with this. I always think of him when writing music, to sharpen your pencil and your mind and know exactly when you have this moment. Today you could go over that and lose it without noticing it.

Not surprisingly, it is mostly younger directors who like to change their films right up until the very end because of their understandable need to prove themselves to the producers and the whole team involved. The mind-set of these directors in most cases seems to be that constant changes mean constant improvement, although that is most likely not the case. Badelt continues,

> In photography, if you take digital pictures you take 20 pictures of one motif. You couldn't do this with film because you only had 24 or 36 pictures in your roll, so you took two. And those were better because you had to think about it. You had to do composition. I always love restriction and limitation. It really helps you to create something special. It takes a good talent to make full use of the technology and not ignore it.

If composers find themselves in the situation of having to alter several cues multiple times, this can eventually—as a worst-case scenario—end in destroying their own musical concept that they set out to execute.

Talking about the downsides of digital editing for composers, Klaus Badelt feels guilty that he was one of the first composers in the early 2000s to encourage changing music as late in the process as possible:

> I got rid of all samplers and all computers. I started writing in 2003 or 2004 on one CPU and mixed in the same sequencer so you could make changes even after you had done the final mix. In the final mix I was on the dub stages with my rig while they were mixing the movie.
>
> I was so pissed off because creation was a one-way street. You could not go back. You had a milestone and when you hit that milestone you could not

jump back over the milestone. You would write something and then record the orchestra. You couldn't go back into your sequencer, into what your writing tool was. Then there was the mix. You would prepare the sync masters. Out of your rig you would record it somewhere and some engineer would mix it. From there it would go to the dub stage. Somebody else would then have 20 tracks of yours but you had no access to it anymore. If they wanted to make changes, they had to cut it from another cue. It was very difficult because it was in another rig.

I changed this whole scenario of writing by putting everything in one CPU including mix and final delivery. The final mix was done, I was on the dub stage, they wanted a change and I could make a change even in the writing. I could change the notes of the orchestra even though it was in the final mix stage.

There are various possibilities for composers to handle the situation as much as it is in their power. Depending on the individual project and the individual director and editor, it can be the "judgment call," which can mean fanning out work to arrangers and assistants by handing over already written cues to adapt them to a new cut. It can also mean refusing to make any more changes and discussing it with the director if composers are established enough to do that as suggested by Badelt: "Say, 'This is it, I won't make any more changes.' Focus on composition, in terms of music as well as on photography. You talk to someone who really enjoys technology but at the same time I am very aware that the key component is the creative responsibility of how to use it. Never forget that content is king."

Not Too Much Content, Please

Pressures on the composer have increased in many other ways with the advent of digital editing. Although temp tracks are ideally supplied by the music editor, the process is also a matter of profound interest to directors, film editors, producers, and even composers themselves. Understandably, this can cause problems for the music editor; Gerard McCann:

When I come in to work, there would be an email with 20 cues that somebody has been listening to over the weekend that they are convinced would be perfect to hear in the film. Even my exploration to put a temp score together is already populated from top to tail and it's more a question of removing material. Usually it's a kaleidoscope of different tastes and that's a harder point to start because even the temp is affected by the temp. You must get to the point to present something that has a cohesive thought to it. It's a battle often with editors and directors who have already established what they think is right for the film. Your role is reduced to tidying up the editing and mechanically finding ways to make the work better.

Since both editors and directors can now easily place a piece of music on a scene and work with this particular piece of music while editing, they do prefer to take the choosing of temp tracks into their own hands. Editing is still a relatively slow process which usually takes several months and gives birth to numerous versions of the film. In the course of these months, both the director and the editor listen to the temp track many times, because they watch the current cuts of the film many times, and therefore get used to the sound and the effect the temp has on a scene. Moreover, so do producers when a cut is being presented to them by the director and the editor—after all, they need to have music on the film to be able to make a judgment about how the film would work when being shown in theaters.

With several parties getting used to this pre-existing, "temporary" music, it becomes increasingly difficult for the composer to come up with a personal concept for the score, or even to deliver music that is close enough to the temp tracks without its being plagiarism. As the composer is usually the last creative force to be brought onto a project, it is an inherent problem.

Temp tracks have also led to film music's becoming more generic, as Rachel Portman recounts when drawing a comparison between her earlier and more recent works:

> When I did *Benny and Joon* there seemed to be very little comedy music out there. That kind of music became quite common for a brief time. [...] Comedy music has changed. I was asked to write comedy music for *A Dog's Purpose*. It's very different from *Benny and Joon*. It's much more generic. I enjoyed doing it a lot but I am less comfortable doing generic anything. The audience sits there and thinks, "This is a generic language." This all comes down to temp tracks. Everything becomes very generic. We think, "Oh, we are going to enjoy the scene because it's funny." The music is telegraphing what the audience needs to feel in order to make them more comfortable. Personally I am more interested in doing things that are more edgy. But it's more and more difficult to make edgy things.

In the case of *A Dog's Purpose*, every scene of the film was temp-tracked. Naturally, all this was down to give more control into the hands of the director, editors and producers, leaving little freedom for Portman. She continues:

> On that film they had a wonderful music editor who worked tirelessly on the temp track for six months. He cut all sorts of pieces of music so that everything would fit, rise up here and hit that. By the time I got around to write the score they said, "You can do whatever you want. We want your voice." I wrote the theme which was fine but when it came to crafting the score I pretty much had to follow the map which had been laid down by the temp. When that came to comedy nobody wanted to stray too far from the thing they all felt safe with or got attached to. It becomes limiting for a composer. It just does.

Editor and sound designer Walter Murch can empathize with the issues a composer has to deal with. He says,

The film emerges into its consciousness midwifed by these temp tracks. The temp tracks are there all during the sculpting of the film. Then the composer is supposed to come in, push the temp tracks aside and produce something that is even better but in the same way as the temp track. The problem is the problem of the missing tooth that the director is so accustomed to what the temp track was doing. Even its imperfections are perfect eventually because you are so used to them that the danger is that you get the Kubrick phenomenon when the director can't just accept the new music.

But which pieces does the editor choose to cut the movie to? A piece with changing meters, complex rhythms and a long melody is by its nature not an editor's favorite. From an editor's point of view this is all too understandable. After all, these are pieces that are very difficult to cut scenes to. A melody very much gets in the way because editors can't cut around it, shorten it easily, or take several bars out in the middle of it in order to make the scene they are editing work. Therefore, it is much easier to take a musical piece with a loop or an ostinato where whole seconds can be taken out if the editing process/scene demands it.

On a flatbed Moviola the editor would simply put a piece of music on without worrying too much about hitting all the cuts of the scene because the technology was not advanced enough to guarantee a satisfying result when trying to do so. Digital editing enables editors to do exactly that. Temp tracks can now be fine-tuned and manipulated in every possible way while having the sound effects and the dialogue playing at the same time in accordance with the music. Says Joe Kraemer,

> It has handcuffed the composer. It has taken a lot of the decision-making about the music for a film out of the composer's hands and moved it into the director's, producer's and music editor's hands. 98 percent of the studio films that a composer gets hired on, the composer walks into a situation where everybody has already made up their mind about all the music in the movie. They are not really interested in your opinion. They want their temp score in a way that they can actually release it.

Music editors have another good reason to choose rather anonymous-sounding pieces of music as temp tracks for the rough cut if they are obliged to provide the temp: music editors quite regularly know next to nothing about the film they just started working on. It is a reason for great sorrow, as music editor Gerard McCann complains: "I'll sit in a room and I'll get a scene from the film. I don't see the rest from the film, I haven't even seen the script because it's too secret for me to know it. What they want is to have a painter to paint a wall without seeing the rest of the room or house."

Another valid reason for the lack of melodies is the problem of association. The cut is being shown not only in a test screening but also to the director and producers. If the director wasn't responsible for choosing the temp tracks and didn't oversee the process, complex pieces which offer more than simply a mood and a rhythm can be distracting as they do not express what the director had in mind in the first place. Moreover, a temp track taken from a classic movie such as *Harry Potter*, *Jaws* or *Star Wars* can be highly irritating for the obvious reason that these pieces are very strongly connected to the movies they belong to. Paradoxically, a more anonymous-sounding cue helps the cause by not having the baggage of being associated with another movie.

To carry that thought further, when you have a melodically-inspired cue as a temp track, the risk of ending up with a rip-off by the chosen composer is much greater, possibly ending in plagiarism. This at least partly explains an anecdote shared by Edwin Wendler:

> I was talking to a music editor whose job it is to cut temp music into a movie before it's being scored. Their instructions were to find music that didn't do much. The less it was doing the better it was. Those same instructions were then given to the composer. The composer was instructed: "The less interesting you can make the music, the better it will be." Without cynicism: it was a straightforward instruction.

John Ottman, himself working as an editor, puts his finger on another issue:

> Film editors aren't necessarily people with great musical sense. Some are, some aren't. They are trying to sell a cut and they just grab something, throw it on a scene and inevitably it's a generic thing because a lot of film music is so generic now. Inevitably they throw something on from a movie that did well at the box office so it sounds like some music from a *CSI* episode. People come in and watch a scene with no music. The moment you put music on, it transforms a scene. Maybe not for the better but it's the only reference anyone has ever had. Therefore it becomes the bible, how that scene must be scored even though it might be completely wrong or just not inspired. So the temp score is being put on a movie from beginning to end and then everyone says, "You gotta do that." So, then that film gets scored in that way and then that score goes on a CD and then the next editor on the next movie puts that score on their temp score and then that score gets ripped off.

With most editors not having a vast knowledge of film music and its history, the easiest way to choose a temp track is indeed to look for currently successful movies that are of the same genre, and put the music of one of these films on as the temp track. Very likely, a finished film then ends up with the bastard child of the temp score—or, as Joe Kraemer puts it,

> You end up with a situation where you have a watered down version of *American Beauty* as a score. That ends up as a temp in another movie and now you have a watered down version of a watered down version of *American Beauty*. We are going to see that with *Mad Max: Fury Road*. Somebody is going to

temp *Mad Max* into a movie and we are going to get a watered down version and then we are going to get a watered down version of that watered down version.

Film music history provides us with several examples of this, a fairly well-known one being John Williams' music for Oliver Stone's success *JFK* (1991). For its most prominent cue, "The Conspirators," Williams came up with a motif imitating a ticking clock. In several movies which premiered shortly after, the same gimmick makes its appearance, most obviously in *Under Siege* (1992), composed by Gary Chang, *Jurassic Park* (1993), composed by John Williams himself, and *The Usual Suspects* (1995), composed by John Ottman. *The Conspirators*, although a rather unusual composition in Williams' oeuvre, made for an obvious choice as a temp track for a thriller: it was composed for a thriller, a *successful* thriller, and it employed a striking motif rather than a complex theme.

In the last few years, something important has changed, which has had its effect on how music editors work with temp tracks. Whereas in the '90s, editors were required to go the nearest CD shop to choose a fitting temp for the movie, they now have access to download services such as Google Play, Napster or iTunes. Now, the range is vast and so are the possibilities.

The problem, though, that composers can encounter when faced with a temp score compiled from various different sources is the difficulty of coming up with a coherent concept for the final score. The most striking example of this might be the case of *The Good German*, Steven Soderbergh's film from 2006 for which composer David Holmes had been asked to write the score. Eventually Holmes' score, a mix of electronica, minimalism, and orchestral elements, got rejected by the producers.

> It was, however, carefully modeled on the movie's initial temp track—which had turned into a disastrous combination of unusual, clashing styles by the time the picture neared completion. Once it was determined that Holmes' strange score failed to fit the picture, the movie's musical concept was rethought, bringing it more into line with the 1940s noir style that informed its plot [...].[1]

Badelt recognizes this issue: "It was always the problem of a temp score that it was a patchwork. It is then the job of the composer—and it's an opportunity—to tell the director, 'I have a really strong theme,' and you weave the themes around and suddenly you have a cohesive sound."

John Ottman gives advice for every party involved when explaining,

> The syndrome gets broken in three ways: you have an editor who is musically inclined not to put this garbage on, you have a director who has a great taste factor for that kind of thing, you have a composer who comes on and actually says, "This isn't right for the movie, let me present you with an alternative

idea." When that happens it's great. The syndrome gets broken from time to time and you get a good film score out of it and you get a good movie.

On a Scale from 1 to 10

If the directors and producers are satisfied with the presented cut of a movie and therefore with the effect the temp score had on the scenes, the movie will then be shown to a test audience in a screening. These test screenings are organized by distributors or the production studios themselves to find out how successful the product is likely to be. While test screenings have a long history, they first caught on in the '80s when the most successful distribution company, Miramax, decided to test their products regularly in this manner.

In most cases several screenings were organized with people from every background and with every taste being invited to rate several elements of the film (including the score) on a sheet of paper. The most perfect rating would of course be a 100. But the fundamental flaw of test screenings soon led to wildly different ratings from screening to screening. So heterogeneous was the audience that viewers found themselves watching a movie they would never pay to watch in the theater (imagine a member of the Hell's Angels watching *Love, Actually*), which soon frustrated directors—understandably, one might say, when a movie is shown to people it wasn't made for.

Test screenings have nevertheless become a standard for Hollywood studios and also another obstacle for composers. In most cases, the composer has already signed on to write the score but has not finished writing or even recording it, meaning that a substantial amount of movies a year are shown not with the final score in a mocked-up version but with the temp score. If the temp music scores high on the rating sheets, it can be a disaster for the composer. Explains John Ottman,

> The whole reason that a movie has to be temped is because the film is not going to work without music on it. So you have to throw music on for a test screening. And then everybody gets used to the music. If the test screening goes really well, everyone is afraid to rock the boat and try something different. The best thing that can happen for a score is a film that tests really badly so maybe the composers can do something different. If the film tests really well, it makes it much more difficult for the composer to make a case to do anything other than the temp score that is in there. It's a difficult thing.

Nobody wants to mess up the film after it scores highly. This also affects the music. When the temp track yields satisfying results, trying to convince the director and the producers to come up with cues that vary heavily from that temp score is akin to the task of Sisyphus. According to Joe Kraemer,

On most studio films by the time the composer is involved the thing has been temped to death. It has gotten its score. The last thing they want is a composer coming in with a vision for the film and changing everything. They want a composer who will make a legally releasable version of the temp score. Because the film has been shown to a test audience and it's gotten a score. That score is a quantifier. If you show a film and it gets a score of 92, and the reason it got a 92 according to 18 percent of the cards is the music and the only people who mention the music mention how much they like it, that music needs to stay as close to the temp as it can. If it doesn't stay close to it and the film doesn't do well, that's bad news for the studio executives. Whereas if you stick to the temp and the film does poorly you can still say, "Look, we tested it, it got these numbers. I can't explain why it didn't do well at the box office but we gave the audiences what the test audience gave a good score to."

If a movie—with either the fully-recorded soundtrack by the composer or, at least, with a mocked-up version instead of being shown with the temp track—scores badly, the blame usually goes on the thing with the least resistance. Very often this is the music because it is one of the easiest things to change at that point. Generally, this means the composer has to go. In one way it can be a great benefit for composers to come into the process at a very late stage and not have their music on a film for the test screening for the obvious reason that they cannot be blamed for a poor rating and still have a hope of keeping their job. There is still a chance.

The Dubious Honor of Copying Yourself

Typecasting is not just a huge problem for actors but to a large extent for composers as well. The reason is quite simple. Here is Matthew Margeson:

> Because of the way films are being made, there are many reasons for being hired. One could be specifically because of your music. People are hired because the filmmakers know they can trust what you are going to do and their baby is in very good hands. Another example where the temp is your friend is when maybe a previous score of yours is temped all over the film. The director then says, "Whose score is this? I want him to score the film." I know this happens with a lot of people. Temp tracks limit your creativity in a way. Even if it's a little bit you can't deny that you are influenced by it. So you are now constrained by an idea that has been there before.

As a result, creative forces are brought together for a certain project if they were part of a similar movie that proved to be highly successful at the box office. For example, Thomas Newman's score for *American Beauty* was one of the most temped compositions in the early 2000s after the film not only made a lot of money but was also hailed as one of the great masterpieces of American cinema. Because the music was, naturally, a big part of the movie's success, not only was the same kind of instrumentation, sensibility and minimalism used for similar productions but Newman was also then commissioned to work on these films with the requirement that he come up with a similar musical concept (*In the Bedroom, The Salton Sea, White Oleander, Cinderella Man, Little Children, Revolutionary Road, Towelhead*). More often than not, Newman was then required to copy himself, as were other composers who were unlucky enough to work on successful movies.

In this instance, temp tracks can be seen as both the best friend and the worst enemy of the composer. They were lucky enough to have gotten the job to work on a new movie because of their previous work's having been used as a temp, but they are now forced to use the same formula, thus restricting themselves from coming up with something new that is satisfying to them as craftsmen (women)—or artists, if they see themselves as such. Music editor Gerard McCann explains in no uncertain terms how quickly composers can find themselves stuck in a machinery that is not interested primarily in challenging them to come up with new musical concepts for their successive scores:

> Jonathan Glazer wanted to have this ongoing laboratory [for *Under the Skin*] which was entirely within his control and came with no preconceptions, including the fact that Mica Levi hadn't even written a film score before. Nobody could grab some of her music from another picture, whereas shortly after one of her *Under the Skin* cues was used as a temp track for *American Horror Story*. Even something as creative and original as that is already becoming part of the temp fabric.

Nick Cave and Warren Ellis have suffered a similar fate. McCann continues:

> They belong to the more original end of film scoring. But when you want to do something else that is as original as that, don't do something that you call original—because it copies something that someone else did that was original. I know A-list composers with a backbone who don't find the opportunity to be original. It's denied to them. You can't just say, "I am so and so, you came to me so you want something original." No. They have harnessed A-list composers because it's an insurance policy. They will say, "We are making a film with so and so who has got five Oscar nominations."
> You can't have the finger pointed at you by the producers and say, "Why the fuck did you employ him or her?" Well, they have status. You still want the insurance policy of them writing something that is not too outside the box. They get just as hampered by the temp track syndrome as anyone else.

There is the potential for a way out though, as suggested by Henry Jackman:

> Occasionally you'll hear, "I love this piece, it's this piece you did in *X-Men: First Class* and we love it!" "Really? Guess what, that piece I wrote for *X-Men: First*

Class was not me copying another piece of music. If you want a good piece of music in your new film you should not be asking me to copy a piece that was written in a creatively free spirit because it will never be as good. It's not artistically honest." I try to remind people that one of the reasons they really like this piece is that it was written by somebody not trying to copy someone else. It happens occasionally when the director doesn't want to let go of something. I tend to find that directors who have creative confidence do not panic too much. One reason to want to copy a temp track is a lack of creative confidence.

The Even More Dubious Honor of Copying Others

If the composer whose work a movie was temped with is either unavailable or too expensive, the next logical choice is a successful (or less expensive) composer who has worked on similar movies before. This composer then finds himself confronted with the temp score of a colleague. After all, it wasn't just Thomas Newman who had to copy his *American Beauty* formula but other composers as well.

The regular experience of having to imitate the style of another composer can understandably be highly disenchanting when one's own style or vision is not allowed to blossom. Says Mychael Danna,

I really feel what people really want to hear from music is *you*. They want to hear you and your inner spirit. If you layer on someone else's spirit on top of it, if you say, "I want to sound like what this film is or that temp score," it's not sincere and I think even uneducated film fans and viewers can sense that. They can sense that it's not emanating from your spirit. People don't want that. People actually want to hear voices of individuals and real feelings and a real take on things. It's something that people need to remember when they are writing. To be yourself is the best thing you can be. I don't believe that audiences reject individual voices in film scoring. I think they are much more open-minded and more receptive to originality than the executives who are controlling that. Certainly the executives are not interested in taking chances that way.

The truth of the matter is that individuality in modern Hollywood productions is not at the top of a producer's list of priorities. If a certain sound is required because of the temp track, a composer will be found who is able to fulfill these requirements. Some composers might argue that temp tracks that differ from their usual style even make them flex their muscles by being challenged to do something relatively foreign to them. Others might find this to be an obstacle they cannot overcome as they find it impossible to renounce their own personal style. Explains Murray Gold,

I can't make things very different because most things I do end up sounding like me. However much I try not to, however much I want to explore something new it somehow always comes out the same. Either that means my range isn't very wide or there's something that I just do that I don't even know. I'm probably mischievous. Sometimes I want to write a very serious piece and somehow I probably can't stop giving it a little wink.

As much as it can be a challenge to find the right approach that fits to the temp score, it can be equally challenging not to stick too closely to the temp and end up plagiarizing it. As directors and producers are usually very fond of the temp score if the film proved a success in a test screening and therefore in some cases ask the composer to stick as closely to the temp as possible, this can result in rather baffling cases where at least sections of the final score sound awfully similar to a pre-existing cue from another soundtrack.

See You in Court

The most famous example of actual plagiarism in a movie score is the case of Elliot Goldenthal vs Warner Bros. Tyler Bates was commissioned to write the music for the sweat and blood epic *300* which premiered in 2007. After its premiere and the release of the soundtrack CD, not only did film music aficionados comment on the similarities between Goldenthal's *Finale* from *Titus* and *Remember Us* from *300*, they also noted similarities between *Victorius Titus* from *Titus* and *Returns a King* from *300*—but so did Goldenthal himself, who filed a lawsuit against his former employer Warner Bros. Goldenthal and Warner Bros settled with severe consequences for both parties. The composer received an unknown amount of money for copyright infringement and Warner Bros released a statement saying,

> a number of the music cues for the score of *300* were, without our knowledge or participation, derived from music composed by Academy Award winning composer Elliot Goldenthal for the motion picture *Titus*. Warner Bros Pictures has great respect for Elliot, our longtime collaborator, and is pleased to have amicably resolved this matter.

Furthermore, a label was printed on the already pressed DVDs, advising the customers to go to the *300* website for "important information regarding the source of the music score."

There were ramifications that were less pretty for Goldenthal though. Having become persona non grata at Warner Bros, not only did he never work for them or any associates again, but Warner Bros has also since prohibited a CD release of his score for *Batman & Robin* (they had graciously allowed a release of *Batman Forever* before but later pulled the plug on its sequel). The case of Goldenthal vs Warner Bros became a textbook example of temp track love and a rare instance where a composer filed a lawsuit—it also shows strikingly why composers usually refrain from doing so.

A rather similar thing happened when Steven Spielberg's *The Color Purple* premiered, featuring an original score by the movie's producer Quincy Jones (and eleven co-composers). Spielberg had temped the main title sequence with Georges Delerue's catchy tune for the British drama *Our Mother's House* from 1967, directed by Jack Clayton. Jones' composition for the sequence bore a striking resemblance to Delerue's theme—and "Purplegate" happened. The resemblance created a stir in Hollywood when both Delerue and Jones were nominated for an Academy Award in 1986—Delerue for *Agnes of God*, Jones for *The Color Purple* (along with Bruce Broughton for *Silverado* and John Barry for *Out of Africa*).

According to *People* magazine, a spokesperson for the Motion Picture Academy commented at that time, "Let's pray to God that *Silverado* or *Out of Africa* wins, then we won't have to worry about it."[2] *Out of Africa* won the Oscar and Delerue won as well: the Frenchman received a large settlement and was shortly after offered the job of scoring an episode of *Amazing Stories* by Steven Spielberg. Delerue went on to score two more episodes of the show in 1986 and 1987.

Bill Conti was lucky when *The Right Stuff* premiered. Not only did the composer win an Academy Award for his effort on it, he didn't get threatened with a lawsuit despite quoting Gustav Holst's *The Planets* in his score (as well as Tchaikovsky's *Violin Concerto* which was no longer under copyright). With John Barry having left the project after disagreements with the director, Conti had only a little time to come up the score for a three hour movie. Orchestrator Angela Morley was careful not to mention names or even the title of the project, leaving it to the reader to figure out that the project she was talking about could only have been *The Right Stuff*:

> The composer's drawn expression suggested to me that he hadn't been to bed for some time. In a weary voice, he told me that a very long cue that we had recorded two days previously, that he had very skillfully composed and that had worked wonderfully with the scene, had been rejected by the director of the film because it wasn't close enough to the latter's beloved temp track!

As a result, Conti had to ask for his esteemed friend's help, which she provided, albeit reluctantly:

> My colleague had now reworked the sketch which he offered me together with the pocket score of the classical work that the director had used as a temp track. My friend gave me an imploring look that seemed to plead for my complicity as one thief in the night to another, apologetically mumbling: "You understand what has to be done here?" I understood, only too well, that I was being required to incorporate the mercifully dead master's engraved, published notes into the new version of the cue. Only thus would the director be satisfied.[3]

(The clue that she was talking about *The Right Stuff* indeed was given later on in the interview when Angela Morley mentioned that her "colleague" later won the Academy Award for said score and "pointedly" ignored the director in his acceptance speech.)

An altogether different problem had to be faced by Nino Rota and the company behind *The Godfather* after Rota had used his own theme for the Italian movie *Fortunella* (1952) as the love theme for the Mafia epic. Unfortunately for the composer, he didn't have the rights to his own theme. *Fortunella*'s producer Dino de Laurentiis had retained the rights as music publisher and brought the case to the Los Angeles court. While it is not publicly known how the case ended, the Academy of Motion Picture Arts and Sciences decided to revoke the nomination for Rota's *The Godfather* as its most prominent theme had already been written for another film.

Disqualified

Of course being acknowledged with an Oscar is a great honor for everybody. Despite constant criticism, the Oscars still draw enormous attention every year. In 2016, a storm in the teacup erupted when it was announced that the score for one of the biggest highlights of the year was disqualified for the award: Jóhann Jóhannsson's music for Denis Villeneuve's *Arrival*, starring Amy Adams and Jeremy Renner. For this project, Jóhannsson had written a complex and at times daring score by recording voices, manipulating sounds and thus creating a unique mix of soundscapes and minimalist music. When the film premiered, it was not only praised for its script, direction and acting, but also for its score which was hailed as Jóhannsson's biggest achievement to that date.

The composer's problem though was that Denis Villeneuve had decided to use a pre-existing piece in two crucial moments of the film by employing Max Richter's *On the Nature of Daylight*. The Academy of Motion Picture Arts and Sciences argued that

> "the credited composer did not write significant and prominently featured music in the film" and, in a letter to Jóhannsson, expressed concern that Oscar voters might be "influenced by crucial music" not written by him. Richter's piece bookends Denis Villeneuve's film, underscoring the Amy Adams sequences at the beginning (for nearly three minutes) and the end (for five and a half minutes). According to Jóhannsson, editor Joe Walker used the Richter as temporary music, and cut the opening sequence to it.[4]

Putting aside the importance of the Oscars for Jóhannsson, it must have felt frustrating to be disqualified for the simple reason that *On the Nature of Daylight* had served as a temp track and was supposed to get replaced by an original score. That didn't happen, though.

During the debate following the disqualification of *Arrival*, Ludovic Bource's score for *The Artist* was an obvious comparison. In 2012, Bource had won an Oscar for his score for Michel Hazanavicius' silent film, despite the fact that a cue from Bernard Herrmann's score for *Vertigo* by Alfred Hitchcock was prominently used in its entirety for one of the key scenes in *The Artist*. In this case though, the Academy had decided that Bource's score was clearly distinguishable from the pre-existing cue.

Considering the fact that Bource's music ran throughout the whole film from beginning to end (with the exception of the composition from *Vertigo*), the Academy decided that even with the Herrmann piece in it, there were still nearly 100 minutes of music to appreciate and warrant an Oscar victory. Ironically though, the *Scene d'Amour* from *Vertigo* had originally been used as a temp track as well, similar to *On the Nature of Daylight* in *Arrival*. Says Ludovic Bource,

> For some scenes in the first rough cut of the film, Michel had used music by Duke Ellington and Bernard Herrmann. Ellington created a whole new musical community and made jazz popular in the USA, therefore it was only logical to feature his work in *The Artist*. When Michel showed the first parts of the film to the producers, only 20 percent of my music had been finished.
>
> However, Michel didn't want to show the film with only 20 percent of music because he was afraid that the producers could be irritated by the musical gaps in the film because certain cues simply weren't ready yet. For this purpose, he used music by other composers. One of these pieces was Bernard Herrmann's *Scène d'Amour* from *Vertigo*. Herrmann was a genius. Michel explained to me that he wanted to use this piece solely for the producer's screening and afterwards allow me to come up with something different. I accepted this, but at the same time I knew that Herrmann's piece would remain in the film. After all, I knew Michel. Furthermore, the use of this particular piece actually made sense for that scene.
>
> I was doomed. Maybe doomed is not the right word though because I knew that I couldn't possibly replace Herrmann's music. That was impossible. Fifteen days prior to the recording of my score, Michel asked me to write my own version for that scene. I knew it was useless but I did it anyway and it was actually great fun for me. It also cost me a lot of energy. I dedicated my version to Michel. I called it *My Suicide*. Voilá!

Bource went on to win the Oscar.

Freedom Infringement

If handled incompetently, temp tracks can destroy even the little creative freedom composers working for movies have. To come up with a personal musical concept turns out to be as impossible as sorting your book collection by color if you are blind—and is as useless. This is frustrating and sometimes even infuriating for a creative person such as a composer. For both the director and the composer, it turns out to be a gamble: will the composer manage to write something that can convince me as the director? Shall I give him/her a chance and spend time and money doing so? Shall I as the composer try to come up with my own musical concept, spending time and money on persuading the director of my vision, very well aware of the danger of being rejected?

John Corigliano, an established and celebrated composer for the concert hall, was aware of this issue when he accepted the job of writing the music for *Altered States* in 1981:

> *Altered States* was a film that allowed me to do this kind of music I wanted to do. Most films do not. In film, the director basically says: "Well, now I want a kind of Beach Boys thing here and I want this other kind of thing here and I want that kind of thing there." Unless you're willing to do that, you really shouldn't write for films.[5]

With the given freedom, Corigliano came up with an original, daring, experimental score which would in turn inspire both composers and filmmakers for years and which was nominated for an Oscar in 1982. As understandable as the director's fixation on the temp track is, it is also highly unfortunate that it does not allow composers to spread their wings as much as possible in line with discussions and naturally the scenes and their demands. Atli Örvarsson, who stepped back from writing music for Hollywood blockbusters in 2013 to concentrate on independent movies, expresses a rather somber view on this topic:

> I think it is very difficult, especially for young composers, to develop their own style. Very difficult. But it depends on whether you work for the big studios in Hollywood or on smaller, independent European productions. With Hollywood productions, it's mostly all about the money. The companies don't want to make any losses, therefore they resort to details which already proved to be successful. In most cases this doesn't work, but that's the way it is. There are hardly any new ideas being developed, let alone tried out. If young composers have an own musical voice and a strong character and if they know what they want, I can only recommend to them to work on independent movies. They will be happier there.

There seems to be a possible compromise both for the director and the composer if the employer turns out to be indeed transfixed by the temp track. Ilan Eshkeri, in recounting one of his experiences, suggests this compromise: "When I was asked to copy a temp track, I asked the director why they simply don't license the cue to be used in the film or even ask the composer whose temp was used to write the music for their production. They did the latter and I left the project. You don't have to copy."

If one of the cues from the temp score is indeed able to fulfill this function (see also Albinoni's *Adagio* in *Manchester by the Sea*), and if this cue works harmonically with the rest of the score, licensing it is indeed a valid option and a way of not getting caught up in copying the piece and enabling the composer to execute their overall musical concept. Alexandre Desplat had his own take on the subject when it comes to the director's obsession with pre-existing music, as he explained about his work on Terrence Malick's *Tree of Life*:

> Terrence has always used a lot of pre-existing music in his films and he has always been very happy with the result. We know that Morricone tried to replace Saint-Saëns and failed. We know that James Horner [on *The New World*] tried to replace Wagner and Mozart but failed. I was in the same position, as there were Mozart, Smetana, and many other composers in the temp. I didn't think I could replace them successfully. And I don't think that Terrence really wanted to have them replaced. I think he uses this music because he really wants it for his film, and it's the composer's job to show him that he was right from the beginning, because otherwise there is not much room for the music in the film.[6]

As tough as it can be for a composer to make their mark in the industry, they do need to speak out to protect their interests—their primary interest as a creative force being to serve the picture and therefore, if necessary, convince the director that his or her concept for the score based on the choice of temp tracks is nonsense and would hurt the production more than help it. Howard Blake remembers when working with Ridley Scott on his first feature film *The Duellists* in 1977,

> I thought the film was wonderful with breathtaking photography! Ridley said: "On this scene I want an electronic sound and on this scene I want music in the style of Stockhausen." Ridley had never done a feature film before and I said to him, "Look, you are not making a series of television-commercials here where it is fine to talk about the use of Stockhausen or Mick Jagger because it is only thirty seconds long."
> When I watched *The Duellists*, it was two hours long and I suggested writing an orchestral score for it because he needed a certain sound that would unify the whole film. David Puttnam [the producer] said, "Do it!" and Ridley agreed to give it a try. Apart from *The Snowman*, this was the most exciting film experience for me because I felt very inspired by the movie and because I was working with a genius director and a very good producer.

With the backing of the producer and his skills for persuading, Blake was able to convince Scott to have the composer take the lead in regard to the music. The more successful and experienced Ridley Scott became, the less successful his composers seemed to become. Jerry Goldsmith's music for *Legend* was rejected in favor of an electronic score by Tangerine Dream, Maurice Jarre was given a wrong direction on *White Squall* and got replaced with

Jeff Rona, parts of *Prometheus* were composed by Harry Gregson-Williams instead of its main composer Marc Streitenfeld, as were parts of *Exodus* where cues by Alberto Iglesias were replaced, while Harry Gregson-Williams had to leave *Alien: Covenant* late in the process.

The most vivid example is *Alien* (1979) where a substantial chunk of Jerry Goldsmith's score was replaced by temp tracks, most notably by parts from Howard Hanson's second symphony—a project Howard Blake was supposed to work on, as he remembers,

> Immediately after *The Duellists* [Scott] was offered *Alien* and he wanted me to write the music. I went down to Pinewood Studios and on the set of *Alien* where we talked a lot about this project. I would have certainly done it and I would have been happy to write the music for all of Ridley Scott's movies. However, the producers at 20th Century–Fox said, "Listen, we have either Jerry Goldsmith, John Williams or the Newman family working for us. Plus, you are not American. So forget it!"

Several high-profile composers have been lucky enough to work with directors who knew how to use temp tracks appropriately without scaring their composers off. Cliff Martinez, for example, appreciates his working relationship with Steven Soderbergh, who had obviously learned a lesson after the *Good German* disaster by using the temp score as a guide rather than a command,

> For the first few episodes of *The Knick* Steven had chosen some temp tracks. He used music from *Contagion, Spring Breakers, Only God Forgives*, and *Drive*. I found this quite daring but in regard to the music, Steven does appreciate unusual concepts. My initial reaction to the temp tracks was quite subdued. The show tried hard to take the audience to the New York of the 1900s. Based on that, I found the temp score to be a violation of the show's concept and it rather bothered me. Using such modern music risked making a colossal mistake. As is usual with music, you get used to a certain language though and will be able to understand it. They tried to attract a younger audience with the music.[7]

Martinez considers himself lucky to be working with Soderbergh, as he added:

> As a composer, you can't completely ignore the temp score if it fits to the pictures. Up until now, I could avoid them more or less. If a director asks me to write the music for their picture, and they ask me for something that is similar to my previous works, I will have to take my own music as a guide, but that is okay with me because at least it's my musical voice. I never had any problems with that.

Music to Act To

At a lecture about temp tracks in modern film music at the University of Utrecht, Netherlands, one student raised his hand and cleverly asked whether these problems can't be solved simply by writing the music before the editing process, even before the shooting by reading the screenplay. This idea seems attractive when one has been exposed to the trials and tribulations of the composer forced to mimic a temp score.

Moreover, it is a technique which has many supporters in the industry, though not necessarily in the Hollywood industry but rather in Europe or artistic circles in the United States. One such being Philip Glass, who wrote:

> In my film work, I continued, to the degree it was permitted, the collaborative approach I had arrived at in my theater and opera work. I made a point of being present through the entire process of making a film, and that included extensive visits on location as well as many hours watching the editing process. My overall strategy was to set aside as much as possible the "normal" role of the composer in the traditional filmmaking process, where the music is considered part of post-production and one of the very last ingredients to be added before the work is completed. In fact, through the 1980s and '90s, I was experimenting with the role of the composer in the overall work scheme. [...] Instead of waiting for the music to be added at the end, during post-production, I had moved it up to the front, before the cinematographer had even shot the film. [...] The main problem is that filmmakers already think they know how to make a film, so changing their procedures would almost always be out of their reach.[8]

Glass gives the example of having persuaded Martin Scorsese to work this way on *Kundun* and sending him some music before the actual shooting. Although supposedly hesitant and puzzled—and even though industry films do not support innovation, as Glass laments—Scorsese agreed.

However, Glass was not the first composer to work in that manner. The best known example of a film score being used during the shoot may very well be Ennio Morricone's music for Sergio Leone's classic *Once Upon a Time in the West*. Morricone explained the benefits of working this way clearly:

> The director's telling of a film's story can be very important, if not actually decisive. In some cases—those in which I have achieved the best results—the composer will record the principal pieces before the film is shot or before it is assembled. This is very useful, because in this way the composer makes the director understand the sense of the music in an unequivocal way. It eliminates at least 50 percent of the uncertainty and surprise that the director might have during a recording session.
>
> I always find it very useful when a director falls in love with a theme or a musical situation. The fact that he listens to it many times over and understands it and makes it his own, and also sings it while he sleeps, means that in a way, even during the elaboration of the film, during the editing, during the mixing, he takes into account the way the music breathes, its tiny pauses. At the editing stage he actually may find strange synchronization points that the composer absolutely never would have thought of. Imagine: the actor in close-

up simply raises his eyes, and the director finds a point of synchronization on that almost imperceptible movement.[9]

If images inspire the music, why can't music inspire the images? It can indeed work particularly well and has the further advantage that the director can abstain from using temp tracks but still has music on the film for the test screening. Early involvement of the composer also has simple practical advantages, as Dimitri Tiomkin colorfully described:

> It is of incalculable value to the composer to be able to sit in on story conferences from the beginning. He will not only better comprehend the total trend, mood or purpose of the story, but he will be able to make suggestions that will enable the music to strengthen and fulfill the story. For example, at random: consider the point in a story at which a man suddenly, without warning, slaps a woman. Let us say the writer's conceived the scene to be with two characters standing together by a window.
>
> Now sudden violence like a slap in the face has more impact if something unobtrusive prepares the audience a second or two in advance. If this split-second preparation is not provided, the mind will resent being taken by surprise. The best "something," it has been found, is music. When this slapping sequence is discussed in a story conference, I might say to the writers, or the directors: "I will have to have a few seconds in there just before the slap in order to prepare for it." And we would talk it over and conclude that the man will have to take a few steps in order to slap the woman. This will give me the time I need to presage the violent change of mood.[10]

As much as Tiomkin preferred that approach, it has rarely been executed in Hollywood simply because it departs from already established conventions which everybody has become used to. The composer's dilemma is that a film is always the work of not one but 100 people whose decisions and points of views all need to be considered and paid attention to by the composer. By reading the script and writing music for it accordingly, the only person whose point of view is considered is the screenwriter's, and in cases where there are careful discussions with the director, also the director's, but the influence of the producers, the most powerful forces in Hollywood, are naturally being neglected.

Also neglected, therefore, are the usual demands for changes after a film has been presented to the financiers, possibly resulting in a new cut which would then result in changes in the music for which a new recording would have to be set up, not to even mention the creative force of the visual effects department which had not been considered when reading the screenplay nor when shooting the film. "We can go through a script and say, 'Oh, this character really deserves empathy,'" explains Richard Bellis.

> But after the shooting and assembly, there may be so much empathy already that the last thing they need is musical empathy on top of it. My concern is

that you create something too early. The process of creating a film has daily periods of diagnosis. "This is working, that's not working, we had to do this shot out of sequence and it was on the morning after the wrap party and I didn't get the performances I wanted." So I, as a composer, need to help if I can. But perhaps the scene as it was first shot didn't need any music because it was a 100 percent effective at that point. [...] It is dangerous to voice an opinion too early or start writing the music too early.

The death blow for the argument of writing the music according to the script before shooting comes from Angelo Badalamenti: "I do receive most of the scripts because the producers send it. I simply scan through them without analyzing. I find with David [Lynch] as a reader what you are visualizing when reading can be totally different than what ultimately winds up on the screen." Intense discussion about music and its role in the film need to be entertained. To find common ground, temp tracks can be a great help and an endlessly useful tool for understanding the vision of the director, who is not musically educated and therefore speaks a language different from the composer. Says Klaus Badelt,

> A director cannot talk to you about music. They don't know. And if they do, they have this half-knowledge, which is even more difficult. I had directors who had a bigger soundtrack collection than I have. They are maybe the more difficult ones. You need to think like a filmmaker. You are one of four people shaping the film: the composer, the writer, the editor, the director. I am not diminishing the actors but that is the core team pulling the strings and making the creative decisions. That's important. It's about the filmmaking process and the collaborative approach, about analyzing the film and the characters.

"The composer has to be responsible for knowing and for educating the film director," according to Richard Bellis.

> I use the term educating carefully because it's like a doctor. The doctor can't tell you about every aspect of the cure. But you have to trust the doctor and the doctor has to tell you in very general terms what the problem is and what he is going to do. The doctor will say, "Here is what I think we should do," as if bringing you into the conversation. As a composer you need to ask questions. What is it about the temp that's working so well for this scene? I can imitate it but I'd like a chance to do something that is as original as your film. An original score that has the same dramatic essence as the temp. That's the conversation that has to happen.

With the temp track as a tool, the composer is able to pull important information from the temporary score in accordance with the director. Matthew Margeson uses them for exactly this purpose:

> We have a temp track. I can't avoid it being there and can't pretend that it doesn't exist. So when I am watching a film for the first time, I ask myself what information can I pull from this? For me, the most important thing about a

movie or even of a specific scene is the pace, the heartbeat of a scene, the heartbeat of a film.

You could have a brilliantly acted film, a brilliantly produced film, but if the pacing is all wrong, you are never going to realize how good the film could have been. Not necessarily the size of the orchestra or the size of a score from a temp track but what I will keep in mind when I am listening to any temp music. Does the heartbeat work, does the pace work? That's the information I pull from it. Then once I have listened to it, I try not to listen to the temp track ever again and not be influenced by it except for how the pace makes me feel.

This advice goes for directors as well as for composers because it is not only the people who write the music who can benefit from using the temp score as a communication tool but abstain from becoming obsessed with it. The obvious advantage for directors and their work is not only to use a score which has its own character, but also to be open to fresh voices and views after the directors have already lived with their work for several years, thus becoming blind to potentially problematic issues, as was the case with Xavier Dolan's *Tom à la ferme* which with its temp score featured music from beginning to end, whereas the final score by Gabriel Yared is much more carefully placed, allowing long stretches of silence which has its own powerful effect on the scenes, therefore enhancing the movie and its qualities.

To guarantee a successful working-relationship with any director, the composer has to make them their best friend by being diplomatic, friendly and persuasive. Christopher Young used these tricks when asked to write the replacement music for *Playing by Heart* after John Barry had been let go, remembering,

Make the director feel comfortable so that he likes you immediately! The director came to visit me for the first time, and he was a chain smoker. I offered him a seat on my couch, offered him a beer and a pack of cigarettes before even mentioning anything about the film or the music. The director liked me already then before I had even started to write the first note!

Turn Down the Sound,
I Can't Hear the Music

Wherever we are, what we hear is mostly noise. When we ignore it, it disturbs us. When we listen to it, we find it fascinating.—John Cage, *Silence*

It was early 2013 and a telephone was ringing in Barcelona. It was late evening. After a few seconds, Javier Navarrete picked up the phone and introduced himself. I was due to interview him about his career as a Spanish composer working for Hollywood productions, about his experiences in La La Land, his hopes, his dreams, his illusions and possible delusions. Javier Navarrete was at the peak of his career in 2006 when he scored Guillermo del Toro's masterful yet disturbing fairy tale *Pan's Labyrinth* for which Navarrete received an Oscar nomination.

A few stints in Hollywood followed: the passable but overlong *Hemingway & Gellhorn*, the colorful yet rather sluggish *Inkheart*, the ridiculous piece of schlock *Mirrors*, the dreadful *The New Daughter* and the big budgeted brain freezer *Wrath of the Titans*. Hollywood (or Navarrete's agent) hasn't necessarily been kind to an original composer who started out in the '70s with a keen interest in avant-garde music and everything that's off the radar. The interview went well enough. I was surprised to find that the composer for these hardly intellectually challenging productions was a shy, thoughtful and introverted artist. He is very much capable of looking back on his past projects without the slightest hint of nostalgia or rose-tinted spectacles.

The biggest blow was yet to come, though. At the time of the interview, Navarrete was working on what would be the most traumatizing experience of his career, the 200 million dollar epic *47 Ronin* starring Keanu Reeves. After Atticus Ross had already been let go, the Spanish composer took over to deliver an orchestral tour de force, filled with muscular action pieces for the numerous battle scenes. His score was nearly at the point of completion, with the assistance of Navarrete's long-time friend Lucas Suarez, when the work was rejected.

Javier and I stayed in touch after our interview. One evening he sent me an email with the news, attaching the photograph of a skeleton to fittingly illustrate his feelings about his rejection. Still, the hope was that his rejection would turn out to be beneficial for him, depending on the film's success or lack thereof. With several re-shoots, a budget that exploded and two fired composers, it didn't look too good for the film. As it turned out, *47 Ronin* bombed like hardly any other studio production had bombed before. That was good news.

After writing the score for the Chinese production *Snow Girl and the Dark Crystal* in 2014, Javier took a break from film scoring to concentrate on what he really wanted to do: express himself. He wrote twelve nocturnes for solo piano, which he wants to find a CD label for, and he wrote an opera which premiered in Spain in 2017. When I was asked by the organizer of the event Media Sound Hamburg whom to invite to give a master class in film music in 2014, I suggested Javier immediately. He did indeed give the lecture to the satisfaction of all attendees and it was here he met Tim Nielsen, the sound designer who worked on such illustrious films as *The Lord of the Rings*, *Avatar*, *Maleficent*, *War Horse* and—surprisingly—*47 Ronin*. Despite the fact that both had worked on the latter project, their paths had never crossed. They never wrote to each other or talked to each other, let alone met in person.

As it turned out, this is not unusual with composers and sound designers. Although music and sound design are both part of the sonic world and are eventually merged during the final mix for the ultimate print of the movie, they don't always interact during the post-production process. It was therefore to the great satisfaction of both Javier and Tim to sit down and talk about their experiences when it comes to the relation between music and sound effects. It is an important topic for any composer and sound designer for obvious reasons.

It is also the reason for grievances on both sides. When it comes to the sound of a modern blockbuster, there are indeed enough reasons to be anxious, and all of these were summarized on a sunny afternoon in 2014 by both Tim Nielsen and Javier Navarrete: there can be too much music in a film, too many sound effects, too much of both. The composer can be asked by the director to mimic the sound effects with his music because the director is either insecure about his film or doesn't know the difference between the purpose of music and sound effects.

Composers and sound designers work separately, rarely have meetings together and thus more often than not have to fight for their work on the dub stage when both elements are brought together for the first time. Composers can be required to record the sections of the orchestra separately, so-called striping, to make it easier for the mixing engineer to delete certain sections of the music if they don't work with the sound effects. Music can clash with the sound effects tonally; it might not work with the frequency range of the effects. The correlation between music and sound effects is an interesting subject. With sound effects becoming more and more elaborate, composers have more to worry about.

"It's not a new tendency to do music with sound design," said Navarrete. "That was done before the actual sound design came up, in the Pirate movies of the '40s. There is not much sound and it's not as elaborate as today of course. We have too much of both now." "Movies are getting busier visually," Nielsen agreed emphatically by explaining the reason behind the constant wall of sound and music in today's studio productions.

> Because George Lucas can do it, there are now 800 space ships in one shot. Everything is speeding up [...]. That's a problem, too. We have an overload. No matter your mentality as a composer, the first time you work with a young director and try to propose to them, "I am going to score only half of your film," they are going to fire you immediately or at least fight with you. You will then end up with 85 minutes of music for 90 minute film. Because the directors don't know anything. It's our job to help teach them that the music and the sound are both tools to use.

More often than not, sound effects and music are being played at the same time, often quite unnecessarily to the damaging effect that the individual scene is not nearly as powerful as it could have been with a more restrained approach. After all, playing music all the time has very much the same effect as using no music whatsoever—without breaks, the effect is lost.

Tim Nielsen recounted an illustrative example when talking about his work on *The Fellowship of the Ring* evoking the scene in which the black riders are out to kill the hobbits and tear down a huge gate to stab Frodo to death. While the hunters sneak in, stab a person and find out it was not Frodo, the sound effects are minimal, creating an eerie and still environment by raising the tension and spooking the audience. Afterwards the music kicks in and carries the scene.

The music was, however, written in a different way. When Nielsen saw the scene with an editor, they reached the conclusion that the scene would be much more effective and in fact quite scary if they played with silence instead of having a large choral piece accompanying the procedure on screen. This was the concept Nielsen and his colleagues pursued, desperately trying to reach Peter Jackson to listen to their work. For reasons unknown to the sound design department, the director was not informed of their request to have a meeting and discuss the approach for the scene. Because of this lack of communication, Howard Shore recorded a massive piece of music, probably at Jackson's request, which was not only huge due to the use of the choir, but also went through the whole scene without giving the sound design department any chance to play with silence and therefore to execute their concept.

In the final mix, Nielsen and his colleagues played the scene with the music and were obviously quite disappointed since they were convinced that their approach would have elevated the scene to a completely new level. Since moviemaking is all about politics and diplomacy, nobody dared to raise any objections. Luckily enough, it was Peter Jackson who at one point demanded to have the music muted. Said Nielsen,

> Here is all this very tonal, eerie work we had done and he said, "This is so much better! That's a great moment! If I had heard this earlier, I would have never scored this part of the movie." If we had made that decision as a group, we could have done something that's even better than what we ended up with. Sometimes there are interactions where this can occur.

"The problem is," said Navarrete, "the directors think they have two elements and they want to play both of them at the same time, saying, 'I don't know what is going to happen, I will ask these guys to do both sound effects and music, so in the final mix I will have the choice.' That's not the best way to do it." It is indeed not. But what to do about it?

The Band Never Stops

Navarrete's observation that music was used to fulfill certain functions of sound effects in the '30s and '40s when sound design was far from elaborate is both true and telling. As mentioned in 'The Sound of Change' above, Hollywood productions from the '30s and '40s more often than not opened in a blast of sound, whether appropriate to the film's subject or not, and the music rarely stopped before the end credits started rolling. The modern equivalent of crowd-pleasers and tearjerkers—superhero movies and family comedies—are very much inspired by the use of music and its constant employment in the old classics.

The New Hollywood in the '60s and '70s abstained from the traditional wallpaper soundtrack but instead placed music carefully in films, often to great effect when they merged with the sound design. The great hits from the '70s use music only sparingly: *The Exorcist, The French Connection, The Conversation, Medium Cool, Paper Moon, The Last Detail, Five Easy Pieces*—the list of films with a sparse soundtrack goes on.

Walter Murch, sound designer and editor on *Apocalypse Now* and *The Conversation*, was dissatisfied with the working process of the studio system and ventured out to San Francisco—where the unions didn't have a stranglehold on the different picture departments—to be able to work together more closely with his colleagues George Lucas and Francis Ford Coppola. "We had not worked that way in film school," says Murch about the old system, "and we didn't want to work that way. In San Francisco there wasn't the same kind of strict division of sound effects editors from music editors to mixers to picture editors. When you worked in post-production on a film you were all in one group. That's what suited us because that's what we wanted to do."

One of the ventures they embarked on together was *The Conversation*, which is now regarded as a cult classic of cinema. Few movies serve as a better example to illustrate their way of working by discussing a common approach with the composer. Murch continues:

> Francis asked David [Shire, the composer] to compose the music before the film was shot based on the screenplay so that Francis could play the music to the actors prior to shooting the scenes, sometimes even during the scenes. This is a great way of working because that means that the actor listening to the music knows intuitively that the music is doing a certain job. Therefore the actor doesn't have to do that job. You can dance with the music in a sense, he doesn't have to cover all the bases because the music is covering that base very well. The actor can shape his performance in a way that collaborates with the music because now he has already heard the music. It's amazing that any other way of filmmaking works at all.

The independent films of the '80s and early '90s continued this tradition concerning the differentiated use of music, although for an entirely different reason—namely to save money. As much as technology, and therefore musical scores and sound effects, have evolved since the Golden Age, we now seem to have come back to the '30s and '40s with a wallpaper sound that simply won't stop, however much we ask it to. George Fenton explains that "There is a certain cyclic aspect to the way films emerge, a reaction not against having music in films all the time but perhaps a reaction against the kinds of films that had music in them all the time, followed by a reaction to the films that don't have music in them all the time." Other trends have arisen as well, namely expensive franchises, which are effects-driven visually and cry out for a lot of music since that is the way these films were constructed.

The spirit of the Studio System of the '30s and '40s went back into action after the collapse of the New Hollywood, although strictly speaking it had never left since it has clear advantages financially, explains Walter Murch.

> The old system is very well suited to a certain kind of industrial product because everything is clearly defined and everything has its box. You wait until this stage and then you move to the next stage. You don't turn the film over to

the composer before a certain point because that's the most efficient way to do it from a business point of view—not artistically certainly. If you gave me a magic wand and said, "You can change one thing in the film industry," it would be to get the composer and the sound designer, who ideally would almost be the same person sometimes, to start working on the film even before the shooting.

Whereas in the New Hollywood the director was the auteur who couldn't be bothered with having powerful producers breathing down their neck, the directors working for American studios now have to compromise with their employers who not necessarily care about the best artistic approach but rather the most financially beneficial approach.

The comparison between the employment of music in independent films and franchises is an interesting one and only a very few composers have had extensive experience in both fields. One such is Klaus Badelt who continues to work with Werner Herzog after having worked on one of the biggest franchise productions, *Pirates of the Caribbean*. While for Herzog, 35 minutes of music in a 90 minute film means wall-to-wall deployment of score, Hollywood producers might argue that two-thirds of the score were missing. Badelt reflects on that:

> Here in Hollywood we literally have more music in minutes than the movie is long. I am still not sure how that works out but there are some overlaps and you have the end credits. I keep saying this for the last 15 years: we have too much music in movies. The absence of music is music. The absence of music is a cue. It has a meaning and an impact just like the use of music has. Here the insecurity of filmmakers is compensated by, "Let's just put music on there." It's not just in movies. The trend has become to have something there, to color the air, as they call it. I keep fighting for a more fine-tuned use of music.

Also, the video gaming industry is not helping that trend since this industry revolves about 99.9 percent around music as coverage. Keeping all that in mind, it is not entirely surprising that the sensitivity evolved to have more and more music in media productions. Nowadays, music is everywhere: in supermarkets, on the streets, in elevators, in video games, on YouTube and Spotify. Says sound designer Randy Thom:

> There is usually too much music in contemporary American films. And often there is too much sound design as well. The urge is to fill every moment with *something*. But the best choice in storytelling is often to starve the audience for input rather than to constantly barrage them with *stuff*. Music, I think, might be the most efficient tool a filmmaker has in terms of how much power you get from it relative to how much it costs.
>
> As with any powerful tool, there is a temptation to use music too much and too often. I do think that the ubiquity of music in the world—ear-pods, clubs,

restaurants, shops, etc., etc.—reinforces this idea that we *must* have music all the time, everywhere, including every scene in every movie.

Sudden silence becomes disturbing because it has become so rare and unusual. While silence therefore can be used to great effect in scenes which are supposed to make the audience nervous, it is more likely to irritate the younger generation when watching any of the currently successful franchises such as *Transformers* and *The Avengers*.

The movies from the U.S. market which either do rely on large stretches of silence or refuse to employ music at all are, unsurprisingly, the unsettling ones: horror movies. Starting with *The Blair Witch Project* right up to *Paranormal Activity*, it is the directors of these works who know how gruesome and anxiety-inducing silence can be, especially in today's environment. European and independent productions have ever since relied on the use of silence, meaning the absence of music, to unsettle the audience.

Movies like Georges Clouzot's *Wages of Fear*, Fritz Lang's *M* and Michael Haneke's *The White Ribbon* use silence to powerful effect, to evoke a sense of doom and dread, as Walter Murch puts it:

> Even in a conventional horror film which was scored by Bernard Herrmann let's say, the presence of that music does scare us but it does so in a companionable way. It's as if your big brother is going to scare you. In a sense the music puts its arm around you and says, "Now I am really going to scare you." And it does.
>
> It does a good job, but you get the sense that there's somebody there, trying to modulate your reactions whereas a film with no music, forgetting the fact that it has sound effects which sometimes act in musical terms, is abandoning you to your own devices so that you have to react and have to come to emotional terms with the film without the music being any guide to you. That's a scarier prospect.

When young people especially are used to having music constantly around them and are therefore afraid of (long stretches of) silence, the use of silence not only has an effect on the theater audience. It starts much sooner and has turned into a vicious circle, because it is especially younger directors who mistrust silence in the 21st century for the obvious sociological reasons. This not only leads to their decision to employ a lot of music in their films but it also affects their whole filmmaking process, with sometimes harrowing consequences for every member of the team. Music editor Gerard McCann offers this explanation:

> What is new in the last few years I have discovered is there are a number of directors who won't even view their rushes. They don't see the dailies. They shoot the film, they will see assemblies of edited sequences. They want the temp track before they see anything. So let's say they shot a sequence on a

Monday, and they might want to see it on the Wednesday. But instead of watching rushes, they are seeing edited sequences that have sound effects and music already because they don't ever want to see it naked because they can't judge it naked. So you are temping rushes. I'll sit in a room and I'll get a scene from the film. I don't see the rest of the film, I haven't even seen the script because it's too secret for me to know it. What they want is to have a painter to paint a wall without seeing the rest of the room or house.

The consequences are obvious: when a director is afraid to view the dailies naked, without music, the music editor is asked to put a temp track on the dailies. As described by McCann, when working on dailies, the music editor lacks the context and is subsequently unable to put together a temp score that has a coherent structure. The temp score becomes a patchwork since the music editor has no chance to see the complete film.

The causes of this rather interesting sociological phenomenon of having a society of people who are afraid of silence are increasing with the constant exposure to music and the need to satisfy all stimuli. With technology enabling us to do several things at the same time, our attention span has gradually narrowed, or, to say it in more friendly terms, we all have become less patient. We can watch a movie, receive WhatsApp messages from friends (and enemies), receive Twitter updates, see the newest Instagram pictures of the celebrity we are madly in love with, write on Facebook that we are doing all of these things—and even smoke a cigarette while doing so.

With lots of things happening simultaneously, it has become harder to concentrate on one thing and one thing only—as Javier Navarrete notes when he recounts an episode from working on a movie where the director asked him to hit all the action on the screen with the music instead of letting the sound effects do the job they are supposed to do:

> I remember a director telling me about a fight scene to hit all the clashes on the screen. We had loops, percussion, brass, and this directors still told me, "I need more, more, more. Let's hit everything." We came in the studio and it was all sound effects. We got all of that atop of the score and we had to improvise that in the studio, doing it in a break. What's the point? Immediately, everything else we had was lost. The music was already so exaggerated. If you do that, the rhythmic part gets lost because there is no way you can push the two of them at the same time.

According to Navarrete, the director never once saw the movie from beginning to end, since he was terrified of it. Instead, he was a man of sequences, who very much liked single scenes from the greatest films ever made but lacked the attention span to devour a feature length film in one sitting—very much like the film studio employees in Robert Altman's *The Player* who walk around the studio lot, discussing certain shots from classic movies, but never the movies themselves.

Have a Seat

Tim Nielsen's anecdote about *The Fellowship of the Ring* shows how important it is for composers and sound designers to work together, or at least have extensive and regular discussions to enable both music and sound effects to be as powerful as possible, fulfill their functions and elevate the film to a higher level. It is also true, as noted by Javier Navarrete, that this rarely happens for the simple reason that sound designers and composers work at the same time and therefore have nothing finished to show to each other because they are both still working on their material. One reason for the necessity of such discussions is to figure out a common approach, especially when creating a new universe that the filmmakers invented and which now needs a suitable underscoring both in music and in sound effects.

If detailed discussions between sound designers and composers are so important, why do they only take place once in a blue moon? Randy Thom provides an answer by pointing out how important these meetings really are:

> Nobody wants long meetings, or lots of meetings, neither the composer nor the sound designer. Ideally the composer and sound designer get involved with the project early and start sending material back and forth to each other from the start. Ideally each gives the other useful ideas. In most scenes and sequences either the music or the sound design should dominate most of the time. The director should figure out as soon as possible which is going to generate the most storytelling bang for the buck. Occasionally the two can be equally present in a scene, but that requires some careful sonic choreography in order to really work.

It is not only the pressures that both departments face that prevent a close collaboration. Logistics also play a part. As detailed already, the pressure for composers has increased substantially within the past 15 years with the advent of digital editing and technology. Particular mock-ups have to be delivered on a regular basis which need approval from not only the director but several other forces in the film studio. When composers need to rely on a team of assistants, how can they possibly find the time to spend with colleagues from another department and exchange ideas with them regularly? Composers are rarely able to do that if the film they are working on isn't a long-term project they have committed themselves to for half a year.

The same goes for sound designers, as Randy Thom puts it:

> In every craft I'm aware of, not only in feature filmmaking but even in the making of commercials, the trend over the last three decades has been toward shorter schedules and lower budgets. The only people who are making more money now than they were in the '80s are the CEOs, and they're making a *lot* more. The most tragic victim of time pressure is experimentation. If you don't

have time to experiment, and make mistakes, it isn't likely that you will break any new creative ground.

In the '30s, although composers and sound designers hardly ever worked together closely in post-production, at least the two elements were recorded at the same time, as noted by sound designer Ralph Ives, who remembered his working process at that time:

> We had two long tables … and these were where all the sound effects were placed, and two mics, one for each of the sound effects tables. They had pots and pans and all different kinds of things, depending on what sounds were needed for the picture. It was an incredible thing. The orchestra sat near the right side facing the screen, the singers and actors on the left side facing the screen. On the left edge of the screen I had mechanically animated a 'bouncing ball' by punching holes in the film to set the tempo for sync, but there was also a conductor who followed the screen. They did a solid reel, which in most of their cartoons ran seven or eight minutes. So they'd start at the top and go all the way through.[1]

A close collaboration between composer and sound designer didn't take place though, and it was exactly this way of working that inspired the artists behind the New Hollywood to proceed in a different direction to pursue their favored method of filmmaking.

Because of technological limitations, sound design in the Golden Era caught only necessary sounds, such as footsteps. But the technology developed rapidly. Possibilities increased to such an extent that soon it was hard for a composer to avoid conflict between their music and the film's sonic effects. The issue became one of making their music heard amid all the crashes and bangs. As early as 1964, John Barry noted how important it had become to work closely with the sound department to discuss a common approach. He said, when remembering his working process on the James Bond venture *Goldfinger*:

> At the time we did *Goldfinger*, certain movies had exaggerated sound effects. But with *Goldfinger* they really, really did it—with the hits and the screeching car sounds and the runaway trains and the fist fights—everything was just way over the top, very noisy. I was frustrated, so I asked if we could have the senior sound editor involved with the music score. […] So, on a lot of Bond movies, I would work side by side with the sound guys. And the formula worked very well.[2]

It also worked well for Walter Murch and George Lucas on *THX 1138* a few years later when sound design and its possibilities had developed but were still far from being as elaborate as they are today. Says Murch:

> When I started out 50 years ago, we would just have a dialogue track and no music and no sound effects as we were putting the films together. We had to

imagine the film with this complement of other sounds to it. As time went on we got to the point where we could run two or three tracks simultaneously—one dialogue track, one sound effects track and one music track. Now of course you can run 99 tracks or even an unlimited number of tracks. Because we *can* do this, this creates an expectation that we *should* do it. Once the expectation is that you *should* do it then to *not* do it becomes a statement.

This exchange of ideas and concepts with the sound department like in *Goldfinger* remained rare and only occasionally were composers satisfied with the result. "Nine times out of ten, you do not have the final effects, and that's too bad," remembered Daniel Licht. "Sometimes, especially in an effects-heavy movie, you need to know what aural space is left to you."[3] In fact, composers were aware of the problems that go with trying to set up meetings with the sound department, as explained by Mark Isham:

> I have actually traded sample disks with sound-effects departments and made musical things out of their effects. And they use some of my musical things as sound effects. The problem with post-production is the time limit toward the end, which, usually, just gets worse all the time. So, a lot of the time, you won't have access to final effects. So you just try and keep them in mind.[4]

Since both sound designers and composers can only fully start to work once the film has been shot and is in the first stages of editing, very little time is left for them. So it happens that both departments work in parallel, often to their mutual frustration. This comes as no surprise, since they start seeing themselves as enemies instead of allies when they start fighting for their work in the final mix. Before composers start working, though, they generally receive a sound-effects guide from the responsible department. How detailed and elaborate the sound-effects guide track is depends on the individual sound-design department and the director in charge. Walter Murch, for example, resorts to compiling a rather rough guide with only the necessary effects to give context instead of providing an atmosphere. Randy Thom, on the other hand, makes his guide track entirely dependent on the director he is working with, saying,

> As with everything else, it depends to a large degree on who the director is, what her/his tastes are, how sophisticated he/she is about hearing unfinished mixes, etc. One of the reasons I've had a long career is that I don't assume I should work with Director Y the same way I worked with Director X. It's a feeling-out process. I know that some directors will be completely thrown if I don't send them something that sounds pretty close to finished, and in context. I know I can send another director raw sounds, and that I'll get meaningful feedback about those raw sounds.

If the guide track is sufficient for the director, it is most likely also sufficient for the composer, as Henry Jackman explains:

It's not the finished thing but you get a pretty good feel for what the sound effects are. It's definitely good enough. The sound effects guys are so proud, obviously their final version is way better than the temp version. But the important thing is the structure of it. You know, simple things. If you are doing an action sequence you make musical decisions. There are certain moments that are obviously going to be so huge sound effect wise that there's no point competing. It's obviously going to be a sound effects moment. They do a pretty good job. The temporary sound effect track gives you an architectural plan of what's going to happen even if it's not the finished perfect sounding effects. It has the correct architecture so you know where you don't stand a chance.

Conflicts can arise when composers discover that in certain scenes their music indeed doesn't stand a chance at all, although they would have liked to have provided music for them because they were convinced that the scene would benefit from a muscular musical piece. It is here that composers and sound designers, or, more accurately, their concepts, clash and a meeting is needed—in the best scenario not only between the composer and the sound designer, but with the director as well, to figure out a common approach that works best for the scene, preventing it from drowning in both music and sound effects. Otherwise composers might be tempted to over-orchestrate their music to make it audible in the final mix. John Barry remarks, "When the effects are that loud, there is no way you can work around them. Seriously, you can't. Range extremes—adding high piccolos, xylophones, bass trombones, tubas, contrabassoon clarinets, that kind of thing—is really the only way to find a register that's not being eaten up by the effects. But it's still too much sound."[5]

"I do, to a degree, understand that comment from John Barry," says George Fenton.

I suppose I feel that we have to try and find a way. I think forewarned is forearmed in many ways about this whole problem. It's quite easy if somebody gives you a film and you have some idea of what the sound track is like. It is not too difficult to invent within the frequency range where you know that you'll be effective. But you have to know what it is because otherwise you can just get wiped out by it. I do definitely think that there is a school of music now which is getting bigger and bigger, on those films—action films—where they, literally, in order to make a substantial enough sound, are using sixteen cellos, ten basses, ten trombones, cimbassos, Wagner tubas etc., and everyone is crashing along in order to compete with the level of sound. It has to end somewhere. The detail gets lost in the music … if there is any detail.

Might the elaboration and foregrounding of sound effects in contemporary cinema be tempting composers into writing unadventurous music, on the basis that anything with detail won't be heard anyway? When Christopher Young talked about the resurrection scene in *Hellraiser*, a darkly ironic orchestral waltz, he mused that most of the music written in the '80s couldn't be heard anymore today with the hyper-realism of current sound design, therefore demanding an altogether different approach.

Composers have to leave it to their imagination and the information contained in the sound-effects guide track to figure our what is musically possible in a scene where twelve tanks, a military troop of 200 soldiers and 20 helicopters are roaring over the film's landscape. Experience is indeed the greatest guidepost of them all, explains Alan Silvestri, who has nearly 40 years of experience in the field of film music:

> As the composer you are in the world of sound. You as a composer share that world with the actors, the dialogue and the set designers through sound effects. And then there is music. It's very reasonable to see the sound aspect of film in a quantifiable sense. There are 100 units of sound possibility at any given moment. At 0.7 seconds if a cannon blast has now just used 85 of the 100 units and then there is a scream along with it and then the scream has occupied another ten units, then there are five units for sound left in the spectrum. There is a high likelihood you are not going to hear anything musically in that moment, so then you have a range of choices.

One choice would be to abstain from the use of music in that scene since it won't be heard or will only double what can be seen and heard on the screen anyway. Often music is needed despite these circumstances for the sole reason of providing continuity. Not only franchise movies tend to be cut with a much tighter pace nowadays to make as many things happen on the screen as possible for the quickly bored audience which expects their money's worth of entertainment. The job of providing a sense of continuity comes with its own set of challenges for the composer, though—challenges that are closely linked not only to the visual components but even more so to the sound effects.

After all, it makes little sense to musically connect two scenes or shots with a rhythmic pulse by snare drums when one of the scenes features a soldier shooting with a machine gun at women and children, grinning with a cold cigar in his mouth. Under the thunder of the gun, the snare drums will not be heard. However if high strings accompany both shots, they will most likely not have a great impact when teamed with the amplified sound of a sword being drawn from its scabbard before cutting the victim's bodies to pieces in the next shot.

This illustrates how important a deep understanding of the visual and sonic aspects of a film is for composers who can consider themselves lucky when being able to set up a meeting with the sound department. All this is useful to avoid aggressive clashes between each party on the dubbing stage when both music and sound effects are joined in the final mix. Silvestri continues,

It's not just the quantified units but also the frequency spectrum. Every music or dubbing mixer knows that you can make room for simultaneous events in the soundtrack by filtering and adding frequencies or adding levels at various frequencies and making that vertical space so that everything has a place to live. That is a challenge especially for someone first going out there to write music for film. There might be a tendency to not realize the impact of the other sound in the film.

The up-and-coming film composer might be surprised to discover that the dialogue of an action movie is indispensable, a sacred cow to be respected in all circumstances. In that regard, both composers and sound designers have as much of a duty to respect the film's dialogue as the director, to make sure that every "hmm" is important and can therefore be heard by the audience without them having to resort to cease crunching their popcorn. If the composer makes the mistake of avoiding clashes with the sound effects by running over the dialogue, it will not be the dialogue that will be removed from the film to render the music audible.

There are more reasons why it makes sense for composers and sound designers to discuss their approaches in detail. The problems that can arise for all concerned parties (including the eventual consumer) run much deeper than having a wall of sound that never stops. Says Tim Nielsen,

> I sometimes think it would be better if we worked linearly, either the music comes first and then I work around it, or the sound design comes first and then the composer works around it. It would be an amazing thing to see what could happen if that was truly the case. If the composer had finished the music, I could very carefully pitch everything I am doing to work with the music. If the composer had the full effects track they would really realize there are moments that really shouldn't be scored.

Nielsen puts his finger on a sore point for most composers working in the industry today: because of the wall of sound and the inability of younger directors in particular to watch their dailies without music or temp tracks, they are often required not only to write music for 90 minutes of a 95-minute picture, but also to underscore the action on the screen by taking over the job of the sound-design department.

If directors watch a scene of their film with music but without sound effects, which are still being worked on full steam ahead, a scene where two people punch each other in the face could and would feel wrong if the composer hasn't supplied these effects musically—the impact of the punches will be diminished, to the great frustration of the directors. Without having the punches marked sonically in the scene, it would be irritating. Something would be missing.

However, foresight should make the director able to relax since these are the effects that would come in later with the finished sound design. In the context of the final mix, not marking the punches musically would work perfectly well since both departments have done their job properly: the sound design adds the hits and punches, the music gives the scene its flow and continuity without doubling up with the sound effects. It also has the benefit for both parties that neither the sound effects nor the musical hits need be deleted in the dubbing when both elements are joined and subsequently clash tonally.

When the sound design is placed on top of the music, more likely than not the latter and its effect will be lost since there is no way of pushing both elements at the same time and giving both equal weight. The important lesson for both sound designers and composers is not to be precious with their work. As soon as the elements are delivered for the final mix, it becomes part of the dialogue. If these elements—sound, score and dialogue—don't work in the service of the movie, at least one element needs to be dropped. And sometimes one element does indeed not work in accordance with the other elements. The hard lesson to learn is that in this case it doesn't matter in the slightest whether the musical piece that disturbs the scene is the best composition ever written. After all, the composer as craftsman doesn't work in a vacuum or for a concert hall but instead for a movie.

Strip(p)ing Down

Digital technology has enabled filmmakers to control individual elements of their work to a much greater extent than before. From a director's point of view (!), it also means that a close collaboration between composers and sound designers during the production is not strictly necessary anymore since the elements of sound and score can be controlled during the final mix instead of spending endless hours in meetings with all parties involved. As with digital photography, the artist now doesn't have to worry about perfect lighting anymore while taking a photograph but can always add the corresponding effect afterwards thanks to Photoshop and similar programs.

The equivalent of this phenomenon in film music is striping: recording the sections of the orchestra separately. Before striping evolved, stemming was done, which means having sections of the orchestra like the brass on individual faders during the mix which allowed for more freedom through being able to mix one section louder than the other. Striping took it to a new level. According to Bruce Broughton,

> Mostly, orchestras are not even recorded the way they used to be. You don't get eighty people in a room and record all the cues. Now you do the violins by themselves, the violas for themselves. You do all the striping. That's the stupidest way of recording music but it's very useful for technology and the control freaks who are the directors or the studio heads who think they know anything

about music. They all know a little less about music than what comes from their iPods. They heard a certain kind of sound or effect and then that's what they want from their composers. Keep the music fresh, contemporary and money-making.

When, for example, Dario Marianelli recorded his score for the adventure film *Everest* in the summer of 2015, the recording of the string parts was scheduled for one afternoon while the recording of the brass took place one day later. This way, the musicians didn't perform one musical piece together as is the case in concerts but split up in several groups, with the separate elements (strings, brass, electronics) put together later during the mix, one element added after the other like building a Lego fire station. It can be done in an altogether different way by recording one section of instruments while the other groups are in the same room but waiting until their colleagues have been recorded, in the meantime checking their phones or reading newspapers. Says one session musician working in Los Angeles, who wishes to remain anonymous: "No one really has a problem with it either way. Obviously at night the studio will cost more for extra hours. If that's what the composer and engineer prefers, the players don't really care."

Striping isn't an entirely new technique in the world of film music, although its earlier manifestation was a little different. A score which consists of several diverse elements and therefore isn't strictly a purely orchestral score but a mix of electronic elements, orchestral elements, drums and guitars, has always been subject to striping due to its eclectic nature as a patchwork. Whereas one can debate how much sense it makes to stripe a purely orchestral score, there clearly is a point in striping more diverse music for conceptual reasons alone since its whole production is generally more complex given the various elements that go into it. Henry Jackman explains:

> If it's a contemporary score with minimal brass and mostly textural, then it makes total sense to pick up the stuff separately because the way the mix is going to work, the score is going to be more like a record and less like a classical, symphonic mix. As soon as something is textural, it makes complete sense to pick up everything in a more individualistic way. Then you have complete control over what you want to do. If you know that the mix is going to have a heavy amount of production, it's different because if you have a cue which is not symphonic the orchestral contribution to that cue only represents 35 percent of what the elements are. It's not really a piece that you play down like a symphonic piece anyway. Then it makes sense to go get your bits like you hang out with a guitar player on a record to get the guitar parts, sort of like an overdub. Then it does help because you are not so committed to the approach in the mix.

This approach also allows for more freedom after the recording takes place and therefore for improvisation. The strings can be distorted, the electronics can be amplified, the guitar can be taken out. The possibilities for production tricks are endless. They stimulate the composer's creativity in the second phase of music-making, after the recording sessions took place.

Needless to say, for this reason alone striping had been a much valued approach long before it started to take hold of the film music industry in the late '90s by tempting the producers and directors to stripe even large symphonic works for the advantages described above alone. Striping has clear advantages not only for the director but for all parties when it comes to the final mix. If the directors find that one piece—which they already approved in the mocked-up version weeks before—is not to their liking for whatever reason, they can always have an element of it thrown out by eliminating either the strings, brass or electronics.

The advantage for the sound designer is very much the same: if one piece of music doesn't correspond with the final sound design, the heavy brass which makes an element of sound design inaudible can be deleted quickly and easily because there is always the option to mute things later in the process. The advantage for the composer therefore is avoiding getting caught up in the battle of sound design versus music. They don't run the danger of having a complete piece of music thrown out.

Striping is, unsurprisingly, quite popular with sound designers, as explained by Randy Thom:

> I think it helps everybody, especially the composer. Often it is only the percussion or the brass in a musical moment that would need to be lowered a bit in order to hear a few words of dialogue or an important sound effect. It's beneficial to the score to just lower that element and not *all* of the music. A few composers have the unfortunate notion that they have handed the director a perfect work of art—the score—which must not be changed at all in order to perform its function in the movie. Bullshit! No craftsperson who works in film can afford to have that attitude. In the end everything we produce is raw material for the director to use, or not use, or ask us to modify. The wise composers know that's the case, and they provide separate stripes.

Tim Nielsen agrees: "It certainly helps us. It's useful to have separations in strings and brass, certainly in some scenes where we can cut around the percussion. A good music editor is not going to destroy your music by doing this."

Considering Thom's and Nielsen's explanations, striping is less popular with composers than one might think. The attitude of the individual composer depends on the kind of score they are recording. While recording an eclectic score with a high production value and with lots of changes and improvisation later on makes sense, it doesn't necessarily have the same value when recording a large, symphonic score which is old-fashioned—or traditional in nature, where the energy flows from one part of the orchestra to another, creating a natural flow in the orchestra and therefore in the music.

Striping could cause a problem by dissecting it like a patchwork, admits Henry Jackman:

> I try to avoid striping. I don't really like that. It depends what you are doing though. If a piece of music is symphonic in nature and quite a lot of the music is grand and symphonic, it's not like a record where you are just picking up textures. The truth is, you speak to any orchestral player—if you want to record a piece of grand symphonic music, there is no denying that when they are all together in the room it is much better. I could bore you with how many reasons there are. Any kind of symphonic music I feel really strongly about.
>
> When I recorded *Kong: Skull Island*, all the players said, "Ah, we love it when you come to London because we get to play as one!" "What do you mean?" "We never…. There's hardly any composers left." Part of it is insecurity because if you don't record everything separately, and if a director goes, "Get rid of that brass!" you have to say, "We can't because it's all one thing."
>
> Some of it ends up being a negative response to the need for flexibility—just in case someone says, "Can we just mute the brass?" If we get everything separate then we can respond to any criticism. The downside to that with symphonic music is massive.

The downside became apparent to Jackman when recording a few takes of his score for *Kong: Skull Island* separately and comparing them later to the takes where all sections of the orchestra played together, describing the separate takes as "ridiculous" while the takes recorded with the whole orchestra in one session "worked like magic." Continues Jackman, "There's something that happens and it beats the other by miles. You can't even describe why. They are all responding to each other in the room. The tuning is better, the ensemble is better. Even the sound is better. When you record the brass instruments on their own, it's always a bit too loud, they need to be with everyone."

Indeed, the lack of the natural flow when recording the different sections separately is a heavy downside as further illustrated by Edwin Wendler who worked with John Ottman on *X-Men: Apocalypse*:

> As I witnessed with *X-Men*, the musicians just sit there in the room while another group is playing. I can only imagine that this is probably the much more expensive solution to this but at least you have the advantage that they can listen to each other. They know what each group is playing before they play their own parts. If you approach film music the way Korngold did, stemming would be impossible because the performance relies on the expression that the conductor gives to the musicians as they are performing whereas now that's not really required. What is required from a conductor is to keep everybody together but there is very little room for flowery performances or overt emotions.

However, whether a symphonic score flows easily and "works like magic" as a listening experience is not necessarily the primary interest of the director.

As with most things in the world of studio productions, the perspective of the filmmaker is a much more practical one, since the venture of producing a cash cow is not about the single elements of the film but about the film as a whole, a film where every step towards its cinematic release is as simplified as possible by taking advantage of the technical possibilities of the time.

If striping does indeed simplify the working process and solve potential issues during the final mix that might have arisen through lack of communication or to the circumstance that the picture is still being re-cut constantly even on the day of the print master, then surely there is good reason to stripe the orchestra and record the sections separately. The same practical attitude has increased the time pressure for composers by working on a film which is re-cut throughout the whole post-production period up until the recording of the score, since digital editing enables editors and filmmakers to do exactly that, regardless of the disadvantages some parties may face. Mistakes are allowed. They can always be fixed later. Don't worry.

Striping plays into the hands of these technical possibilities. It is even a consequence of it, in part: if one scene of the movie was shortened after the recording because the director wasn't satisfied with it, the score would need to correspond to that change, and be shortened. Such a change would be easier to make if the elements had been recorded separately in the first place; more difficult if the cue had been recorded as a symphonic whole requiring complex reediting. Lorne Balfe doesn't mind:

> The reason for striping is, when you get to the dub stage and there are picture cuts, it makes mixing very difficult if you have got just the two mixes. If you have all the elements separated, you are able to make it unnoticeable to the viewer so they are not aware that that scene just lost seven seconds. We have to look at the bigger picture. I would love everybody to play at the same time. But we have to think further than that. We have to think about what's best for the film. And depending on your schedule. If your picture is locked and you are at the last minute, then you can do it. But if you record in advance it's safer to record separately. It's all about trying to think ahead and it's not just about writing a good melody now. On *The LEGO Batman Movie* we did a lot of splits because they were still cutting when I was recording. In that case it was essential.

Sound designers, composers and directors are not the only people affected by striping an orchestral score or striping in general. It has consequences for the musicians too, since they don't get to play with all of their colleagues but only a handful of them. Their attitude towards this new phenomenon of recording the constituent layers for a large-scale orchestral score separately is of no interest to the people who pay them. For the musicians, striping is exactly as unpopular as one might think. Richard Bellis explains:

The musician's job is too often boring, it is abusive in many cases and striping is yet an additional abuse. It is unnecessary, but the information the directors get very often from their fellow directors is, "You have got to do striping, because it gives you control in the dub and isolation." Isolation and control in the dub means you can play with the music in the dub, which burns up a lot of time in the dub. It is a very expensive place to be. You can stripe a couple of action cues if you want but it doesn't mean that you have to. The musicians hate it, the mixers hate it, everybody hates it except the directors.

We have to know how to phrase the questions such as, "What is it about striping you like? Because I do provide control with stems that I deliver to the dub. And we have isolation booths. Now, we can certainly do it on a couple of cues but you have to understand that doing a whole film that way will cost you three times as much as a traditional recording."

You need composers to say it. But composers are not saying that, even the ones that are mid-level to high because there is competition or because they haven't thought about how to say that. When we merely accept the way things are we are promoting the status quo. We are not moving forward.

Striping is indeed at least twice as expensive as recording everything in one go for the obvious reason that more recording sessions need to be booked, with the possibility of facing extra costs if a recording takes place during the night. Says arranger Nan Schwartz: "You have to imagine they have to spend up to three times the money with an orchestra when stemming. Instead of having an orchestra sitting there for three hours, you have strings sitting there for three hours, then brass for three hours and woodwinds sitting there for three hours. You are tripling the cost."

Furthermore, it has created increased dissatisfaction among the musicians chosen to perform on the scores. They do suffer when they are not playing with each other but with only their sections or even performing a solo for an over-dub. The biggest issue can be the tuning, as explained by a British woodwind player who doesn't want his name published:

Often you end up playing a solo over something that has been pre-recorded. Let's say the strings have already recorded it. When you are playing with headphones on, you don't get all the information. You don't get much bass. If you don't get much bass, you don't have the full spectrum. To play in tune you need to have the full spectrum of all the harmonics. You don't get it. Also, you got a click, which we have most of the time. So, as far as music making is concerned, it's relatively thankless because you are on a hiding-to-nothing.

That's where I am sitting. Now, no musician will talk about this in this situation. Of course they are not going to say anything because it's all been decided for them. It's pointless. You are not going to complain about it because you can't. It wouldn't change anything. But the reality is it's not a very satisfactory way to produce the best results. They are obsessed with control though, these people.

I quite often think it's counter-productive. I am wondering how many people in the control room have ever thought about that. I bet you that has never occurred to them. They sit in their control room with banks of speakers with all the frequencers. If I go into the control room after playing something I can then hear what I have not heard in the cans. That makes a huge difference. But I don't suppose that they would be aware of that because they don't spend their lives with the headphones on. I don't think they care about the musicians. We are cannon fodder, soldiers on the front line.

Recording with a playback can lead to further irritations. One musician, who recorded a score of Gabriel Yared's over a decade ago, noted:

There was a piano on the track already, which I think Gabriel had done. There was a click, there were strings and then three or four woodwind players with us playing atop of everything that had been done before. It wasn't together. The click from the strings and the piano were not together in my can. There was already a problem. I said, "Gabriel, I don't know who to follow. I don't know who to play with." The engineer got a bit cross with me because he thought I was unreasonable. "We are here to do an overdub session." As if I didn't notice.

That put me back in my box. That was the end of the conversation. The recording engineer complained to the fixer who in turn got very, very upset with me that I had upset the recording engineer. I have worked with this fixer for 25 years. I got into terrible trouble. I thought, "This is crazy. I am trying to talk to this fixer who doesn't understand a single word I am saying. It's ridiculous." Sometimes Gabriel has been put in a position where he has to do stemming. It's not very satisfying. He is much too natural a musician.

Gabriel Yared himself confirms this: "It doesn't make any sense for me, or for the musicians." He continues:

A compromise would be to have two or three sessions with the whole orchestra playing together, and then move to recording in stems if absolutely necessary. Then, at least when the woodwinds are playing alone they would be able to remember how they were playing with the rest of the ensemble, and how the music will sound as a whole. The advantages of this are only to have more control during the mixing and dubbing of the film, but actually this can still be achieved by recording the whole orchestra with a professional engineer and mixer.

After recording in stems, a director could completely remove a certain woodwind line if they felt it was interfering with the dialogue, but this should be a decision that is made before the recording rather than afterwards. We should not necessarily give the directors the comfort of being able to change the balance and certain aspects of the music as they feel after the recording, but decide beforehand so that the musicians can play as an ensemble and produce the best possible sound.

Another issue arises when musicians suddenly discover during the recording that they are playing with an instrument that was recorded before—without having been notified about the deployment of this instrument.

One musician openly expresses his frustration that they weren't fed the information of having, say, a harp as a playback since the harp was tuned for the session. If a section of the orchestra isn't able to play in tune with the instrument that the players have to listen to through their headphones it makes it necessary for the recording engineer to manipulate the recording later on to make everything sound harmonious. The phenomenon of striping has become so frequent that recording with the whole orchestra has become a rarity for the musicians, who can be overheard screaming out in joy when turning up for a session with the rest of the orchestra sitting in their chairs.

The situation can be summarized by quoting Nan Schwartz:

> I thought it was the stupidest idea ever when I first heard about it. I am the kind of person who stands in front of the orchestra and wants to hear how it all sounds together. Don't forget, I am the daughter of a studio musician. I come from that place of, "How are the musicians going to relate to this music?" It has changed so much. Imagine you are used to playing with other musicians and suddenly you got to put on headphones and see everyone else walk out—and you have the metronome going on. How unmusical is that?
>
> Add to that equation the fact that you are not even playing with the rest of the orchestra but just with your own section. You just become sort of a robot. They try not to be but I find it dehumanizing. Stemming seems really dumb to me and it also seems amateurish to me. It seems like these are people who can't write for a full orchestra. But I know the motivation for it was to have full control over it so they can take sections out. I know that's what they are thinking.

Battle Cry

After the recording, the composer and the sound designer meet at the final mix where both music and sound effects are being brought together like a spoonful of chocolate sprinkles on an ice cream cone. The final mix usually, at least for American studio productions, can take up to three or four weeks and is largely spent with discussions between the mixer, the sound designer and—if present—the composers. If composers choose not to attend the final mix, they are usually represented by the music editor, the "best friend" of the composer, as described by Lorne Balfe.

Since there are more elements in the sound effects than in the music, the sound designer outplays the composer by far in the pre-mixes, usually bringing 250 to 350 tracks into the final mix (often reduced from 600 tracks originally) with seven to eight background pre-mixes, each being eight channels wide, laid out left and right in 7.1 with 12 to 14 effects pre-dubs, while the music editor is content with having 16 tracks at his display.

The time that wasn't spent on intense discussions between the composer and the sound design department during the scoring process is then spent during the final mix. Henry Jackman describes the arguments between the two forces with a comparison to the Brexit negotiations in the United Kingdom, saying,

> Usually, somewhere along there are lots of fights where the sound designers say, "No, no, no, but we designed this whole amazing sound effect thing for that scene," and you say, "Yeah, but it's not heroic, it's just loads of noises. The feeling of heroism comes from the music, the music is not loud enough, the sound effects are killing everything." "Wait, the music is way too loud, you can't hear the smash of metal...." It's a bit like in Parliament. You have the ruling party and the opposition and after that the democratic process of to-ing and fro-ing and the decision, "Okay, this is a sound effects moment." Then I find the right moment for music later.

"Most composers on big budget movies," says Randy Thom,

> don't even hear most of the sound design for a movie until the cast and crew screening, when the film is finished. The music editors hear it, and they sometimes report to the composer the state of things. Often there is, unfortunately, an atmosphere of competition between the sound-design department and the music department, competition for sonic space or sonic dominance. It's tragic, because music and sound design should really be one thing. Each should reinforce, reflect, and counterpoint the other.

Understandably, composers most often fight to make their music heard because to their ears it is in most cases not being mixed loud enough and is being overtaken by sound effects. Meanwhile, sound designers fight to make their sound effects heard because to their ears it is in most cases not being mixed loud enough and is being overtaken by the music. The director or the picture editor stands between them and demands that the levels of both elements be quietened since the dialogue cannot be heard. Also, composers might be tempted to fight for the actual sound of their work if they find too much reverb on it in the final mix. Would the process of the final mix be shortened if composers and sound designers were to sit down with the director beforehand to discuss a common approach?

Interestingly enough, Henry Jackman suggests that directors listen to the sound effects before the final stage since his complaint is that most directors he has worked with heard the sound effects in the final mix for the very first time, even though endless meetings and exchanging of notes had taken place concerning the music and getting it approved. This probably says more about the directors in question than about the sound designers, since the technical possibilities are at hand to have the sound effects approved before the dub. Randy Thom recalls that

In the bad old days, especially way back in the 1970s and '80s, the director and the editor of the film would put together a temp track consisting of dialogue, music and sound effects while they were editing the film. This was typically referred to by the sound crew as the "guide track," the implication being that it was the sound editing department's job to replace it with something "better." Well, that was often a disaster. The sound department would work diligently cutting hundreds of tracks, most of which the director and editor never heard until the first day of the final mix. *Very* often, when they did hear those sounds they hated a high percentage of them. It was often a massive waste of energy, and very depressing for all involved.

Thom credits his employer, Skywalker Sound in California, for improving the situation by having a small sound-effects crew start work on a movie not long after the picture editor:

That sound crew is feeding sounds to the picture editing department from the start. Temp mixes get done along the way, using material the picture editor has found, in addition to material the sound crew has found. This way there is no big surprise on the first day of the final mix. The final mix is just a more elaborate or more finely tuned version of the most recent temp mix. Digital technology has made this sort of incremental work flow possible.

This also says more about the directors Thom worked with than about the development of technology, since the directors of the New Hollywood consciously decided to work differently by listening to both music and sound design continually during the process so as to avoid being surprised in the final mix. Why the directors whom Thom and Jackman worked with refrained from listening to the sound effects is open for discussion. Their decision was by no means rare, bearing in mind that even Peter Jackson wasn't informed about the call for a meeting on *The Fellowship of the Ring*, as described above by Tim Nielsen, since the director was busy with other commitments deemed more important than having to deal with the elements at that time which are reserved for the final mix.

The frictions between the sound design department and the music department become clear when Jackman claims that sound designers are often overcompensating by

coming up with noises for absolutely everything. That all arrives pretty much at the beginning of the dub, so actually quite a lot of the dub is clearing out the sound effects and deciding what is really needed. It's a real shame that the sound effects scenario isn't like the scoring process. Imagine I wrote a score that was 90 minutes long and it was approved, but suddenly when I get to the dub stage, I just show up with an extra 50 minutes of music that I throw all over the movie. Then you'd have to spend time at the dubbing to decide, "We don't need that piece and that piece..." That takes time. It doesn't happen with music, but the sound effects should be taken creatively almost as seriously as music, meaning I don't know why it is considered fine that the sound effects just show up.

The implications are clear: if the director listens to the sound effects for the first time in the final mix, a substantial amount of time will be spent wading through all the material to decide what is really needed for the film, a process which has already taken place with the score, making it unnecessary to figure out which pieces will work in the movie at the dubbing stage. However, as sound effects are discarded, so will some of the music. Composers would do well not to be too precious with their work as craftspeople; but then again, their working conditions don't allow them to feel too precious anyway.

Let's Do It Together!

When I do it, it's not gossip, it's social history.—Saul Bellow, *Ravelstein*

When I spent a few days with composer Christopher Young in the summer of 2016, I managed to upset him ten minutes after we had first spoken. We had briefly chatted about his current projects before I made the mistake of mentioning a video of the Academy of Motion Picture Arts and Sciences: the organization had published a five minute film of him a few weeks before, a mixture of interview and showing Young at work during his composition process. In the short film, Young can be seen sitting at his piano, watching a movie and simultaneously banging on the instrument, before getting up and humming melodies into his phone.[1] As shown in the video, he then talks to his assistants about the concept of the score and lets them make suggestions. As to how the written score got to the recording stage (and how much was actually composed by Young) remained, in the clip, a mystery.

I mentioned to the man behind the *Hellraiser* music that I had seen the video and asked him how it had come about. For reasons undisclosed to Young himself, the Academy had approached him for the project, and after having filmed it, sent it to him for approval. Without really paying attention, Young signed off on it, and that was that. As he doesn't use the Internet much, apart from writing the occasional email, let alone visiting Social Media sites or music discussion boards; he hadn't read any reactions to it. When he eventually asked me what I thought about it, I hesitated briefly before saying that the video failed to deliver an insightful view and—worse—made the viewer wonder how much his assistants actually did for him.

Stupidly enough, I didn't stop there and mentioned some comments from friends and acquaintances of mine who had also seen the clip, dismissing it saying that Young probably didn't write any of the music himself. It was instantly evident that he was devastated. I saw him leaning forward and his head shaking before he hit his right fist hard on the table in front of me: "You know, I didn't really examine the footage that closely. They had spent hours

130

in my studio and shot an endless amount of material. I just signed off. This breaks my heart, you know? This breaks my heart because it isn't true." He cursed several times before storming off with his assistant to investigate the reactions on the Internet.

The next morning, he was quiet and thoughtful. At one point, he took me aside and said, very calmly:

> I read some comments on Facebook last night and it broke my heart. There was one guy who was suggesting that I don't write my own music. This is just not true: 95 percent of all the music for the movies I worked on was written by me. This is a blessing and a curse. It is a blessing because I can be really proud if it's good music. It is a curse because even the bad parts are by me.

He confided in me that his unwillingness to employ ghost writers had caused him big trouble in the industry. As he recalled, his agent used to call him up constantly, and at one point even screamed at him for not using other people to write music for him. The advice was simple and without ambiguity: "If you do not work with ghostwriters you will never make it to the top!"

That is truer now than ever: movies used to be locked before composers started to work on them, meaning that they didn't have to deal with sudden re-cuts, and could concentrate on developing themes which would work with the cut. Nowadays films, especially blockbusters, are rarely locked, and the edit is often being changed until a few days before the theatrical release. One of the main reasons for this development is the elaborate nature of special effects and, of course, the plurality of producers and financiers who have to agree the final product.

To be able to keep up with the workload of a modern production schedule it is near to impossible for one composer to work on a big project without the help of orchestrators, assistants and ghostwriters. If Christopher Young refused to employ ghostwriters he could find himself in serious difficulty when working on a large scale project. Young made a compromise with his agent. In 1998, Young had already finished his music for the Matt Damon vehicle *Rounders* and started working on the horror movie *Urban Legend*. While busy on the latter project, he received a phone call from Harvey Weinstein's secretary. Weinstein was the producer of *Rounders* and he was dissatisfied with some cues. The movie was to premier in a few days and a quick solution was needed.

First and foremost, the powerful Hollywood figure demanded a new love theme. Young was open to this request: "I can write something and send you some ideas in a few days." "No. You are going to write it now," Weinstein replied. As the story goes, Weinstein sat down with the composer at the piano and was present the whole time while Young came up with a new theme on the spot. This caused problems as *Urban Legend* still needed a massive amount of music.

It was something Young's agent said that did the trick: "What costs more time? Getting the ideas or writing them down on paper?" Young pondered this only briefly. The ideas came quickly. He then agreed to employ assistants to help him with the less creative aspects of the process: making suggestions, reviewing the material he had written ("because I am very insecure") and working closely with him by sorting out his sketches and voice recordings, discussing them with him and getting them ready for the orchestrator.

In 2016, Young employed six assistants and was able to keep up with large projects such as the Chinese hit *The Monkey King,* despite, as he put it, being "pathetically old-fashioned." For several years he has given classes on film music throughout the world, granting his students a generous view of his own sketches and partly handwritten scores.

With Some Difficulty

Arrangers and ghostwriters are imprecisely defined terms in the field of film music. When composers mention their arrangers, they often mean people who help them out by writing music. Matthew Margeson recognizes this:

> The terms ghostwriter and arranger or score programmer or additional music are all slightly interchangeable. The process may be slightly different but it's all the same thing. The composer is hopefully responsible for the sonic color of the score and the pace of things, the themes and motifs. But you may write or program something that consists only of strings because of the time constraints and you may hand that off to an arranger or a ghostwriter who then will start orchestrating it for the full orchestra. The job descriptions are very close to one another.

A clue to find out who did what can be found in the credits though, as John Ottman explains: "If it's 'additional arrangements by,' it's someone who helped with the programming or did a few cues. If it's 'additional music by,' that's the differentiation. That means the person did a lot of shit and way more ghosting than is normal. That's where I draw the line."

Writing music can also be done by orchestrators, even though that is not, by definition, their job. But composers facing a lack of time rely on help from other people—rarely, for this simple reason, is a modern film score orchestrated by the composers themselves. As James Newton Howard remembered: "I had composed *Alive* in five weeks, then wrote out the full score in six weeks—longer than it took me to compose it."[2]

Orchestrating, meaning assigning notes for an orchestra to play, takes time. Time is money in the movie business, so composers usually hand their sketches (however detailed they might be) to an orchestrator to write out the full score, and in most cases to add some details. While some composers reject this way of working, and some strongly-opinioned aficionados of classical music despise it outright, it had already been done occasionally in concert music, e.g., by Franz Liszt, and on Broadway by George Gershwin, both of whom gave some of their work to orchestrators. It is a controversial matter because how much the orchestration adds to the composition depends on how detailed the composer's "sketches" are.

Aaron Copland famously made the following comparison, defending the practice of having his music orchestrated: "If I dictate a letter and it is typed for me, who actually wrote the letter, me or my secretary"—and André Previn wasn't shy to reply: "It's a valid point but only if the composer's sketch, or short score, is as complete as Copland's obviously was."[3]

Previn, who used to orchestrate a lot for other composers during his early days in the business, was not a hardliner on the topic. He put it rather simply: "Given the hair-raising shortness of time allotted to the completion of a score, if help is needed, then that is fair dues. On the other hand, if orchestrating help is sought by a composer because he doesn't know how, then that is meretricious."

A distinction has to be made between orchestrating and arranging. While orchestration means that all notes for the final score are already on the short score provided by the composer, arrangers have in some respect an even more difficult job because they have to add musical elements to the actual composition. Arrangers are needed when a composer hands in an unfinished score with several parts for the musicians and orchestra sections missing, left to be completed by the arranger.

This can mean that the short score has only three or four staffs, consists of only a melody without accompaniment, and might, for one reason or another, not be suited to being played by an orchestra. Dimitri Tiomkin, for example, was primarily a pianist and, while his short scores were almost complete, his compositions were pianistic in nature. His arrangers had to rearrange his scores and figure out what the composer had intended so that the end result worked as orchestral music. Bernhard Kaun, who worked with Tiomkin on one of his earliest projects, *Lost Horizon*, explained the process: "Since he was a pianist, one had to rethink his ideas in an orchestral way. I did that in the few musical numbers that I did for him. He would give his pianistic sketches to a good arranger who would make the best of it. But it was still Tiomkin's music."[4]

Two examples show how difficult it can be to make a clear distinction between orchestrating, arranging and ghost-writing in today's film music business. Gerard Schurmann was busy working as a composer in England and Hollywood in the 1950s and '60s, occasionally helping out friends and colleagues by writing music for them without receiving credit. In the new millennium, he published an article in which he elaborated on his experience orchestrating *Lawrence of Arabia* for Maurice Jarre. In the article, Schurmann explained that the sketches he was given by Jarre consisted mostly of five or six staffs for the percussion part and only one or two staffs for the other instruments (woodwinds, brass, strings), giving Schurmann the impression that Jarre had an "astonishingly inarticulate musical technique."[5] Schurmann, as the contracted orchestrator, proceeded to add the other parts for the orchestra.

Gerard Schurmann is still bitter about the experience:

> Maurice Jarre made a fortune with that movie. You have to remember one thing: when one writes music for a film, one never knows whether that film is going to be successful. If I had known that *Lawrence of Arabia* was going to be *Lawrence of Arabia*, I would have insisted on my original contract as co-composer. But you don't know. When you get paid an enormous sum of money—and I got paid more money than [Maurice Jarre] did—you don't worry about that. But then Maurice made a fortune with the royalties. He became a millionaire. That was the first film that made him very successful.

Bitterness is not rare among ghostwriters or arrangers. In his memoir *No Minor Chords*, André Previn shares an anecdote from his time working for Herbert Stothart, one of the most successful composers working in film music in the 1930s and '40s:

> His method was to devise pretty themes and melodies which were then turned over to one of the musical drones for metamorphosis into something orchestrally usable. I was assigned to concoct the title music to an "important" epic, and Stothart had been explicit in his instructions to me. He handed me his tune, which was very nice indeed, and said, "Big! Big! Impressive! Use a huge orchestra! Add a chorus if you want to. Or an organ. Or extra brass. Big!!" [...]
> On the day of the recording, Mr. Stothart was on the podium, his gestures reeking with authority, his head leonine. [...] I was sitting, as invisible as possible, on the bottom step of the conductor's rostrum, following my score. As the music headed for yet another fortissimo wallow of excess, Stothart leaned down toward me without missing a beat. "Young man," he stage-whispered, "did I write this?"[6]

Ghostwriting is vague term in itself, it being generally accepted that a ghostwriter is somebody who authors works that are credited to other people. This definition remains particularly blurry in regard to film music, not only for musicologists but for the collaborators themselves. Said Bill Stinson, a music editor during Hollywood's studio system years: "Victor Young had a couple of orchestrators who knew his style and they really were his sound. You would turn lead lines over to them and tell them to score the picture, then he'd come in and conduct it."[7]

A composer who worked mostly for television during the 1960s and '70s remembers:

I worked at CBS during a time when Maurice Jarre was very popular because he had done *Lawrence of Arabia* and *Doctor Zhivago*. He was hired to write a theme for a new western we did. We thought that he was going to provide an orchestral theme. What he provided was simply a melody. So the orchestration and the arranging had to be done by somebody else. Maurice had somebody else figure it out. That does happen.

Blockbusters Versus B Movies

As ghost-writing is not a new phenomenon—neither in film music nor in any other profession—it is worth taking a look at what has changed over the decades. It is probably fair to say that time pressure was especially tough on composers during the studio system when working on B movies.

One of the most well-known composer collaborations came out of this period. Frank Skinner and Hans J. Salter formed a duo in the 1940s and '50s working in the Hollywood studio system by composing scores for cheap projects. Although they were both credited and thus didn't ghost-write for one another, "their" films needed (at least) two composers to get the job done in time. Salter remembers:

It was the beginning of a long friendship [with Frank Skinner] and a great working partnership. We worked on many pictures together, and it was a matter of close teamwork. I recall one stretch in scoring *Son of Frankenstein* in which we didn't leave the studio for two solid days. Frank would sit at the piano, compose a sequence, and then hand it to me, and I would orchestrate it. While I was doing that, he would take a nap. Then I would wake him up so he could write some more, and I would take a nap. This went on for forty-eight hours. We had no choice because the recording date was set.[8]

In today's film music scene, this approach is still being followed, albeit now on high profile big budget productions, as Matthew Margeson remembers from his days at Hans Zimmer's Remote Control Productions:

With Jim Dooley, not immediately but soon after I had started working for him, he let me start doing some arranging. So it was 80 percent technical and 20 percent creative work. I worked with Jim for about two years. That percentage shifted to where by the end of my two years there, we had one or two other technical assistants and I was basically coming in to the studio at 10 p.m., picking up where Jim would leave off in the driver's seat and write all throughout the night. Then he would come in at 8 a.m. and we would switch. So it turned into a full time creative role to help with his arranging and writing.

Hardly any composer who is commissioned to write the music for a small film can afford to work like that. This not only has to do with the fact that they are being paid less for an independent movie, thus they have no money to pay any possible ghosts (as composers are freelancers nowadays), but is also a factor of the schedule, which is in most cases less rigid than it is on today's massive studio productions. When composers enter a big budgeted Hollywood project in post-production, the release date is already set in stone and cannot be moved. The later composers enter a project, the less wiggle room they have, timewise.

Conversely, deadlines on independent movies, especially those which are due to be submitted to festivals, are somewhat more flexible, offering more freedom for everybody involved. Composer Edwin Wendler explains why:

> Festivals loom large in the indie movie world, especially the high profile festivals that could get you distribution. Although there are festivals that will accept works in progress, filmmakers are always very nervous to submit those because somebody who looks at submitted movies cannot say, "This would be so much better if the sound was fixed or if there was an actual score instead of temp music." It's impossible to make that judgment, so filmmakers are very nervous. Sometimes they say, "Why don't we take another year? We can't possibly meet the deadline this year, so let's wait another year. It might be frustrating for everybody but we will have a much better product. Everybody can relax and make it the best it possibly can be and we will submit it next year. No big deal."

The pressure for composers on B-productions in the 1930s, '40s or '50s was therefore higher and help was often desperately needed. When time and money were especially tight in the early days, the studio—or the music department to be exact—would turn to library music, having a composer go through the studio archive to look for cues which would fit to a certain scene and, if necessary, re-arrange them for a new recording. When Henry Mancini worked under contract at Universal from 1952 to 1958, this was one of the tasks he was assigned. Bruce Broughton elaborates on a practice which was very common during those days:

> At Universal Studios, you used to see the credit "Music Supervision by Joseph Gershenson." What that meant was that that film [...] was composed by a handful of guys, one of whom was Henry Mancini. Somebody would write the themes and then hand them to the composers. Everybody would take a reel of film and knock out the score based on these themes. I think they got their credit as composers, but they didn't get a film credit. The credit went to the music supervisor. [...] Nobody had over 50 percent of the music so no single composer got credit.

However, this practice was employed not just for B-productions, as the schedule could be tight even on prestige releases. David Selznick was described as being especially difficult by several composers, and didn't make a new friend in Max Steiner when he assigned him to work on *Gone with the Wind*. Selznick demanded several changes throughout the production of the movie, even in the post-production stage, and granted the composer only twelve weeks to write more than three hours of music.

Steiner had to go to extreme lengths. In order to be able to finish the work, he had a doctor who would come to his studio and regularly inject him with vitamins and Benzedrine so that he could stay awake to be able to continue working. This was after Selznick had threatened to hire Herbert Stothart if Steiner was not able to finish the score in time and in accordance with his demands. Even so, Steiner had to offload some work to colleagues, giving them sketches and themes to form into orchestral score, sometimes even letting them write pieces without handing them sketches of his own. Among them, Hugo Friedhofer wrote several cues, and Walter Scharf was responsible for one of the biggest scenes in the entire movie, the burning of Atlanta. For Steiner, it was humanly impossible to do everything himself.

A similar approach worked on other big budget productions. Even though Alfred Newman received Oscars for "Best Music, Scoring" for *Alexander's Ragtime Band* in 1939 and "Best Music, Scoring of a Musical Picture" for *Mother Wore Tights* in 1948, he barely wrote a note for each project, but rather supervised a staff of eight composers for each movie, among them David Raksin and David Buttolph. Alfred Newman, though respected by every colleague and admired for his craftsmanship to this day, had to regularly rely on ghostwriters, especially after 1940, when he became the head of the music department at 20th Century-Fox.

With this new position, he had understandably less time to write music himself. David Raksin was one of the colleagues he regularly turned to. As Raksin explained:

[Alfred Newman] would give me five reels out of a ten-reel picture, and [David] Buttolph would sometimes do a few reels.... We used Al's material, but we composed—he didn't sketch the cues. [...] It nearly killed me. [...] He'd give me some of his early sketches—he would show us what was going on— but even they were very sparse. They would contain a melody, and sometimes a few bass notes. But it was all there, if you knew what he was doing.... We would actually harmonize them ourselves.... We were working day and night. Sometimes this went on for weeks [...][9]

Together with David Buttolph and Cyril Mockridge, Raksin formed a reliable trio of "ghosts" who could be trusted to get a quality score done in time. Raksin had, after all, in 1936 gained a huge amount of experience by turning the humming and whistling of Charlie Chaplin into an orchestral score for *Modern Times*.

All That Pressure

Several things have changed that explain why film composers nowadays regularly have to work with a team on a big budgeted production. Whereas in the early days composers usually worked on a locked cut, meaning that the picture was unlikely to be changed, composers nowadays are faced with the issue of digital editing, a technology which allows the movie to be constantly changed right up until a few days before its theatrical release.

There are other recent technologies for the composer to contend with: producers and directors usually demand to hear the score as a mock-up before it is recorded by the orchestra. They will make their notes and then usually "suggest" changes. Composers, even on a TV show, find themselves writing a score two or three times. This has led to it becoming common practice for a composer to hand a piece over to somebody else to fix, either reworking it, or writing a new cue based on the first attempt.

The days are long gone when one director or one producer was in charge of musical decisions. Now there are countless different producers and decision-makers who attempt to guarantee that a movie, with all its ingredients, is marketable. As Bruce Broughton puts it:

> In the last few years, they have wanted it fast and cheap. Because of the schedules and all the silly previews, they make the composer rewrite cues several times for no reason at all. This has made it economically difficult for composers and nearly impossible to work on their own. Today, I would go home, start to write and then I would have to put it into the synthesizer. Somebody would then send the file to the producers or directors and I would have to wait for their notes. Then I would send the new file of rewritten cues and they would send their new notes.
>
> I'd be working endlessly just to get ten minutes of music done. I would need somebody else to help. Nobody is on salary nowadays and very few are getting a fee. They are working from a "package." They get a music budget to pay for all the expenses themselves. Some guys do very well with that. Others are terrible with that. It is a very difficult time. I don't think it is a happy time.

Producers and directors expect the composer to work as quickly as the quickest person in town, never mind how many assistants are necessary to employ to get the job done. This increased pressure in the industry has lead composers who value working on their own, rather than relying on a team of arrangers, interns, assistants and orchestrators, to reject offers that would require them to work as the head of a team to get the job done in time. As Rachel Portman admits:

> It is really sad—or not. It probably isn't when you are a young composer trying to get in. I think it can help them if they get a break. It's not something I am interested in doing, really. I have been quite purist about it. When I have been offered projects where I know I would have to have a number two composer underneath me for me to do it, I turn them down. I want to write music that is bespoke. All of it. When I did *Used People* and *Benny and Joon* I orchestrated every note of it. I loved it. I am not interested in handing things over. That's not me.

Bruce Broughton recounts a rather amusing anecdote about a director's expectations:

> Years ago, a director came over to my house. At that time I had a piano in the room where I was working. I had some synthesizers in another room. He came into my piano room, looked around and said, "Is this your stuff?" I said, "My stuff? Yes, this is what I write on." Then I understood what he was talking about. He expected to come in and see what a lot of composers were getting in these days, all the hardware. So I had to show him "my stuff." Well, I have now heard: "Where is your team?" They expect you to show up with other people. If you just come up with yourself that's very old-fashioned. Do you still write with a pencil? Do you ride on a horse and buggy? Do you have color photographs or just black and white? They expect you to have a team. Everybody has their team.

Are most directors and producers aware of the fact that the composer they commission works in a team rather than writing everything themselves? Not necessarily, as one composer and arranger, who wishes to remain anonymous, says:

> I don't think many producers and directors know about the extent of composers farming out work. Composers make sure that their clients never interface with the people who are actually writing the music. Especially in the context of television series, producers must be aware that the composer they are hiring is already working on five or six other shows. It's easy to look up that information on IMDb. Yet, they seem to be convinced that the composer *alone* is going to have enough time to address their every need, while simultaneously working on five other shows and maybe also on two features and a video game. Occasionally, you hear a story of a director asking a composer to not employ ghostwriters on a specific project, but that seems to be rare. In most cases, composers are scared of their clients finding out that someone else has been writing their music, and the arrangers are scared of telling the truth, in fear of never again finding work in an industry that will shun them.

Yet Broughton argues that today's producers are more ready to accept the idea that they also hire the composer's team when they hire a composer.

> They may not think about what the team does though. What the team does varies from composer to composer. What happens as well is that after you presented the score, the producers or director decide to use the score in a completely different manner and they rearrange the whole score on the stage. Is that ghostwriting? As a composer, you can never be sure how your score gets into the film.
>
> I'm under the impression that people are now used to seeing the composers' team. You walk on the stage and you have at least an orchestrator there, likely a technician running clicks, likely some software or hardware programmer. There are video monitors everywhere, running all kinds of software all at once. It's obvious that the composer is coming in with a team. Who did what, I

don't know. The producers and directors care about the name of the person they hired.

Matthew Margeson has had a slightly different experience as a composer in Hollywood, which leads him to assume that producers and directors are now very well aware of the fact that only a few A-list composers in town are writing everything themselves:

> Especially in the studio system no one is oblivious to that any more. Directors and the heads of the studios know that it's a team effort and that there are maybe some young composers that are just trying to make their way. It's a beautiful thing because it's giving a lot of young people a chance, and because everyone is aware that it happens maybe the need from the composers perspective to hide isn't as great as it once was.

Yet the revelation that a composer's work was partially written by ghostwriters may not only anger directors and producers, it can also be disillusioning for young composers who grew up as fans of film music. Here is John Ottman:

> The whole factory mentality is still weird to me. When I first started I was like, "Wow, how can a composer go into a meeting and people know that other people are writing for him?" Now people just know it and they accept it. As a composer you are now seen as sort of a director. They are basically an architect or a contractor who has his workers around. We know when that whole factory mentality started. It was just so in the face that everybody just accepted it. To me it's still weird. But I'm an old fart. Now it's necessary for composers. Even if it's just a few cues, you got to have some help.

The Fear of Unemployment

Another reason for composers not being able to finish a score in time is simply accepting too many movies. During the days of the Hollywood studio system in the naively named Golden Age, composers were on the staff of a studio and were simply assigned projects by the head of the music department. Now, with composers being freelancers, they have different reasons for working on a substantial number of movies each year. "There are people who make very good money with films. In television though they pay much less now than they used to when I began," says Bruce Broughton.

> What is the reason for working on more movies? More money is a good reason. Trying to be popular, trying to make it look as though you are very, very busy.... Composers do that. Some composers just like to work a lot. By any way they can, they will just continue working. If that means they have to hire some people to get the job done, they'll do that. If it means hiring somebody to write the whole score for them, they will do that. That happens.

To put it simply, during the early days of the studio system, composers wouldn't earn more money by taking on more projects. These days, as freelancers, they do. Having worked on as many as seven movies in a year, James Newton Howard shared familiar sentiments about the competitive nature in the industry. He is also grateful: "There is so much work here, so much money to be made here, and so many great opportunities here. It sounds like a cliché, but this business has been so wonderful for me."[10]

In an industry like the Hollywood movie business, where everything is about money, composers are naturally pressurized by its capitalistic nature. After all, so far as the companies are concerned, the more money, the better: "You can only do so much, and you want to be your best on each movie," lamented Howard Shore.[11]

> Some people churn 'em out and do three or four movies in the time I might take to do one or two, but they often have a team of people working on a score. If you look at the numbers of movies being made in Hollywood, compared to the number of composers who are scoring them, not that many guys are doing them—it's the same guys over and over again.

Working in the movie scoring business is now more precarious than ever. While composers on staff were paid whether they worked or not, composers today have to compete for projects. This causes great additional pressures. As typecasting still predominates in Hollywood, if they don't become known for a particular type of score then most successful composers usually develop long-term working relationships with producers or directors. Ironically, the more relationships of this kind a composer has, the more difficult it can become. What happens when the composer says no to their producer or director friend because they are busy working on another project? Eventually, the producer or director will turn to another composer, possibly forming a new working relationship and therefore replacing them.

Being out of work is an ever-prevalent fear for freelancers, especially in the movie industry where a composer's success is dependent on the success of the movies they have worked on. If composers want to sustain a relationship with directors but are busy on other projects they may resort to ghostwriters. A regular arranger and orchestrator for established composers in the industry remembers:

> The largest amount of music I wrote as an arranger was 86 minutes out of 94. Something like that. The vast majority, between 80 and 90 percent. On this project, the reason was that the credited composer wanted to retain a relationship with the director but was physically unable to write all the music himself for scheduling reasons. This was beyond his control.

The arranger/ghost can never know how much music they are going to write in total. The anonymous source continues:

In many cases you might start with one cue. If that goes over really well you might be handed more cues. Even if the sole credited composer takes all necessary precautions and gives you as much information as is possible in the initial phases of a project it might turn out to be a completely different animal once the music is being delivered. Sometimes there is a domino effect. You might deliver one cue, it gets approved. You get more cues and in the end you thought it was going to be a project where you compose ten minutes and it ends up being much more than that, maybe even five times as much.

The downside for the arranger, of course, is that situations like these make life nearly impossible to plan:

As an arranger you just say yes to everything. Even if you have another project lined up you might be inclined to just say no to that project because the more lucrative project is the one that's being offered. Of course you don't tell the composer, "Hey, I had to say no to this project so I could do more on your project." That would be politically incorrect. But sometimes that might be the situation you are faced with, especially if you have a lot of bills to pay or you might want to buy a car. These are very pragmatic decisions that you might make. Of course nobody will ever find out about your personal decision-making that you do in your little microcosm.

One Problem, Several Facets

All these reasons for taking on ghostwriters are aspects of the same problem—a lack of capacity. Like an airplane which doesn't wait for one late passenger to show up before taking off, the release of a movie with a multi-million dollar production cannot depend on the composer alone, who is by profession near the bottom of the creative food chain.

One example of personal problems preventing a composer from fulfilling their duty was given by Joel McNeely. During his work on *Terminal Velocity*, his son was born but turned out to be sick, necessitating that McNeely spend more time at the hospital than working on his assignment:

In the case of *Terminal Velocity*, those guys were more than orchestrators—they actually wrote some cues. [...] I just called in and said, "Guys, you have got to help me get this done." I would write fourteen hours a day and then go down to the hospital and spend the night there. It was a real stretch to get that movie done. In the end, it affected my health. I ended up in the hospital with heart problems. As a result, I was a completely wrung-out wet rag at the end of it.[12]

The lack of capacity to finish a score in time doesn't necessarily have to do only with increased pressure during post-production, but can take on several forms. Indeed, the lack of capacity to finish a work in time illustrates the priorities of composers working in movies: to serve the film, to get it done, to not indulge in complex writing just to satisfy your own standards and ego.

Jerry Fielding (*The Wild Bunch, The Outlaw Josey Wales*)—a composer respected for his challenging scores, his method of composition and the intellectual concepts in his music—was especially prone to setting the highest standards for himself, which forced him to rely on his loyal colleagues Lennie Niehaus and Greig McRitchie. As the latter recalled:

> I remember *Straw Dogs*. The rape-scene—[Jerry] must have taken two weeks. And I used to say, "Jerry, what are you doing?" He was involved with tone rows in those days. I said, "Why are you experimenting with this right in the middle of a picture, Jerry?" But he used to do that. Then, at the last minute, he'd call me in, and Lennie Niehaus, and he'd just throw stuff at us—just timing sheets and the themes—and say, "Here, *you* guys figure it out."[13]

Composers sometimes need a "ghost" even when they have sufficient time if they are faced with writing music in an unfamiliar idiom. "Billy May was a terrific arranger," says Bruce Broughton.

> Billy May's music went into an awful lot of films in the '70s and '80s when they needed big band stuff. There is a movie [score] by James Horner called *Cocoon*. There are some big band pieces in it which sound absolutely great. Because there was nobody better than Billy May to do that. Well, if you wanted to sound like that, you better get that guy.

Bernard Herrmann approached Christopher Palmer and Howard Blake to do jazz arrangements for some of his late period compositions, while Miklós Rózsa turned to André Previn: "In the early fifties I wrote some big band jazz for Miklós when he composed the score to John Huston's *Asphalt Jungle*, for the simple reason that Miklós asked for my help. His musicological education was vast, but I think the last time he had heard a dance band was in a tearoom in Budapest," confessed Previn.[14]

Matthew Margeson gives another example:

> If there is a director that hires me because they like my vision, my music or my approach, they then say that the score needs a quality that can only be conveyed with the use of a choir. I can do my own choir research, but I can also hire someone who's a really great choir arranger to help bring in their influence and expertise on what the choir can do and how to write for choir. As long as it is my vision, that's fine.

Then there are stories which show how dangerous the idealistic determination of composers to write and orchestrate all the music for a film score themselves can be. The experience of Joel McNeely on *Terminal Velocity* is one example—another is given by Howard Blake who worked on *Flash Gordon*:

> Dino [de Laurentiis, the producer] said to me, "I have got a fifty million pound film and we have got to get a score." On Thursday afternoon he said, "Do you think you could write a new score by Monday?" I said, "If you had

Tchaikovsky, Beethoven and Bach and everybody else, they couldn't do it by Monday. It would actually take until Monday to look at it." I asked him if he had a music-editing bible. He said, "What's that?" I said, "Sounds like you haven't."

"How long will it take you to write one?" "Well, it would take a month." He said, "We can't do that. Because we want to incorporate some songs by Queen." I said, "That makes it even harder." Eventually, I agreed that I could do it in three weeks rather than four weeks. But in fact what happened is that by the time I had measured the film and by the time they had organized every-thing, I had ten days left to write an hour and a quarter of music for an 80 piece orchestra. It was a very chaotic production.

I always insisted on doing my own orchestration. I guess I just thought it would be quicker. I didn't know who to get for help. I hadn't realized the enor-mity of it until I started. I was living in Mortlake with my wife and two chil-dren. She moved out the day after I had started because it was hell. People were ringing up at three in the morning and everybody was asking where the score was. All hell broke loose. At the end of the first day I had written about a minute of music. I just had to write like crazy. I needed to write something like eight minutes of music a day. I had never worked so hard in my life. I worked the last four days without sleeping because I had to finish it. They said, "If you don't finish it, we will sue you." I did finish the work.

We were supposed to start recording on a Monday and I remember living off coffee and biscuits the last days. I had nothing else left because my wife wasn't there and I didn't have time to go shopping. The weird thing was I found it really easy to write at some point. I wrote in the speed of light, run-ning on adrenaline. I remember finishing the score at six on the Sunday morn-ing. It was a beautiful summer day. I took a great walk down the riverbank. Then I went off to the studio and conducted for three days. I seem to remem-ber feeling all right when going out to dinner. Then I remember arriving home on Wednesday evening. I crashed out.

The next thing I remember is my wife saying, "I thought you were going to Paris." I said, "I am going to Paris on Thursday, tomorrow." She said, "It's Satur-day. You have been asleep since Wednesday." That was very dangerous. She couldn't wake me up. She got a doctor who injected me drugs to wake me up. He said, "If your wife hadn't called me, you would have never woken up. You are suffering from acute exhaustion, double pneumonia and double bronchitis." In the end, they dropped most of my music from the movie and never thanked me.

A Promising Start?

With the studio system long defunct, composers have to assemble their team themselves, mostly relying on aspiring composers who hope for their big break, or even students who are lucky enough to get an internship at the composer's studio. Bruce Broughton teaches film music at USC and has seen many of his students working for major composers in the industry:

What the collaborators are doing is a murky thing and depends on the individual composer and collaborator. [...] Some of my students get jobs interning for composers. Sometimes they get hired by the composers. Generally, as an intern your job is making coffee. But they usually get to do proper work. Sometimes they are working with digital files, improving the sound of the samples, preparing samples, finding or making sounds the composers can use. This is creative stuff. Sometimes they are composing for them by writing bridges and small cues which are not really important, but which give them something to do. Sometimes they are cleaning up the tracks. When the composer knocks out his score on Logic, the tracks have to be cleaned up before they can be orchestrated or looked at or assembled by people who are going to give it to musicians to play.

There are all sorts of things to do. If one of these people should suddenly write an extra cue, then it's probably ghostwriting. But it's necessary for the composer. Experience is experience. It is always good to get experience. And to get experience by having a guy looking over your shoulder and helping you with your mistakes and helping you learn is very valuable.

If you are in a position where you are writing the music for a lot of shows without getting credit for it but just a cash buyout, the advantage is you learn to write but you are not advancing your career because your career is partly based upon your reputation. And if your work has somebody else's name on it it's not going to do you any good. Most interns would love to write for a successful composer. They then start doing things with supervision. That's good. Most interns do rather basic tasks though.

There is no way to predict whether aspiring composers will make their break in the industry by starting out as interns or ghosts. Ironically, approaching the business this way can have a reverse effect, says John Ottman:

Sometimes ghostwriters are not actually in the studio. They sit at home and you can direct them just to do a cue. You still have to present the cue. You will go down in flames with the cue because it's your name. Part of the comfort of being a ghostwriter is they don't have to deal with the politics. They are just helping you behind the scenes. I work with a couple of guys and they say, "Man, we would never want to do what you do. We are happy just helping you out." Because they see all the hell a composer goes through. These guys help me on a couple of cues and they have a mentally healthy outlook on it. They think, "We get paid well to do this. We can sit at home and have a normal life, not having our hair ripped out by someone all the time." Most ghostwriters don't want to climb up the ladder and get their own movie. A couple of my guys just saw what I go through and they said, "Fuck that."

There still many examples of people who started out as ghostwriters or assistants and became successful composers in their own right—Matthew Margeson for example, who reflects:

After I worked for a couple of years for Jim Dooley, I then had to face the decision of whether I would like to do this for the rest of my life with Jim. The answer was making an investment in gear, computers, samplers and synths. That was a bit of a scary moment because it was a big investment. After that is when I really started to work with Hans Zimmer a bit and Brian Tyler, Harry and Rupert Gregson-Williams and just being a guy that would float around from movie to movie.

Because on a lot of these things there is no time for one person to write all the cues themselves. There are very few people in Hollywood that really do every single bit of music themselves. Meeting people like that was really the seed of my career. This kind of apprentice thing worked for me and I advocate that because you learn so much by being a fly on the wall. Not just writing music but also how to run a meeting, how to talk to a director, how to gauge all these other bureaucratic issues that come up.

Some composers are very supportive when it comes to enabling their helping hands to develop their own careers, be they arrangers or ghostwriters. "[Bill Goldstein] got the *Fame* series over at MGM, and I started working on that," recalled Alf Clausen.

I did a lot of orchestrating and ghost composing. At the same time, I did some ghost composing for David Rose on *Little House on the Prairie* and *Father Murphy*. One thing led to another. I started orchestrating for Lalo Schifrin and Lee Holdridge. Lee and I struck up a really, really close friendship, which still exists to this day. [...] His focus with an orchestrator/composer is that if he finds a guy with some talent, he finds a way to help him work his way into the system and get his own gigs. His whole focus was to find a television series, write the theme, and then turn it over to me. This was without me asking![15]

Other composers can be more demanding and trying to hide the fact that they are employing ghosts as best as they can, remembers Matthew Margeson:

I know certain people that I have worked with that are the most generous, kind, creative composers to work with and for. And [then there are] other people where it's all about the ego. It's all about making people believe that it's all a one man show and they do it all themselves. That's one of the beautiful things that I feel I've been blessed to do when I was still making my way into the industry and work with 15 different A-list composers by being their ghost-writer. I got to experience all sides of that, and as my career was developing to pick and chose how I want to run my career, what kind of artist and business-man I want to be and how to run my ship.

Paying the Rent

One obvious reason to accept a position as a ghostwriter is money. "When I was starting, I wasn't starting as a youngster—I was already in my thirties," recalled Shirley Walker.

But I had that incredible enthusiasm that you have when you discover a whole new world that you didn't even know existed. And you're just sort of blinded by the enticement of the money. You're just staring into those headlights, not realizing that there's a car coming at you from behind those headlights. I was quite happy to be standing out on the highway there for a while. But then, ultimately, the impact happened—I realized that I had had too much of making other people look as great as I was making them look. So at that point, I said, "Boy, I just don't have the tolerance to continue doing this much longer." And I found that I could step into the role of being strictly an orchestrator and a conductor for composers. [...] Actually, I had to say no, stop doing things. And a little, terribly frightening, dry period was the result. This town likes to just eat people up. When you have specific abilities and the studios get used to being able to turn to you for specific things, they don't want you to change the role.[16]

While ghostwriters can acquire their own scoring gigs as a result of proving themselves to be reliable and efficient, it can, as Shirley Walker explained, be a disenchanting experience. Ghostwriter are always at the mercy of their employer. Whether an arranger/ghostwriter will receive credit or royalties depends on several factors, as John Ottman explains how he approaches paying his staff:

Everyone is treated the same. But I don't have a massive team. It all comes down to the project, whether I am paid well or not, and how much I am paying this person as well. I feel horrible subjecting anybody to writing ghost music. I know how agonizing it is to write music. I almost feel terrible when asking anyone to do it. I pay really well upfront because I feel bad. Then I put them through hell. I don't think any writer writes a cue for me less than ten times, sometimes more than that. So I pay them a lot because of the hell I put them through.

It really depends on the project. Then I treat everyone the same. On *Non-Stop*, Edwin Wendler wrote a lot. That was a different situation. When I work with people, they do a couple of cues. But Edwin wrote the music for a couple of reels because I was busy doing *Days of Future Past*. I had written three reels of *Non-Stop* before I had to go to Montreal, so Edwin worked with me on a couple of reels. I am not going to hide it that someone helps me out so much.

Matthew Margeson makes the payment for his arrangers and ghostwriters dependent on the actual work they contribute, something which differs from project to project. He elaborates:

I like to keep it a very static system. If I have written a piece of music, fully orchestrated it myself and I then get an updated version of the film three weeks later where they removed 30 seconds of that scene, I won't have time to adjust that music accordingly. So I may have someone come to my studio in the middle of the night and remove that 30 seconds and musically connect the tissue, so it still sounds like a piece of music. That may be slightly less of a creative job than me sketching out a piece and having someone else orchestrate it.

I take all this in consideration when giving out the royalties. [...] There are definitely composers that I worked for who will say, "This is something that I can't give any royalties out for," or, "I need you to do this under the radar." I think that in some cases, in their defense, that maybe it's the first time they work for a specific studio or a director and they do want to keep that relationship with that director close and not let them through the smoke and mirrors completely.

An unusual example of a composer giving credit to a helping hand who is an aspiring composer is Michael Giacchino: his son Mick is credited for 52 cues of the complete score for his father's *Jurassic World*. Giacchino has never hidden the fact that he is a family man: in both *Star Wars: Rogue One* and the multi-million dollar flop *John Carter*, he has the chorus singing the names of his children. The cue *Apes Past Prologue* from Giacchino's score for *War of the Planet of the Apes* is credited to Giacchino himself and his son Griffith. Similarly, Basil Poledouris gave his daughter Zoe a credit for a melody on *Conan the Barbarian*. As the story goes, Poledouris was playing the music for a scene he was working on when his daughter came in the room playing a counterpoint on her recorder. Poledouris was so enamored of what Zoe had spontaneously improvised that he incorporated her melody in his composition.

Keeping Your Mouth Shut

When composers let students or interns ghost for them they have several things to consider. One is whether the person assigned is able to fulfill the tasks they are given, meaning that they have to have both a dramatic and a musical understanding of what is required. But another quality is almost as important—discretion. Despite ghostwriting always having been a common practice in film music, and in the arts in general, it still is very much a taboo area which is best not talked about.

Shirley Walker, composer of *Final Destination*, as well as an orchestrator and ghostwriter for several composers, explained why in the simplest terms: "I came into the business at a time when the nature of ghostwriting was that you were paid big money not to talk about the fact that you were doing it and to support the illusion or delusion, whichever you prefer, that composer × was actually doing the work that they were being paid for."[17] One ghostwriter who broke with that rule and eventually made headlines (which didn't further his career) was Daniel Kolton, who had helped out composer Joseph LoDuca on his scores for the series *Xena: Warrior Princess* and *Hercules*.

Like many ghostwriters working in the industry, Kolton was denied authorship of the cues he wrote and therefore didn't receive royalties for his work. Instead, the royalties were paid to Joseph LoDuca, who had put his name on the cue sheet and was therefore legally the author. In fact he wasn't the author at all, and had never made any such agreement with Kolton, who he had asked to provide the additional music. The ghostwriter claimed he had never transferred the copyright to anyone else and therefore was due to receive royalties. After seven years without a single royalty check arriving, Kolton approached the U.S. Copyright Office, which after a lengthy investigation awarded him the copyright for his compositions he had provided for *Xena* and *Hercules*.[18]

This caused a new problem: Universal Studios was now broadcasting the series with his music, although Kolton hadn't given Universal permission to do so. Consequently in 2003 the composer sued the studio for copyright infringement, a decision he would soon regret. In 2004, the court ruled in favor of the defendants (Universal Studios, Joseph Lo Duca, Anchor Bay, Oxygen, and Renaissance Pictures), determining that by his conduct, Kolton had given LoDuca a nonexclusive license to Kolton's copyright interest in the music. Because of said agreement, LoDuca was free to take any action consistent with copyright ownership, including having the works broadcast without infringing Kolton's copyright interest. The case never made it to trial, and yet Kolton as the plaintiff was left with a seven figure sum to pay for legal fees.[19]

In the course of the investigation, details about his working-relationship with LoDuca as his employer came to light: Kolton had begun working on *Xena* and *Hercules* in 1995, before the shows became international smash hits. Because of the success of the shows, Kolton asked LoDuca for a share in the royalties a year later, which his employer refused. Instead, he gave him a raise in his salary and provided him with recording equipment in order for Kolton to work comfortably from home. In 1999, LoDuca was asked to provide the music for the new shows *Cleopatra* and *Jack of All Trades*. He asked his ghostwriter if he was willing to write additional music. Kolton, though, was only interested if his employer would share the royalties. Again, LoDuca refused. As a result, Kolton ended their working relationship that year.

Sometimes ghostwriting has simply been referred to as "helping out," and not seen as a big deal. Gerard Schurmann explains:

> What we did in those days is no longer applicable today because it's different. We, the composers working on films, mostly knew each other in England: Walton, Britten sometimes, Rawsthorne, Alwyn, Constant Lambert. We all knew each other. If one of them got into trouble and said, "God, I can't finish this," we would help out. We all got into trouble because of the lack of time when working on a film. What are you to do? You talk about it and, as a friend, you ask: "Can you do that for me?" And as a friend you do it. I did it

for others to help out. I don't say, "I am the ghostwriter." You just help another composer. And hope you do it properly. Sometimes it's good, sometimes it's not because it's so unlike what the other composer did.

There is a big difference though in the practice of helping out friends between Hollywood and England—or basically between Hollywood and the rest of the world. First and foremost, studios in England didn't have music departments that assigned ghosts to composers. As a result, a composer would turn to friends to help out, which has never be seen as an issue—so why talk about it? It was an arrangement between friends, usually rewarded by them helping back in return on some later project.

John Addison, a British composer who became successful in Hollywood after he won the Oscar for his music for *Tom Jones*, was quite amazed by the highly elaborate organization in the country of unlimited opportunities:

> I get the impression that in Hollywood film composers are expected to take every job as it comes along. Fortunately, the pressures were not quite as great in England. [...] Having come to know Hollywood better, I now appreciate the advantages of the system as it works today, which is less rigid than in the past. The composer is provided with every kind of assistance regarding the administrative side of scoring—copying, music editing, all the devices of the trade, even what I would not have believed possible in my English days, having one's score proofread by a librarian before it goes to the copyist.[20]

Ghosting as a practice has been as common in Europe though as it has been in Hollywood. For instance, Ennio Morricone worked closely with and for Mario Nascimbene and Giovanni Fusco, contributing jazz pieces for Nascimbene's *Morte di un Amico* and score cues for Fusco's *Violenza Segreta*. Morricone's friend and colleague Angelo Francesco Lavagnino made his reputation by writing music for film composers in the '40s, before himself becoming a household name—a fact revealed by Italian film music expert Stefan Schlegel.

Vladimir Cosma (*Le Boom*) "helped out" renowned composer Michel Legrand in 1968 by writing the majority of both *Le Plus Vieux Métier du Monde* and *L'Homme de Buick*. Cosma later became successful as a film composer himself. Jean-Claude Petit and Michel Colombier composed for Michel Magne on several occasions including the 1967 movie *Les Grand Meaulnes,* for which Petit actually received a credit for orchestration.

Nico Fidenco, well known for scoring several Italian softcore productions in the '70s, was not able to read music, and thus heavily relied on first Gianni Dell'Orso and then Giacomo Dell'Orso, the latter being the husband of Edda Dell'Orso, who can be heard singing on countless soundtracks by Morricone—perhaps most famously on *Once Upon a Time in the West*. As explained by Gianni Dell'Orso, Fidenco would give him a tune by singing or whistling, then leave everything else to his "orchestrator," while all the pieces that didn't rely on a musical theme, mostly suspense cues, were composed entirely by Gianni and Giacomo Dell'Orso.[21]

Renowned German composer Hans-Martin Majewski relied, sometimes heavily, on helping hands, namely Gert Wilden and Peter Sandloff, who later became sought-after composers for German films themselves. Producer Arild Rafalzik wrote:

> Gert Wilden once told me the following story: "I sat on a plane from Munich to Berlin, and next to me a young man was sitting who had woolly, dark locks of hair. During the whole flight, he browsed musical scores, made notes and added something to the scores. At some point, I asked him what he was working on and he replied proudly, 'I am the ghostwriter of Hans-Martin Majewski!' I said, 'But that is me!' As it turned out, we had often worked on the same film score while each of us thought that the other part of the score had been done by Majewski. It was strange though," Wilden said, "that when I worked and composed for Majewski, it always sounded like Majewski."[22]

A risk always remains for any composer relying on ghostwriters—the risk that their "helping hands" will boast about their work. Recalls Schurmann:

> When these ghostwriters talk, why did they do it? I suppose they knew they were not getting the credit. They were not getting the royalties. You just help out for money. If you complain then it's because you want to be taken seriously. What about your own stuff? When you are a ghostwriter, when did you write yourself? They themselves have no kudos to lean on. They go to other composers and say they wrote for others. Don't believe it. Every composer I have ever met has at least one detractor, a person who claims to have written the music for him or her.
>
> I don't know a single composer I have ever met who hasn't gotten into trouble one way or another, having to sue somebody for putting out rumors about ghosting or stealing or plagiarism. They only do it when you are successful, mind you. If you don't have money, it's not worth saying. [...] I have helped out friends occasionally and I got paid for it. Sometimes they would say, "I owe you something," and I would say, "Forget about it."
>
> It's different when you do a substantial amount of work like I did on *The Vikings*, though. But I thought that people had found out about it by now. I had to write the action sequence because Nascimbene couldn't write any action music at all. Nascimbene did not know his job at all. He had an army of ghostwriters. He tried several times to write action music but it didn't work. In the end, they brought the whole thing back to London and I wrote it. It was recorded in London. Come to think of it, I did not get paid for it.
>
> He said to me afterwards, "Oh, but you used my material, didn't you?" Because if you use their material then it's their copyright. I said, "No, I didn't use any of your material!" It really is a piece of mine. You can hear it. You can hear the piece over the scenes when the Vikings are rowing. I am not boasting

about it. It had become public knowledge, people came to me and said, "You wrote that, didn't you?"

Recently, somebody came to me and said about *Richard III* with Laurence Olivier, "You wrote that piece, didn't you?" I said, "How did you know?" He had recognized the style. I must have a personal style. Malcolm Arnold helped William Walton a great deal. He was the main person who helped, mainly because of time pressure and because William was getting on a bit. So what?

The Hans Method

I'm Your Man.—Leonard Cohen

How does Hans Zimmer work? How is his company Remote Control Productions set up? What tasks are the composers, assistants and interns at the facility given on a day to day basis?

Many rumors and myths have swirled around the German-born composer and producer for decades. This is not surprising, considering Zimmer has long been a driving force in the American film music industry, putting his stamp on many of the most iconic films of the last 30 years. The overwhelming majority of composers who have worked at Remote Control Productions (formerly Media Ventures) and whom I interviewed for this chapter looked back fondly at their time in Santa Monica, admiring the skill and efficiency of Zimmer and his colleagues.

Not every employee of Zimmer's company is suited to work in such a demanding environment, though. Music needs to be delivered promptly, efficiently, and above all, in a way which satisfies the producers of the project. Christian Halten experienced how stressful this method can be. Halten is a German-born musician who briefly worked for Media Ventures assisting Henning Lohner. Halten recalled his first day when he arrived in Santa Monica and barely had time to introduce himself before he was instructed by his employer at that time—a colleague of Zimmer's—to rush to the airport and deliver music recordings on a hard drive to a plane which was due to take off in less than half an hour. This was well before large uncompressed music files could be sent over the Internet.

As it happened, Christian Halten didn't have a car. This was not of interest to his employer, whose only concern was to get the hard drive across the Atlantic. Halten rushed out of the studio and tried to find a vehicle that could bring him to the airport. The clock was ticking relentlessly. After some minutes of pure panic, he recalled with laughter, he grabbed the first person in the Media Ventures parking lot and persuaded her to let him borrow her car.

Because the people at Media Ventures know how the company works, his new colleague was happy to help, letting him drive off in her car as if he was about to replace Keanu Reeves in the *Speed* franchise. The new employee at Zimmer's company managed to deliver the hard drive to the plane at the last minute, caught his breath and returned to the studio. He had proven to be reliable. Welcome to Media Ventures!

The idea of working with other people comes naturally to Hans Zimmer. He started out as a keyboard player in bands where music is made in a group, as opposed to a traditional composer sitting in a room alone. Apart from which, he himself made his break as a film composer by being part of a team. The British composer Stanley Myers was key to Zimmer's early opportunities in the business. Myers had made his break in the British film industry working on classics like *Sitting Target* and *Kaleidoscope*, often fusing jazz and symphonic music. In the early '80s, Myers decided to update his studio by buying various electronic musical equipment, including several synthesizers. This was despite the fact that, according to Howard Blake, a close friend of Myers and a successful composer himself, his colleague was well aware of the fact that he had "no clue" about working with modern electronic devices. So, to take care of his new acquisitions, Myers employed Hans Zimmer, who was living in London at the time.

Zimmer had had a rough start in the UK. He recalled:

> I was playing in bands in England—pubs, colleges, working men's clubs, strip-joints. Always late with the rent, and worse—always ran out of shillings for the electricity meter. [...] I lived mainly off the kindness of friends [...]. Always owed the bank money—but the bank manager sort of believed in me, and let me overdraw. I borrowed a synth from the good people at Argent's Keyboards and Syco Systems. Fell in with the jingle crowd, which was a regular check (I used to do two or three a week, sometimes as a composer, sometimes as a synth programmer for other composers). Started working with an equally poor Trevor Horn and Geoff Downes. Made a song we couldn't give away. Went to number one the week before my twenty-first birthday. Still waiting for the royalties.[1]

In the early '80s, despite the revival of orchestral scores brought about by the success of *Star Wars*, many filmmakers were turning to electronic music. Myers needed to keep up with these developments and so the relationship with Zimmer was forged, with Zimmer contributing electronic elements to the symphonic or jazzy compositions of his employer, and even writing whole pieces on his own. This latter venture was immediately successful, as Zimmer explained in an interview for *Sound on Sound* in 2002:

> I was working as an assistant for another film composer, Stanley Myers, and he would just let me write film cues. He'd never tell the director what I'd written and what he had written, and inevitably, in the beginning, everything I wrote

was always chucked out and had to be rewritten. After a while, I got better at it, but I don't know how or why, other than by doing it—you sort of get an instinct for it.[2]

Through this process it didn't take long for the young German musician to form a friendship with Myers, with whom he eventually built his own studio in London.

It didn't seem likely then that Zimmer would eventually become one of the most successful film composers in the industry. Howard Blake was assigned as musical consultant on the film *The Hunger* in 1983, a production directed by Tony Scott. At one point, Scott wanted to hear some electronic music, which Blake had no experience with. But he remembered the young guy working for his friend Stanley Myers who was very clever with synthesizers. Remembers Blake,

So I rang Hans Zimmer and asked, "Can we come and see you?" He said, "Sure." Hans sat at his synthesizers and Tony said to him, "I want to hear something spiky, something modern, something electronic." But Tony didn't like anything that Hans came up with. Tony then turned to me and said, "Howard, you are wasting my time. This guy is never going to amount to anything." I think that's how Hans met the Scott brothers.

However, film music was not the only avenue that Zimmer was exploring. Tim Bevan and Sarah Radcliffe, good friends of his, had started a film company under the name of Working Title and the young composer saw himself getting involved in production. It was an adventurous time for him, as he explained: "It was all just a different form of the world of entertainment, and the rent was cheap. Still owed the bank a fortune. I kept telling them that a synth could buy a house, not the other way round. That one idea, one tune would make the difference between ruin and being able to pay the banks back."[3]

If his dream of becoming a film producer came to nothing, following his big break with his electronic score for *Rain Man* in 1988, Zimmer was established as one of the most sought-after composers in Hollywood, leading to gigs on movies by established directors such as Ridley Scott, Nicolas Roeg, Mike Nichols, Bruce Beresford, and later Terrence Malick, Michael Bay and, of course, Christopher Nolan. However, Hollywood was not at first the dream he had imagined it to be:

It was very talented people writing on paper, with their arrangers and orchestrators in some dingy back room with neon lighting and cottage cheese ceilings. Not really my thing. Stained, cracked linoleum floors and water-damaged ceilings ("but that's where Orson Wells cut *Citizen Kane!*" "Yeah, great, but can you at least change the light bulb?") So, I build [sic] myself another studio and other people wanted to be part of it—like Mark Mancina, Harry [Gregson-

Williams], John Powell ... and because we had all that rather cool, yet primitive technology, directors actually liked coming over and hearing mock-ups of a score, discussing the music to picture without a hundred-piece orchestra waiting outside. And we had an excellent drinks cupboard.[4]

Early on in his career, Zimmer wasn't a director's first choice, but with the German composer's star rising, producers became increasingly interested in his skills. Bruce Beresford, who worked with Zimmer on the Oscar-winning *Driving Miss Daisy*, explains that he originally wanted to continue his working relationship with Georges Delerue, but relented when the producers pushed for Zimmer, who had just had a big success with *Rain Man*.

Team Building

Throughout his career, Zimmer has proven himself to be unusually adept at assembling a team to assist with the process of creating a film score. As Zimmer has repeatedly explained, he had had no experience working with an orchestra when he was assisting Stanley Myers, who wrote the symphonic parts of their collaborations. Furthermore, Zimmer wasn't able to read music.[5] To be able to cope with the demands of a symphony orchestra Zimmer relied on musicians with experience in the field, namely Shirley Walker, who gave an example of their way of working in an interview:

> Hans had asked me to help him in London with a replacement score for Disney's second *White Fang* film. In an emotional climactic final cue, Hans wanted to have a soaring fast woodwind line added over several phrases of his theme. We had a brief discussion about the difficulties involved. Hans played a section of Berlioz' *Symphony Fantastique* to demonstrate what he had in mind. I could see that Hans thought perhaps I doubted the ability of the London players.
> I think I spent almost three hours with my woodwind fingering charts figuring out a line that would be performable as well as work harmonically with Hans' tune. As we rehearsed the cue, I was relieved to see that my intricate trading off between all the upper winds was going to work. When I came into the booth to listen to a playback of our final take, Hans turned to me and said with a tone of triumph in his voice, "See, I told you they could play it!"[6]

Walker is credited with additional music for projects as varied as *Black Rain*, *Pacific Heights* and *Radio Flyer* as well as for being an orchestrator and conductor for *Renaissance Man*, *A League of Their Own* and *Toys*. However, she was clear about her actual involvement, saying: "Hans Zimmer was the first major-star composer I worked for [...] where I wasn't ghost-writing." Rather, Walker acted as a "teacher. Although neither of us would describe it that way, necessarily."[7]

Among the assistants on Zimmer's scores from the late '80s to early '90s were artists such as Alex Wurman (who contributed to *The Lion King* and *A League of Their Own*), Nick Glennie-Smith (conductor on *The Lion King* and additional composer for projects such as *K2*, *True Romance*, and *Drop Zone*), and Richard Harvey, an additional composer on *Beyond Rangoon* and the later *Inferno*, and who was recited as co-composer with Zimmer on the 2016 version of *The Little Prince*.

Zimmer has continued to work with a substantial number of artists from the early days of his Hollywood career right up to the present, such that if he deems himself not sufficiently well versed in a musical style he instead trusts another composer to supply the required material. In this way, Conrad Pope wrote the cue *Love* for *The Boss Baby* in a late romantic style as an homage to Howard Hanson. Benjamin Wallfisch adapted Edward Elgar's *Nimrod* from the *Enigma Variations* for *Dunkirk*, while according to director Christopher Nolan (in the booklet notes for the *Dunkirk* soundtrack album) Lorne Balfe supplied some "finishing touches" during the last weeks of mixing. On *The Lone Ranger*, the adaptation of Gioachino Rossini's overture to *William Tell* wasn't written by Zimmer but by Geoff Zanelli.

However, for many years the most significant person at Media Ventures, Zimmer aside, was Jay Rifkin. He had been a close friend of Zimmer's for years—together in the late '70s they had set up a studio in Brighton, England. When Zimmer was offered *Rain Man* and moved to Hollywood Zimmer called him and they were reunited, as Rifkin remembered in the expansive joint interview the two men gave *Sound on Sound* magazine in 2002 (cited above). The latter then co-produced, engineered and mixed the electronic score for the Tom Cruise film, which led to a string of high profile movies with Zimmer providing the score and Rifkin writing songs, e.g., for Iggy Pop on *Black Rain*.

The success of *The Lion King* was a turning point for them, leading to the building of their first studio in Santa Monica to house their equipment. As Rifkin recalled, it couldn't possibly have been a wiser choice: "We finished *Lion King* and we had five rooms immediately busy working on one project and thought 'We're on to something here.' As post schedules are more and more compressed, you just need to be able to throw a lot of firepower at a project, or else really hurt yourself doing it, having a very small team with just a limited number of workstations."[8]

With an extensive team on all their projects they were in a good position within the industry and their respective careers were at a high point. Indeed, based on the description in *Sound on Sound* in 2002, Media Ventures seemed to provide exactly what it promised: "Media Ventures is a unique collective, providing filmmakers with a one-stop shop for music production, and composers with all the musical and technical support needed to complete a project."[9]

The Rise and Fall of Media Ventures

Shortly after the *Sound on Sound* interview with Zimmer and Rifkin had been published they broke off both their professional and personal relationships, with Rifkin suing Zimmer in December 2003. Rifkin claimed his business partner had conspired to take over the entire Media Ventures company himself. The report published by *Variety* that month gave an insight into the business:

> By the late 1990s, the company had hired numerous "resident composers" to assist with Zimmer's scores and other composing projects. The composers split fees with Media Ventures and left once their own careers were established. The suit alleges that in order to keep the talent it nurtured, Media Ventures decided that the composers must sign management contracts with the company and that, to set a precedent, Zimmer would be the first to sign a formal agreement. Although Zimmer did not have a contractual obligation to use Media Ventures, the suit alleges that the company relied on Zimmer's use and gave him substantial benefits such as increasing his fees and improving his deal with ASCAP. Zimmer, however, informed Rifkin that he would no longer commission Media Ventures to work on his scores and allegedly encouraged other composers, via a series of secret emails, to break their ties with the company and join his new composer fraternity.[10]

Rifkin sued his (former) business partner for $10 million. It didn't take long for Zimmer to file a counterclaim. In early January 2004, he sued Rifkin for $20 million, accusing him "of secretly embezzling money from their business to support a lavish lifestyle," as the news agency *Reuters* put it. According to Zimmer's lawyer at that time, Bonnie Eskenazi, her client had decided to end the 15-year relationship with Rifkin after Zimmer allegedly discovered that his business partner had used money from the company to support his lifestyle. Zimmer's suit accused Rifkin of "plundering their company to pay for home renovations, his car, furniture, lavish meals and expensive hotel stays for himself, his family and his mistress, and of extracting exorbitant fees from the studios who hired the composer."

Eventually, both parties settled out of court for an undisclosed sum and went their separate ways, with Zimmer changing the name of the company to Remote Control Productions but otherwise retaining its working methods. Zimmer did not respond to a request for an interview.

In interviews Hans Zimmer repeatedly claimed that his reason for setting up Media Ventures, and later Remote Control Productions, was to give back what had been given to him—a chance for aspiring composers. The Media Ventures/Remote Control way of working also enabled Zimmer to take on more gigs than a sole composer could ever manage, often supervising the productions rather than writing every note of the score himself. At the same time he helped various young composers establish their careers, making his company an attractive place for those who wanted to make it big in the industry.

Quite a few succeeded: Trevor Rabin, who following his score for *Con Air* became one of the most popular composers for action movies in the '90s and early 00s; Atli Örvarsson, who contributed additional music to *The Holiday* and *Angels and Demons*; Ramin Djawadi, who assisted Klaus Badelt and Hans Zimmer on Sean Penn's *The Pledge* in 2001. Badelt himself, after providing additional music for projects such as *The Thin Red Line*, *The Prince of Egypt* and *Gladiator* (the later as co-composer), got his big break in feature scoring with the epic blockbuster *Pirates of the Caribbean*.

Originally, Alan Silvestri had been assigned to provide the score for the movie. Producer Jerry Bruckheimer wasn't happy with Silvestri's demos though and turned to Hans Zimmer, with whom he had worked several times in the past. Unfortunately, because of contractual commitments on *The Last Samurai*, Zimmer turned out to be unavailable. How the problem was resolved demonstrates the advantages of a company like Media Ventures: Zimmer was able to forward the project to his team, while he wrote sketches and the famous theme based on a motif he had employed in *Drop Zone* in 1994 (the cue *Too Many Notes*) and *Gladiator* in 2000 (cue *The Battle*). At this point Badelt took over, along with his colleagues Geoff Zanelli, Blake Neely, Steve Jablonsky, Jim Dooley and James McKee Smith, who also wrote a substantial amount of music.[11] Badelt received sole composer credit for the score, which became a smash hit, astonishing many in an era when pirate movies where considered box office poison.

Badelt parted company with Zimmer a few years later. In 2017, when asked if he was willing to talk about his experiences at Media Ventures/ Remote Control, Badelt said,

> I left there 15 years ago. After 15 years I have cleansed myself. It's a great place to be an up and coming composer, it's not a great place if you are a strong composer and if you have established yourself. It's all geared towards one guy and they all serve that one guy. [...] You have to leave as soon as you can to do your own thing. I have a very different style I think, not necessarily when it comes to music, but I like to be challenged all the time. I don't like to repeat myself. I like to swim against the mainstream. Instead of doing *Pirates of the Caribbean 4* I would rather do an independent film in China.

Despite Badelt's departure from Remote Control, he has gone on to work on many other projects. Other composers who worked for Media Ventures were not as lucky and couldn't gain a foothold in Hollywood, among them Henning Lohner and Ian Honeyman. One successful composer was Atli Örvarsson. After working with Hans Zimmer, he scored big budget movies such as *Hansel and Gretel: Witch Hunters* and *Season of the Witch*. Örvarsson is grateful to his mentor; he described the way of working at Remote Control Productions:

I rented a studio at Remote Control and found a home there. I never worked for Hans per se, but was an independent composer without a contract within Remote Control and had the pleasure of working with Hans on some projects. Because I was always an independent artist I had to pay rent for the studio there. Hans always writes a lot of music at the beginning of a project. Sometimes he assembles a band and they start jamming to get ideas and develop them. Artists have worked like that for centuries, when someone comes up with the main idea and then has other people fleshing it out for him.

The main idea is that Hans writes the themes and ideas and then relies on other people to help him apply them to the film. I think one of the things that Hans really thrives on is cooperation. [...] Most composers work more or less alone, but it has been incredible to get to know the "Hans Method." You need solutions. And there is room for creativity. Hans is really successful with combining his own creativity with the input of other people. You are more likely to win a war with an army than just one general.[12]

The set-up of the studios is explained by Matthew Margeson, who started his career with Zimmer before venturing out on his own and writing the music for productions such as *Eddie the Eagle* and *Kingsman: The Golden Circle*:

When I was working for guys like Klaus [Badelt] and Jim Dooley, it was just an employer-employee relationship. I was brought on and paid as an assistant. As long as you didn't mess up too bad and you got the job done in time you were welcome to stay. In a lot of the composers' suites, not only at Remote Control, there is maybe a writing room for the composer and then an assistants' room which may have a smaller set up in it, or a place for you to do administrative tasks. But then of course when the composer leaves at the end of the day, that's a lot of the time when my job would start. I would then go into the writing suite and clean up what he was doing as far as backing up things, or finishing arrangements, or uploading a finished cue to the server, or emailing it to a director, or doing the preparations for the next day.

When working with a team on a film score it is essential to make each piece of music fit homogeneously into the overall sound of the score, rather than having a mixture of styles and different approaches by the various composers contributing to the project. Nothing is more irritating than a patchwork score which actually sounds like a patchwork.

The approach to resolving this potential problem is elaborate, as explained by C., a former assistant at Remote Control who wishes to remain anonymous. At the beginning of each project, Zimmer has a meeting not only with the director of the movie and perhaps some of the producers, but also with the composers who will contribute to the score, as well as a music editor and possibly some assistants—a group of not more than ten to fifteen people overall:

In a production meeting, the division of work is being scheduled. As a composer, after you return from the meeting and go back into your studio, there are already several messages on your computer with detailed notes about the production which was just talked about a few minutes ago. The work flow is absolutely amazing and necessary. It is incredibly quick and one meeting is not enough for that.

Indeed, in the course of the production of the score for a movie there will be several meetings at regular intervals. C. continues:

> Even when Hans is mentioned as the main composer on a project, the director talks to all composers involved in the team during a production meeting. As the music is being presented in a meeting this makes sense. At the end of a production such a meeting is likely to be held every day, or at least every other day. Sometimes Hans asks a question during the meetings and sometimes you do better not to answer. Because sometimes he just wants to have your skills proofed.

The amount of music Zimmer writes himself varies from film to film, but the process itself is always the same, with Zimmer exploring new, unusual sounds:

> Before writing a single note, my team and I spend a lot of time programming new sounds, sampling new instruments. [...] The moment I start writing, I start mixing. Since I don't write on paper, I spend a long time making each note and sound convey the right emotion. It helps later with the live musicians. I can be very specific in my language (and I use English, not Italian) to convey to them why I want a note or phrase played a certain way. I don't make changes on the scoring stage, I don't let directors make changes with the musicians there. The recording is about getting a performance, not re-writing the cue. Nothing sounds worse than a bunch of bored musicians that had to wait while someone's changed an arrangement.[13]

After programming new sounds Zimmer writes a suite of music for the movie. C. elaborates:

> This suite is based on his talks with the director and the musical ideas he got from them. The vision is his. Of course, he asks for opinions from people at Remote Control, but the overall concept is his and his alone. Some composers who worked for Hans were not able to deal with the stress. You can't solve problems with logic. You need to solve them psychologically to be able to survive there.

After each production meeting the composers who have been assigned to write parts of the score retreat to their individual studios and work on their cues, which are based on the themes by Zimmer. To be able to work as efficiently as possible in a team, Remote Control has its own internal server. During the night, everything that had been written during the day is synced to all the computers so that every composer has the same data available when they come into the studio the next morning. Every composer not only has all the music written by every other composer, but also has all the materials created, such as virtual instruments and samples. There are people working at Remote Control whose job is to build virtual instruments, manage the samples and ensure this content is available to the composers.

With this way of working, every new production has a set of new sounds, ensuring that each project is distinctive. As elaborate as this technology is, it can cause problems, as recounted by C. in a rather amusing anecdote:

> One night, I was in charge of the back up. But I needed some material from the computer which I wanted to put on my private hard drive. I put my hard drive in and pulled it out again afterward. Or I thought it had been my hard drive. As soon as I had pulled it out, an error message of the sync software appeared on my computer, saying that the back up could not be completed. I looked at other computers in the studio as well and found that the message appeared on every single one of them. I had pulled out the wrong drive! This meant that every computer had a different amount of material. I panicked. I then had to do a night shift to repair the damage by walking into every studio and checking every computer to see what the individual status was and if any material had been damaged.

Competition in Town

Hans Zimmer combined synthesizers, beats, loops and pop music sensibilities with symphonic music, creating a hybrid that quickly caught on with producers and audiences, especially so because many of the movies for which it was composed were hugely successful commercially. Then as the '90s went on, with the team at Media Ventures/Remote Control, Zimmer was able to produce many more scores than a single composer could ever craft in the same time.

This way of working had several effects on film music: first and foremost, it inspired producers and directors to commission similar sounding soundtracks, doing so even when Remote Control was not employed. Patrick Doyle, for example—considering his earlier work—delivered rather unusual sounding scores for films such as *Rise of the Planet of the Apes* and *Jack Ryan: Shadow Recruit*. Abandoning his familiar style of long, memorable orchestral melodies, he adopted electronics and penned short motifs that could easily be edited to fast-paced action.

Secondly, it became much more difficult for lone composers who were not part of Remote Control to deliver commissioned scores on time, as postproduction schedules became significantly shorter. Instead of working with a team like Hans Zimmer, they still tried to work alone. Zimmer's company, though, is much more effective at dealing with sudden changes in the editing process because (quoting again the description of Media Ventures as given by *Sound on Sound* cited): "Media Ventures is a unique collective, providing filmmakers with a one-stop shop for music production, and composers with all the musical and technical support needed to complete a project." This is not something a single composer can deliver. So why would a producer commission an individual rather than Remote Control, a company which could fix issues much more efficiently?

Mychael Danna experienced these changes in the movie industry and has had to adapt:

> It has become a very hard career, in that you have to do so many things. Writing music is one thing. You have to be good at managing your staff, because there is no way that one composer could work on a major film by themselves. It is impossible. You need a team, even if it is an orchestrator or technical assistant, because nowadays there is so much technology that we have to work with in order to deliver mock-ups. Then you need to have people skills in order to have these meetings. You need to be able to delegate because there are so many picture changes that you have to chase, and which is a very common thing now. It is impossible to keep up with the writing. So you have to have other writers on a big movie. [...] Two good composers can do a big score. But otherwise you need ghostwriters or assistants filling in. The system is set up now that the Hans Zimmer model has become the expected model.[14]

Mychael Danna's comments are not about the music itself, but about the actual way of running a business. Zimmer himself is rather open about his working practice—when asked about his earlier days at Media Ventures he said:

> We very much worked like a firm of architects. One main designer, with us all helping each other out. People are still confused about the "additional music" credits. If it sounds like me, it's probably me. Head Architect. But how can my collaborators ever get a career going if they are just "ghosts"? If it sounds like John Powell, it's probably him…. Same rules apply. Personally, I couldn't give a flying fuck about credits. I'm in it for the process. That's the part I love.[15]

A striking example of Remote Control's efficiency was recounted by C.:

> In one of the meetings for *The Ring 2* the director disapproved of one cue which Hans had wanted to include. During the meeting, Hans had the idea to replace the piece which had just been thrown out with the end of a certain cue. Dan Pinder, the music editor for the project, then received the task of opening another session in his already packed ProTools arrangement with the same amount of tracks to cut the last minute of the replacement cue into the beginning of the replaced cue and sync it.
>
> All this had to be done during the meeting while the whole team sat around him and waited. Every 30 seconds Hans would ask how long this would still take and if they should have a break. Everybody suffered with Dan who then got help from some assistants who brought additional USB sticks and who coupled the computer with another computer via LAN to finally solve the

problem. Remember, this all happens live with the director being present. And what happens if you screw up and the new cue is being thrown out as well? Hans won't accept that.

In the previously cited interview with Atli Örvarsson the composer mentioned that he didn't have a contract at Remote Control, but rather worked as a freelancer. However, some Remote Control employees (composers included) are required to sign a contract, which includes a confidentiality clause that prevents them from talking about their experiences. Zimmer's protégé Lorne Balfe flat out refuses to discuss his work at Remote Control and his relationship with Zimmer: "I don't want to talk about Hans. I am not too sure how that's relevant. [...] I just don't know what it's got to do with it." When pressed about the lessons he has learned at the Santa Monica based factory, Balfe relents:

> There is no one thing I have learned. There are many things. The biggest thing I learned from him was the role of filmmaking. The majority of the time is not spent writing. It's spent listening and talking to the filmmakers and understanding what the journey is. It's not necessarily about writing music, which one may think it is. It's not. It's a bigger thing. It's about being able to sit back from the keyboard and talk to filmmakers about what the story line is and what needs to be said. [...] Neither of us were classically trained musicians. It's not that you learn how to orchestrate or write. It was the process of the interaction with directors and producers and editors.

"I would say that the difference is that the people working directly for Hans have much more pressure on their backs than the people who just rent their studio there," says C.

> It's a difference in the quality of life. As a person working for Hans, you need to have a certain coolness about you to not let Hans' energy get to you. Andrew Zack was responsible for the administrative side at Remote Control. A classic example of Andrew's attitude was Hans' lunch routine. Hans received his lunch but was dissatisfied with the quality of some of the ingredients. Hans threw a tantrum and accused Andrew of bringing him bad food. Andrew then asked in all calmness how the dessert had been. Hans got quieter and admitted the dessert had been fine. The debate ended there and then. You need these tricks and attitudes to be able to survive at Remote Control. Being an assistant there involves extreme pressure. When working on a score with him, he gives you a to-do list of countless items, and then asks you randomly whether you have completed these tasks. If you haven't, he will make life hard for you.

Regarding financial rewards, C. explains: "Some of the composers working on a score with Hans receive royalties, others don't. This depends on several factors,"

> It depends on how long you have worked for Hans. In this regard, it is a kind of a "thank you" from Hans. It also depends on how much you contributed to

the score. If you contribute more than just additional arrangements, as it is called, then you receive royalties. I worked for Remote Control for quite a long time without receiving royalties. There are quite tough negotiations about royalties. Even while working on a production there are negotiations about who contributed how much.

I remember that there was some confusion about *The Ring 2* because it was a follow-up and Hans had written all the themes and established them already on the first movie. For a long time, Henning Lohner and Martin Tillman didn't know if they would get a mention on the cue sheets. In the end, they contributed their own themes and received royalties. When Hans' *Ring*-theme was featured, he received the royalties. When there was a cue where other composers contributed, they received a share.

In a lot of cases, the cue sheets say: written by Hans Zimmer, arranged by XYZ. Sometimes, even when the score is being compiled and readied for print, it still isn't clear who will receive the credit on the cue sheet. If you want to win an Oscar, you have to make sure that not too many names are mentioned on the cue sheet and in the end credits, otherwise your score will not be eligible for a nomination. If you score a film which seems likely to be an Oscar contender, you do well to minimize the staff of composers. This happens. It doesn't mean that fewer people worked on the score than on other soundtracks. They are just not mentioned.

Even without the European Tour he made in the spring of 2016 and a subsequent World Tour in 2017, Zimmer has cemented his image in the public eye by venturing into other fields in a way that seems unusual for a film composer. Indeed, Hans Zimmer's business tactics and ventures, as discussed in the following sections, read like a manual on how to remain successful and famous once you are at the top.

Giving Young Artists Hope

In February 2014, a competition was launched which piqued the interest of both aspiring and established composers, agents and publishers. This event bore the irresistible name, Hans Zimmer Wants You. As stated on the competition's homepage, it was organized by Bleeding Fingers, a "joint venture between Extreme Music, the production music arm of Sony/ATV Music Publishing, and Academy Award° winner Hans Zimmer's Remote Control Productions."[16]

Bleeding Fingers is a company which specializes in library music for program makers and broadcasters, employing composers to write music cues which can then be licensed for use in various media. It is a joint venture between RCI Global, a company owned by Zimmer and Steven Kofsky, and Extreme Music, a production music library (and part of SonyATV Music Publishing) which has been a close ally of Media Ventures/Remote Control Productions since its beginning.

Bleeding Fingers had just been founded a few months earlier, in 2013. As Russell Emanuel, CEO of Bleeding Fingers and Extreme Music, said in a statement published in December 2013: "The custom-scoring business is long overdue for a major shake-up and we fully intend to bring it. This is a natural evolution for us and represents major incremental growth and an exciting next chapter in our story."[17]

The idea was to find and recruit promising talent through the contest. The contestants had to download stem files of the cue *Destiny's Door* composed by Hans Zimmer and write a variation on it. The panel of judges comprised Zimmer himself, Lorne Balfe, Junkie XL (both composers experienced at working for Remote Control Productions), Steve Kofsky, Russell Emanuel and Jacob Shea, a composer at Bleeding Fingers. Successful contestants would have the "opportunity of a lifetime," as the campaign put it: "The prize includes the opportunity for full-time employment, including a full benefits package, plus the use of a fully equipped studio in Bleeding Fingers brand new state of the art facility." The prize would then be awarded to the eventual winner from a shortlist of three.

The word "opportunity" was carefully chosen—there was by no means a guarantee of a job from Bleeding Fingers, as a look at paragraph 6.2 from the Terms and Conditions shows, which promises any selected winners a three day trip to Los Angeles, including an interview with Bleeding Fingers for a possible paid position as a composer at the facility. Included in this package was an economy flight to LAX, standard hotel accommodations, $500 pocket money, and a Visa/Mastercard gift card: "For the sake of clarity, the Winner(s) are not guaranteed to receive an offer of employment with Bleeding Fingers, rather, the Winner(s) shall solely be guaranteed an interview with Bleeding Fingers, which may or may not result in an offer of employment."[18]

But what had the contestant to agree to in order to receive the chance of an interview with Bleeding Fingers? Let alone get a job with them? Any composer taking part in the competition had to surrender all rights to their entry, as was made unambiguously clear in paragraph 3.2: Bleeding Fingers would be the owner of all rights to submitted pieces, with the possibility of using them in any form in every part of the world, "solely as part of this Competition," and without granting the composer any fees or royalties. To quote the rules:

> For clarification, Bleeding Fingers will therefore own the Composition and have the sole right to exploit it, including the right to amend the Composition and transfer any and all rights in and to the Composition, Amended or not. However, Bleeding Fingers shall not exploit any Composition, other than as described herein, in any manner or media other than as part of this competition.

Was it maybe still worth it? The winner of the contest was Daniel Suett, a UK citizen, 22 years of age at the time. Says Suett: "It's not every day a top Hollywood composer opens the floor for unknown composers to share their work in this way. I saw it as a career opportunity worth pursuing—evidently I was right! After all, the competition pieces have not been used for anything else and are unlikely to be used in the future."

Indeed, it seemed to have been worth it for Suett since he is now living most of the time in Los Angeles and has been busy as a composer, working on his own projects—and for Bleeding Fingers. How did the interview with his future employer go after he had won the contest?

> They didn't really need such a formal interview at that point. The music had already served as the audition, but we did have a general chat to gauge how I would fit within the work environment at the company. I suppose they saw how eager I was and that I could create music that met their requirements, I also think my age was a contributing factor, as well as having just graduated from university. Whereas some of the other candidates already had established careers. I guess they felt that I was at the perfect stage of development to join the relatively new company.

Bleeding Fingers offered the composer the chance of full-time employment, for which Daniel Suett had to sign a non-disclosure agreement.

Bleeding Fingers has since secured several high-profile gigs. One was David Attenborough's hugely successful TV series *Planet Earth II*. While the first series of *Planet Earth* had been scored by Attenborough's longtime creative partner, George Fenton, Zimmer and Bleeding Fingers took over for the 2016 return. Moreover, after 27 years, Bleeding Fingers replaced Alf Clausen as the composer for the long running animated sitcom *The Simpsons*. This change caused some controversy, not least because of the way Clausen was let go: one day, the composer received a call from producer Richard Sakai who informed him that "a different kind of music" was now required, and that therefore he was being replaced.

One colleague of Clausen's, who wishes to remain anonymous, criticizes the way the situation was handled:

> The way it was done was inappropriate. [...] Now, I love Alf. I have known him since he was a copyist. That was a long time ago. Alf [...] has never been out of work a day in his life. It's a little hard to feel sorry for him, but the way it was done was inappropriate. I am not surprised. I am not shocked. I am disappointed the way it was handled, but you saw that *Dancing with the Stars* cut their band [when the rating went down]. That's what happens over time. Something is bound to happen.

After 27 years, it was Bleeding Fingers that took over from Clausen, who was by then suffering from Parkinson's Disease. Perhaps in hindsight it was inevitable—it was after all Zimmer, not Clausen, who had gotten the gig to provide the music for *The Simpsons Movie* in 2007.

The Hans Zimmer Wants You campaign wasn't the only competition Zimmer and his team launched. In 2017, Zimmer and Lorne Balfe provided the main theme for the National Geographic series *Genius*, starring Geoffrey Rush as Albert Einstein, with Balfe providing the underscore. After the show's airing, a competition called Show Us Your Musical Genius! asked participants to create their own version of the show's original theme. The top prize winner could look forward to attending a recording session with Zimmer or Balfe, either in Los Angeles or London.[19]

For his music for *Genius* Balfe received help from colleagues at 14th Street Music, a company which was founded in 2010 by Zimmer, Balfe and Steven Kofsky to create production music for video games, trailers, TV shows and commercials.[20]

There is always the possibility for those sufficiently talented to work as an intern at Remote Control. One student (S.), who was living in the UK, was lucky enough to have his application accepted and spent several weeks at Remote Control in the second half of 2017. What S. learned was that working his way up the system at Remote Control was not the path he wanted to pursue after all:

> Many people go to Remote Control and want to start working there as assistants. That's great for them. But you have to be aware of the fact that you might spend five to ten years cleaning up the Logic projects of the various composers. There are people there who haven't done anything else for ten years. That's not a creative job, it's a job you are assigned to do. You have to clean up after people. You lose the time to write music for yourself. I don't want to start as an assistant and crawl up the ladder. As an assistant, you have to come into the studio before the boss does, and you have to leave after he left. Your whole life consists of making his life as simple as possible.

Despite the fact that he was only there as an intern for a few weeks S. was fortunate enough to gain some insights into the Remote Control way of working, and this regardless of the fact that Hans Zimmer was not even in Santa Monica during that time since he was busy touring:

> I could watch Hans' composers a few times. It was very interesting to see how Hans would send them a theme and how they would then take it and develop it over the course of a few days. I remember one theme was for *The Lion King* and I asked one of the composers where in the movie the theme was to be used. He answered that no one could tell if the theme was ever going to be used at all. It was helpful for me to see how the process is—how the cues are sent from the boss to the assistants, from the assistants to the orchestrator before they are recorded.

Observing how the different processes work was made easier by the fact that S. had no assigned place for himself. Instead, he would walk around and watch the employees writing music—"giving comments was, of course, not appreciated." The atmosphere was comparatively relaxed and S. had many inspiring chats. This was partly because of Zimmer's absence: "Hans is incredibly busy and heavily involved in the whole process. Many people told me that it was much more relaxed because he wasn't there. It is incredibly busy and hectic when he is in the building because he is very much in demand."

S. estimates that during his time at Remote Control ten to fifteen other interns were working at the company at any given moment, the numbers varying depending on the time of day. Of these interns, two were fortunate enough to be offered jobs shortly afterwards, but are, of course, prohibited from talking about their experiences. Even S. had to sign a non-disclosure agreement which prevents him from talking about "how the people behaved. Private stuff."

Hans Becomes a Brand Name

People working in the film music world are rarely well known to the general public—Hans Zimmer is an exception to the rule. After all, he has worked on several of the highest grossing blockbusters in recent memory. And that fame has allowed him to associate his name with brands quite a few times.

The most obvious examples are the sample libraries on the market that feature some of the trademark sounds Zimmer has employed in his sound-tracks. Spitfire Audio, a library company based in London, released five products with samples created by Hans Zimmer to be used by other composers in their projects: Hans Zimmer Percussion London, Hans Zimmer Percussion Los Angeles, Hans Zimmer Percussion London Solos, Hans Zimmer Strings and Hans Zimmer Piano. The London Percussion product is advertised as

> a product produced by Hans Zimmer and his diamond class team of Grammy winning engineers, musicians and technicians. [...] Herein lies not an emulation or synthesis of his approach, but a recreation. The same studio, musicians, instruments, signal chain and talented engineers, sitting alongside a decade of experience, innovation and refinement overseen in every detail by Hans himself. The same excruciating attention to detail, perfection but most importantly the endless choice for tweakability and customization you'd expect of the greatest of sound-smiths.[21]

Producing sample libraries is not new for Hans Zimmer, after all he started recording instruments for use in his own studio early on. As he explained in an interview with the software company Steinberg:

I use very few (virtual instruments) now. [...] There's also my sampler which we had to build from scratch. Mark Wherry has been building it and it's slightly over the top as far as the technology is concerned. And we've been creating our own library and that project just goes on forever because we keep on adding to it. The problem with samples is that you get bored. Unfortunately, every time you press the same note, the same sound comes back at you. I've never understood why people don't make their own sample library because it's really not that hard, it just takes a bit of time and having a few friends who can play instruments extraordinarily well plus a hall for recording. And it's so much better because it's custom-made.[22]

C., who worked as a composer's assistant at Remote Control, suggests that Zimmer's influence is the prime reason for the development of the library market in recent years, although it needs to be pointed out that other companies had already put out samples in the late '80s (such as the Rack Module Kit):

The structures he has established were trendsetting. That starts with the technology. 95 percent of the library technology we have today goes back to ideas which were developed by Hans Zimmer. At some point, someone looked into Hans' way of working. This was then brought to the attention of library developers through word of mouth propaganda. If I am not mistaken, he already produced his own library in the late '90s by recording samples with the musicians in London. [...] At one point after a very expensive library recording, Hans turned to Jeff Rona to ask him what would happen if the library wasn't successful. Jeff Rona looked into the costs and answered: "If we drove three expensive BMWs down the cliff, this would equal the costs of this recording" to which Hans replied: "Ah well, this is okay then."

These libraries are not only used for demos and mock-ups, but are used in the final recordings of a film's score—Zimmer always employs a fusion of real musicians and samples for his soundtracks. Says C.: "During my time at Remote Control, the composers who used these libraries for their projects had to pay an annual sum to be able to do so. This amount was quite expensive. They could only use the samples after they had paid for the licensing."

It is not only composers at Remote Control who can rent Zimmer's own sample libraries. Harry Manfredini used a library called Hans Zimmer Guitars for the horror film *Jason X*, effectively crediting Hans Zimmer as a musician on a score despite his having nothing to do with the project.

Zimmer also lent his name to a rather unusual extra included on the two disc extended edition of *Angels and Demons*, available on DVD and Blu-ray. The extra—available on discs in the USA, Germany, France, Italy, Spain, Australia, as well as New Zealand—is called Hans Zimmer Music Studio—Powered by Sequel 2, a trial version of a program for music production developed by Steinberg which is similar to Apple's Garage Band.

Zimmer is an advocate for the products of Steinberg and has repeatedly stated his love for Cubase—Steinberg's most popular product—in interviews, a program he uses himself. It is not surprising then that Remote Control and Steinberg worked together in promoting Sequel, a much less popular product from the company. And it is clever advertising indeed: whoever installs Sequel 2 from the *Angels and Demons* Blu-ray or DVD gains access to three pieces from the soundtrack, consisting of stems of strings, choir, percussion, brass and synthesizers. By opening the three projects, the user can get an impression of how the cues were arranged. Enthusiasts can also play around with the different instrument sections and create their own pieces with the tools provided.

Zimmer provides this caveat: "And no, you can't sound like me. You are not me, you are you. Just like I can't sound like any other composer. Not with any degree of authenticity."[23] Even so, to a certain degree Hans Zimmer's customers and fans can successfully sound like their role model by using previously mentioned Spitfire Audio libraries.

In 2018, Zimmer teamed up with Range Rover and branded content studio Atlantic Re:think for a campaign entitled *Land Rover Presents: Scoring the Drive with Hans Zimmer*. In the video, the composer drives around in a Range Rover, while explaining how he scores his drive—the curves, the landscape, the smell. The music playing in the short film was written by Zimmer himself. And so it happened that he became an ambassador for Range Rover and the magazine *The Atlantic*:

> The project comes from *The Atlantic* magazine's marketing arm, Atlantic Re:think [...]. Execs said this kind of branded content drives 75 percent of the pub's digital revenue, which surpassed print revenue nearly a decade ago. "Scoring the Drive" aims to "capture the experience of driving a Range Rover," said Michael Monroe, vp, marketing at *The Atlantic*, "and connect with the audience through the power of (Zimmer's) cinematic music."[24]

Playing to the Fans

Part of Zimmer's continuing success comes through making his fans feel close to him, and one way of doing this is through giving concerts. After decades in the music business, Hans Zimmer decided to go on tour in early 2016. The tour took him to London, Brussels, Hamburg, Krakow, Prague, Rouen, Dublin and other cities. The tour was produced by Steven Kofsky and Harvey Goldsmith, a promoter whose main business is large scale rock 'n' roll concerts. He is "the impresario behind some of the biggest live music events in the country," as reported by the British newspaper *The Guardian*.[25]

Goldsmith had already promoted Zimmer's two London concerts in October 2014. The 2016 concerts proved to be a huge success, with several giant halls sold out. For these concerts, Zimmer assembled an impressive list of musicians, notably Tina Guo, who had played cello on several of Zimmer's soundtracks. A young musician, Guo moves fluently between genres, having performed in classical, rock and jazz concerts, but recently has been concentrating on writing and producing her own music. She made it clear that her involvement with Remote Control helped her a great deal in getting new gigs, and not only on film scores. As she recalls, very little music that she was required to play had been written out by Hans Zimmer. Rather, the music making proved to be an improvisational process, with Zimmer discussing a general approach with her. He would then oversee Guo's playing by encouraging her to "show her balls."

Another member of the team for the concerts was a close friend and collaborator of Zimmer's: Richard Harvey, who played clarinet on several of the pieces that were performed. Harvey, himself a renowned composer for concert hall, film and TV, was, as a close friend of Stanley Myers, one of the first contacts Zimmer made in the world of film music. Also part of this musical family were Johnny Marr, who had played guitar on the score for *Inception*, and who joined the group in several cities, and the singer Lebo M., the voice of *The Lion King* and *Tears of the Sun*. Finally, Mike Einziger, a member of the group Incubus, was featured on guitar, having previously co-written the music for *The Amazing Spider-Man 2* and performed on the score for *The Lone Ranger*.

As noted in several reviews, Zimmer didn't stage stuffy, elitist film music concerts. Instead, he went for a rock 'n' roll atmosphere—people could eat and drink during the performances—displaying an impressive technical set up and telling anecdotes about his professional and personal life as part of the performance.

However, despite making appearances on the red carpet at the premieres of the movies he has written the music for and giving interviews at film festivals, Zimmer has rarely attended other film music-related events. Along with his busy schedule working in Los Angeles, this probably has to do with the fact that, as he has said, "parties scare the living daylights out of me."[26]

Rather than public appearances, Zimmer has chosen to have an extensive series of videos recorded of him talking about his approach to film scoring. These videos were shot for the company MasterClass, which provides paying clients with access to esteemed names in the industry—Annie Leibovitz has given virtual classes in photography, Aaron Sorkin in screenwriting, Ron Howard in directing, Helen Mirren in acting, and Hans Zimmer in composing for media. In these recordings "Hans Zimmer teaches you how to tell a story with music in 31 exclusive video lessons."[27]

As an instructor Zimmer went for a hands-on approach. The advertisement made it clear that students looking for lessons in composition, counterpoint or harmony were in the wrong place. Instead, Zimmer concentrated on how he "works with directors, including what he needs to learn from the director in order to start writing—sometimes even before the film is shot." Additionally, he gave an insight into how he "uses synths, as he creates a song from his starter patch for us."

Aspiring composers struggling to come up with memorable themes, on the other hand, were told Zimmer could help since he "has created some of the most memorable themes in film. Learn how he creates a theme, and how simplicity is his best tool to maintain a theme." In this way, for only £70 [~ $92] anyone with internet access got the chance to be as close as possible to Zimmer without being able to touch his lilac corduroy jacket.

Following Trends and Collaborating with Hip Artists

Hans Zimmer, as a composer and musician who started his career playing keyboards on The Buggles' hit *Video Killed the Radio Star*, has closely followed developments both in the worlds of music and technology. As shown above, he has increasingly surrounded himself with outstanding artists, be it composers, orchestrators, musicians, as well as people from the business side of the industry. His background in pop music is evident in most of his scores, and one of the reasons for his success is his ability not only to pick up current trends in music—underscoring dramas from the '80s and '90s with the hip music of its time (*Rain Man*, *Black Rain*)—but to mix pop elements with orchestral music. He has employed various methods to achieve this, such as adding electronic percussion and synthesizers to largely symphonic works; including unusual sounds in scores via his sample libraries; taking orchestral recordings and changing them electronically in the musical post production process electronically; and—most importantly—working with artists who are currently the most sought-after and at the top of their game.

The most obvious example of this is probably Zimmer's work for *The Amazing Spider-Man 2*, where he worked with not one but two famous artists, who had their names on the film poster and CD cover next to his. Pharrell Williams had been a successful music producer before he wrote the hit song *Happy* in 2013 for the animated blockbuster hit *Despicable Me 2*, a film which was scored by Heitor Pereira, a longtime friend and collaborator of Hans Zimmer and a member of the Remote Control team. *Happy* sold more than ten million records worldwide, a No. 1 hit that was never off the radio. In fact, Williams had already written a couple of songs for the first *Despicable*

Me in 2010, tracks featured on the soundtrack album produced by Hans Zimmer. From there it was only a small step to their collaboration on *Spider-Man*.

Zimmer recalled,

> I was talking to Pharrell about it. It was around the time he was writing *Happy* and we talked about the power of music. What if we did *Spider-Man* as a band? Spending time with Pharrell is experiencing a hurricane of ideas. His music is borne out of a thirst for the knowledge of everything—painting, writing, science, psychology, history. But it's not a cold intellect that informs his art. At the center is a steadfast real concern for the human condition, and the charm he brings to his work is grounded in genuine love for his fellow man.[28]

The other members of the band were not unknown either: Johnny Marr founded the long-running band The Smiths with singer Morrissey and is considered one of the most important musicians of the British new wave movement of the '80s. He had already played guitar on the score for *Inception* and now became a member of the *Spider-Man* band, sitting in the studio with Zimmer, Williams—and Junkie XL. The latter musician has made a name for himself as a film composer in his own right since then, garnering mostly positive reviews for his score for George Miller's *Mad Max: Fury Road*. At that time though, he had primarily been known as a DJ, having started out as a performing musician in 1988. In 2012, he had already released six albums, with the track *More* featuring Lauren Rocket reaching number 11 on the Billboard Electronic Album chart in 2008.

Working with such successful artists was naturally beneficial for everybody involved: fans of Pharrell Williams were introduced to Hans Zimmer, fans of Hans Zimmer were introduced to Pharrell Williams, and so forth. Similarly, Zimmer worked with Radiohead on the music for David Attenborough's series *Blue Planet II*, rerecording Radiohead's song *Ocean Bloom* (originally called just *Bloom*), which had been recorded a few years prior and was now to be recreated for the opening of the show.

According to Thom Yorke it was a dream collaboration from beginning to end:

> *Bloom* was inspired by the original *Blue Planet* series so it's great to be able to come full circle with the song and reimagine it for this incredible landmark's sequel. Hans is a prodigious composer who effortlessly straddles several musical genres so it was liberating for us all to work with such a talent and see how he wove the sound of the series and *Bloom* together."[29]

The song was produced by Russell Emanuel from Bleeding Fingers, which also provided the musical score under Zimmer's guidance.

In the course of his career, the German-born producer has worked with several artists from fields other than film music and, naturally, the more successful he has become, the more powerful the artists he could sign for film music ventures: Art Garfunkel, who sang *Always Look on the Bright Side of Life* on the soundtrack for *As Good as It Gets*, produced by Hans Zimmer in 1997; Lisa Gerrard, providing vocals on the soundtrack for *Mission: Impossible 2* in 2000; Robbie Williams performing *A Man for All Seasons* for the soundtrack of *Johnny English*, with the song being produced by Hans Zimmer in 2003 and, more recently, Lang Lang playing the piano on the score for *Kung Fu Panda 3* in 2016.

Seizing the opportunity to popularize your own brand is always a good move for a businessman, though in Zimmer's case this doesn't have to happen through working with international stars of the music world. In early 2017, for example, Zimmer took to the stage on Stephen Colbert's highly popular *Late Show* to perform the theme from *Planet Earth II* alongside his protégés Jasha Klebe and Jacob Shea from Bleeding Fingers. That same year, Zimmer was guest at one of the most beloved music festivals in the world: Coachella. No composer working mainly in film had ever previously been invited to the prestigious event in California. Reviewing Zimmer's performance, the *Los Angeles Times* wrote: "It was a stroke of mad genius to put him out here at primetime, and the literal squeals of delight coming from teenage ravers when they recognized his film themes rivaled any reaction to anything else all weekend."[30]

It only shows that Zimmer has always had an eye and an ear for current trends, a gift which has enabled him to remain at the top now through four decades.

A Secure Position in Powerful Companies

Today Hans Zimmer is not only head of Remote Control Productions, but is the co-founder of RCI Global (which produced his concerts). Long before this, but vitally important in the development of his career, he served as the head of the music department of DreamWorks, for a time one of the biggest film studios in Hollywood. Steven Spielberg, founder of the studio, employed Zimmer in 1997. The first movie produced by DreamWorks was consequently scored by Zimmer himself, a thriller called *The Peacemaker* starring George Clooney and Nicole Kidman.

In quick succession, Zimmer also provided the music for the first two animated projects at the studio, *The Prince of Egypt* and *The Road to El Dorado*. In the course of 20 years at DreamWorks, Zimmer has composed the music for more than a dozen productions (among them *Gladiator*, *The Ring* and *Kung Fu Panda*), while other DreamWorks projects scored by composers working for Remote Control include *Transformers*, *Shrek* and *The Island*.

When he was appointed as head of music Zimmer said: "I am not going to be scoring everything at DreamWorks. The whole point is to find interesting young composers to do things. [...] Most films today are done by the same five composers, and I'm one of them. It's really tedious. [...] I want to hear other people's ideas."[31] During Zimmer's association with DreamWorks all hiring decisions naturally went through him. One of the films financed by Dream-Works was *Wallace & Gromit: The Curse of the Were-Rabbit*. It had quite a troubled post-production history. Composer Julian Nott was close friends with director Nick Park, with whom he had gone to film school, and for whom he had also written the music for the *Wallace & Gromit* short films. Naturally Nott was Park's first choice to score *Chicken Run*. Alas, it wasn't to be. DreamWorks rejected Nott's main theme when it proved not to the taste of Jeffrey Katzenberg, one of the three founders of the company and the head of animation.

The job eventually went to Remote Control, thereby letting Harry Gregson-Williams and John Powell provide the underscore for this unofficial remake of *The Great Escape*. A few years later, Nott was asked to provide the music for *Wallace & Gromit: The Curse of the Were-Rabbit*. Since it featured the same characters as in the short films, Nott was in a stronger position this time around. It didn't help him much, though. After he had written the score, test screenings were arranged by the studio, and unfortunately the audience didn't react to the film as the executives had hoped. According to several sources, it was then Zimmer who suggested he could "improve" the score as means of improving the film's testing.

Nic Raine had orchestrated Nott's score and went on to work for Zimmer's team, whom he met in a hotel room in London to discuss a possible new approach:

> I met for the first time Hans and the four composers who were going to be working on it. We all sat around a table and Hans said, "I feel like we are the American army and we are flown into a third world country and we are here to save the movie." He talked about doing the film and said, "They don't really like Julian's music and we have got to save this. I trust you all. It's all going to be great."

The decision to let Zimmer and his team work on the music went down well with Julian Nott, who was no longer able to cater to the demands of DreamWorks. They were requesting changes to the score around the clock. A deal was struck that Julian Nott would get the composer credit and a large percentage of the royalties, with Zimmer and his team handling the changes the studio demanded. Nott appreciated Zimmer's handling of the situation and was glad that his name was still attached to the project, considering that Zimmer was in a position where he could have had him fired.

For orchestrator Nic Raine it was the start of several hectic weeks:

> [Hans] is the producer of the score and he delegates. One guy is going to do the love theme, some guys are doing the action, another one is going to do the comedy, [Lorne] Balfe does the wall of sound. It was all delegated like that and

I was orchestrating for everybody. This really was the Hollywood way. There were so many changes, I must have written that score two times at least. I was earning a fortune because they were paying something like £12 [~$16] a bar. It was real Hollywood rates.

In the course of that work I once spent 48 hours working with two hours of sleep. It was that bad with the changes and the rewrites coming in all the time. Hans was the conduit. The composers would send their demos to wherever and then all the people in the team made their comments about the music. The notes go to Hans and then he disseminates it back to the composers, saying, "You have to change this and that." I then received the music from the composers who had received the notes from Hans. They were the ones dealing with me. Each composer individually would say, "On this cue we change bar 48. That's pizzicato now."

Working in a team like Zimmer does isn't a new phenomenon. What is new is the technology he has at hand to develop and deliver a score efficiently. As he admits, his job is sometimes more about doing PR for the movies, as per requests from the producers and directors, than writing the actual music: "I have a deal with one film company where they pay me next to nothing for the music, but a shitload of money for doing press. Press is hard work [...] and premieres are only great for being in among a big audience for whom, ultimately we made it, and enjoying the movie with them."[32]

Two reasons why Hans Zimmer has become so powerful and successful are his communication skills, and his abilities as a professional and efficient team leader. These skills have helped him enormously in his rise to stardom. As C. elaborates:

What makes Hans unique is not only his craft as a composer but also his communication skills. This helps him a great deal both during the production process and when he is watching a movie he is about to score. Of course, he watches the movie differently than anybody else. We may catch some connections, but Hans catches much more by paying attention to body language, for example. He also has very detailed discussions with the directors about their intentions. He is able to catch a lot of information by simply paying attention to the body language of the director, which he himself might not even be aware of.

Without discrediting his musical achievements, as this chapter shows through interviews with Zimmer himself, as well as his colleagues and members of his team, the Oscar-winner can in some ways better be described as a producer than a composer. In this position he has acquired not only stardom but also power, enabling aspiring composers to pursue their own projects (John Powell, Harry Gregson-Williams, Junkie XL, Atli Örvarsson). By now, Zimmer has nearly a monopoly position in the Hollywood film music world, farming out countless projects to the dozens of composers at Remote Control. Such a situation raises the question, is competition good for business?

Instead of a Fireman

Time has a way of demonstrating the most stubborn are the most intelligent. In Galileo's day, a fellow scientist was no more stupid than Galileo. He was well aware the earth revolved, but he also had a large family to feed.—Yevgeny Yevtushenko, *Career*

People who move in the same realm as Gary Yershon can observe one fascinating fact: everybody loves him. It is easy to see why. The composer, who made a name for himself by working with acclaimed director Mike Leigh, is modest, funny, supportive and artistically inventive. Yershon is also a late bloomer. He wrote his first film score when he was over 50 and received his first Oscar nomination (for his work on *Mr. Turner*) when he was 60. Before he embarked on his career—although he himself would only use the word in jest—Yershon was busy being an actor on the stage and writing music for plays.

In 2015, he was sitting opposite me in a noisy cafe in London, having lost the Oscar for Best Original Score to Alexandre Desplat for *The Grand Budapest Hotel*, attacking a vegetarian sandwich and sipping tea. Chirpy and charming as ever, he was not in the least disappointed by the fact that he had come home from Los Angeles empty-handed. The nomination? It was certainly nice to receive, but how foolish it would be to expect an influx of work—not that he was craving more film work—from an Oscar nomination at his age!

Anyway, being as independent minded as he is, he wouldn't necessarily be comfortable working on studio productions. His work with Mike Leigh puts him very much where he wants to be—Leigh is just as independent, rejecting Hollywood's standard procedures outright. There is no place for temp tracks, or a multitude of producers who all want to have their say in the music, on his films: "Mike is the only person to have a conversation with," explained Yershon. "He is an independent filmmaker. There is no studio, there is nobody to tell you what to do. There are just conversations with Mike."

The only film Yershon was offered that was not directed by Mike Leigh was Stanley Tucci's *Final Portrait,* about the renowned painter Giacometti. Yershon found that Tucci favors a rather different approach to music than Leigh. While Leigh rejects temp tracks and electronic music, Tucci carefully assembled temp tracks for every scene and insisted Yershon follow them as closely as possible. It soon became clear that this wasn't going to end well. After working on the project for several weeks and submitting a handful of pieces that weren't to Tucci's taste—because they were not close enough to the temp tracks—Yershon left the film.

Age had afforded him very much a laissez faire attitude to work. Certainly, he wasn't willing to bend over backwards to satisfy the director, essentially copying the work of other composers. Instead, Yershon concentrated on writing a ballet score, *The Boy in the Striped Pyjamas,* planning an opera based on a story written by his mother-in-law, as well as writing articles and monographs and giving lectures.

Although the Oscar nomination didn't bring him any work as a film composer, as a new member of the Academy of Motion Picture Arts and Sciences, he was put in touch with the London branch of the Academy. This not only meant being able to attend early previews of films and receiving screeners to watch at home—no small thing for a film aficionado such as Yershon—but more importantly, opened up the possibility of working closely with the Academy to promote the work of artists all over the world. This new association with the Academy has led him to host several master classes and lectures in London, celebrating the work of his colleagues with insightful talks and presentations.

Yershon had long since taught at the Royal Academy for Dramatic Arts and given lectures at the Royal College of Music where, naturally, he is in close contact with numerous students with one goal: to make a career in music for the media. Of course, his students all love him—not least because he brings composers such as Michael Giacchino to share their knowledge with them. His students are always eager to listen to the wisdom of established experts who can show how to get a foot in the door.

This is difficult though, for the obvious reason that there is no secret recipe that guarantees success. Film music is not the niche it used to be, but has moved more and more into public awareness in the past few years, not least due to concerts. It has become a viable career path that many young people desire to follow. It is exactly the competition that makes it hard for graduate students to secure their first gig. "It's common knowledge that starting out as a young aspiring composer is as difficult as it gets," said Charlotte Raven, who is the assistant to composer Guy Farley. Indeed, Raven, bright, young, motivated and creative, is one of a large pool of bright, young, motivated and creative people who are only waiting to be discovered, score their first gig and find their place in the business.

The creative industry, however, is not like other industries. Here, nothing is traditional. There are no traditional promotions, no traditional pay rises, no traditional working hours. Similarly, entry into this working life is by no means traditional. Aspiring composers can take several routes in order to obtain their first gig: going to film festivals in the hope of meeting producers and directors who are looking for fresh musical voices; starting an internship with an already established composer; enrolling in film music competitions; meeting young filmmakers at university; putting their music on YouTube or Sound Cloud to gather attention, or pursuing all of these options at the same time.

But while bright, young, motivated and creative composers can pursue more job options than people who wish to engage in non-creative work, it doesn't make it necessarily easier. Be it film music, television music, production/library music, game music or concert music, the competition is stiff in any area. Whereas film music up until the '60s was simply *there* in films (being released only rarely on LP), pop musicians engaging in film work, concerts of film music, and the catchy tunes of the Spielbergian blockbusters of the '80s have all worked to spawn a new fascination for pieces written for film. In turn, more universities than ever offer courses in film music, with more and more students pursuing the field as a viable career option.

The road is often difficult and, as in any creative field, many are left behind—the room at the top has always been limited. To develop perseverance and never give up is easier said than done, as many formerly enthusiastic and motivated composers seeking a career in the media have found out. Creative people are often sensitive by nature, easily affected by sudden setbacks and a lack of success. But while there is nothing to prevent setbacks, it is always good to be prepared for the worst, as well as for an incoming gig.

There Is No Ceiling

One of the ways to make connections is to enroll in a university—preferably in a university that also teaches filmmakers, who can then reach out to their fellow students on the composition courses whenever they need a piece of music. Needless to say, a course at a university can always be useful in learning the tools needed for the job—there shouldn't, after all, be a ceiling on education. There is one particular problem, though: which university? It is a question not to be taken lightheartedly, since composers seeking assistants, and therefore giving important job-experience, are very much aware of the shortcomings of individual universities, and can be careful to avoid employing someone who studied at the same place as a former assistant who, due to educational failings, proved to be inadequate in the position. As Klaus Badelt explains:

When I get students or interns, most of the time I have to make them forget what they learned at school. I am not saying they teach them the wrong stuff, but it's not relevant to what we do. There is a discrepancy between what they are teaching and what the practice is. I believe more in this 17th century master-pupil-relationship of teaching and handing it down to generations than maybe in the institutional teaching.

Mychael Danna has clear preferences when it comes to the educational background of his assistants:

[The students at Columbia in Chicago] have been taught so well there. And then there is Berklee, people that I have worked with. I am very conscious of the school they come from and what they learn there. It's incredible what they come out knowing technically. Also, they have a pretty good grip on how things are and how things work. I have been really impressed with the quality of the people that are available. Not all of them. You once in a while have some millennial issues, but honestly the people I am working with from Berklee are amazing and they have this great energy of being young and excited. The knowledge base is really good. [...] I am certainly open to other possibilities but those are the two schools that I have had experiences with. [...] I have no reason to think that USC would be any different.

Universities offering courses in composition for media have to incorporate different disciplines in order to prepare their students for their future job. It is no longer enough to teach composition, since students can enroll in traditional composition classes if they so choose. But certainly composition, counterpoint and harmony alone don't provide all the necessarily skills. A graduate who is not familiar with the technical gear that is used by the established composers in the film music industry will have a hard time finding work or maintaining a career within it.

It is highly unlikely that a new composer working only with pen and paper will have a chance in the industry, first and foremost because of the demand for electronic demos. As composer Gabriel Yared muses:

Nowadays, directors and producers want to hear the music before going into the studio to record, and the only way to do this is to produce demos. The best way is to make them yourself, rather than to give this responsibility to someone else. The melody, counterpoint, harmony, variations and orchestration should already be thought of and written before you create a demo, so that when you come to make it you have all the ingredients to work with.

A graduate who is adept at working with the technology and software and knows how to write a piece for orchestra without getting ridiculed by the musicians who are due to perform said piece will still also require a grasp of the history of cinema and music. Moreover, in order to discuss musical approaches with directors and producers, to find out what they want or don't want, graduates entering the industry need good people skills and at least a rudimentary understanding of psychology and diplomacy.

A knowledge of film history, filmmaking and the mindset of a director or producer often go hand in hand in the job of a film composer, "The more a composer is a filmmaker at heart and understands the filmmaking process," John Ottman says,

> The more flexible he is going to be because he is going to understand that there is more than one way to skin a cat. A scene can be scored 150 different ways, but at least ten of those ways are just as good as the others. A composer has to know that. You have destroyed yourself in writing the music for a scene and everything is perfect and you love it. Then the filmmaker comes in. If he is able to communicate why he doesn't like it, then you as a composer have to say, "Oh yes, that's what he is trying to say!" The more you can put yourself into the mindset of a filmmaker the more you are going to be successful doing your job.

Offering courses in film music is especially difficult for universities because of the diverse range of musical skills the job demands of a film composer. Since film music is not a genre per se, and doesn't have a certain sound, students will never know when they may be called upon to provide anything from orchestral music to electronica, pop, rock, jazz, world music or any style in-between. Juggling all these different disciplines is not only a challenge for composers, who cannot allow themselves to concentrate solely on one of these skills, but also for their professors.

Since different universities follow differing approaches when teaching their students composition for the media, it is not entirely surprising that established composers, arrangers, orchestrators and conductors have a variety of complaints concerning the education being offered to the next generation. Composer Nan Schwartz says,

> the craftsmanship has gone down. Technology is a big reason. But it's also because schools are not teaching music anymore in the same way. They used to teach harmony and counterpoint and all that. [...] Having gone to some of the well-respected music programs and universities and listening to some of their concerts, I think the attitude now is [about] self-expression. It doesn't really matter if it has any form.

Meanwhile Jeff Rona says that too many universities teach the students to write "like Stravinsky," but leave them in the dark where the importance of technology is concerned. He notes that:

> Especially the young composers who have had the most training, went to conservatory, for some reason put the least amount of effort into the technology. They have learned their modes and scales and all of that, but there seems to be an amazing disinterest in what is easily the other half of the equation. I try to remind people whenever possible that a film composer's job isn't to write the music. It's to produce the music—it's to deliver a recording.

Klaus Badelt, who never trained as a composer at university, goes a step further, saying that assisting ten different composers will teach an aspiring musician more than five years of intense study: "I totally generalize now but let's talk about film music students. They learn writing music. Film music is not about music. It's not how you write music. It is how you create film. You have this one different brush than the director. Like a director should be taking film scoring classes, the film scoring should be 70 percent film classes." It is a sentiment Gabriel Yared tends to agree with:

> It is not necessarily the fault of the composer, but the institution where they have learned. They are led to believe that you can be a great composer simply by learning and studying music to a high level. While this is important, I completely agree that it is only half of the equation. A great composer should get their hands dirty, embracing technology or any other aspect [of the craft] in order to learn and better themselves. It is impossible to be a good composer if you believe that there is nothing left to learn.

Students should, therefore, be aware of the different disciplines they will need in the job and look for universities that satisfy their needs accordingly— they should seek to learn about filmmaking at least as much as about composition. As Jeff Rona points out: "What would be the point of hiring a genius who doesn't know how to produce music properly? It's better to have a mediocre composer with great technical ability and who understands budgets and schedules than to have a better composer who fucks up."

Even if students learn composition, filmmaking, film history and diplomatic skills, there is still one more thing to consider—contracts. In order to navigate through the pitfalls of a composer's working life, understanding contracts is essential. This can cover everything from how to budget a score—if the composer is given a package deal—to how to negotiate royalties and mechanical and publishing rights. It would be naive to think that a composer who is well-schooled in the creative aspects of the job is necessarily sufficiently well educated in other matters to sustain a career. As Marco Beltrami warns:

> I would say thirty percent of the job is enjoyable. That is the creative part, coming up with ideas and writing the music. But so much of it is not creative. It's dealing with budgets and contracts and problems, dealing with too many producers. It's the normal bullshit. It just saps your energy. By learning to remove myself a little bit from that and by saying, "Whatever happens happens," I find that I am able to deal with it a lot better and have a more healthy relationship with my job.

But even within a carefully crafted university course there will be a disparity in knowledge among the students. Students are a diverse group after all, with some who are more electronically oriented, and others who follow a more traditional, classical approach to music. It is a challenge to teach a class where everybody has a different background and therefore different interests. This bridge could be crossed by following the advice of Richard Bellis, who has regularly given guest lectures at USC:

> I had suggested that the first two or three months the people be separated into two groups. Those who were less electronically edified go to classes with a focus on electronic music while the students without a deep knowledge of acoustic music go to classes which teach the basics of acoustic music. By the third or fourth month at least we have a balance of knowledge, because otherwise people are getting frustrated.

Studying at a university does have clear advantages over aspiring composers teaching themselves. A good university course can both enable the students to discover music they would otherwise be unaware of and expose them to subjects and skills they might not otherwise have encountered. This prevents students from potentially limiting their options by concentrating too much on a specific style or approach—the more technique and range composers have, the better off they will eventually be. In this way, if a university can broaden their horizon, it has already achieved one major goal.

Nevertheless, in an age when music technology enables everybody to produce music to some level it is tempting to forgo an academic education. Such a decision doesn't necessarily hinder one's chances of having a career in film music, as successful composers such as Danny Elfman prove. Even so, composers without a formal musical education have regularly been attacked by academics.

Few examples of the differences of outlook between self-taught composers and academic scholars are as well illustrated as in Danny Elfman's letter to Micah D. Rubinstein, who in 1989 bitterly accused *Keyboard Magazine* of "glorifying musical ignorance" after the magazine had published an interview with Elfman. Rubinstein said that Elfman didn't know how to read or write music, arguing, following Elfman's success with Tim Burton's *Batman*, "In the complex world of film and orchestral music, there are no shortcuts. If you can't do it yourself, you have to have the money to hire competent, conservatory-trained people such as [orchestrator] Steve Bartek or [conductor] Shirley Walker." Elfman replied:

> There isn't any one "correct" way to score a film. Each film is a world unto itself, with its own unique strengths and weaknesses which must be addressed. [...] On *Batman*, as on many films, there was a team effort to pull it all together on time, and I'm fortunate to have very talented people on my team. [...] I am self-taught, and although that's not something I'm proud of, neither am I ashamed of it. While you, Mr. Rubenstein [*sic*] are incorrect in stating that I studied with Christopher Young or anyone else, you are absolutely presumptuous in assuming that Mr. Bartek and Ms. Walker are conservatory-trained. In fact, Mr. Bartek never attended a conservatory, and Ms. Walker,

who in addition to being a great conductor and orchestrator is a fine composer in her own right, never finished college, and considers herself to be primarily self-taught as well.

A musical education, Elfman continued, "is something for which I have great respect. It can, I'm sure, be a wonderful thing, and provide all kinds of invaluable tools with which to work. It is not, however, the only way to acquire tools, or to learn."[1]

One can ask whether it is necessary for a composer working in media to be able to read and write musical notation. Because of the development of composing technology, composers now more often than not send MIDI files of their compositions generated from their DAW (Digital Audio Workstation) to their orchestrators for printed score preparation. The assistants responsible for the score preparation in turn import the MIDI files into a notation software program, clean up the music and turn the material into actual musical scores. These are then sent back to the orchestrator and/or composer, who will check them to see whether any mistakes have been made in the process. If a composer delegates the reviewing of the written score to the orchestrator, then it makes any skill the composer has in reading and writing musical notation redundant.

Being a masterful sight reader is a valuable skill for any graduate who wants to embark on a career of his own, but it is not an essential qualification to get a job in the 21st century film music world—as Marco Beltrami points out after highlighting the benefits of writing music the old-fashioned way:

> When I sit down at a keyboard or at any particular instrument I begin to think in terms of the sounds I am hearing. The only way to get something pure is to think about it in your head and figure it out there first. [...] Buck [Sanders, Beltrami's co-composer on numerous projects] is fair at reading music. I wouldn't say he is a masterful sight reader, but I guess it's not super-important. I think it's more important that he has the skills that he has.

Considering the skills composers for media should have at their disposal (a knowledge of different film genres and of film history, an awareness of the pitfalls of contracts, a facility for psychology and diplomacy, the ability to work with a tight budget on a short schedule, to be gifted in using musical technology), it is surprising that the number of media composers looking for a job is as large as it is.

Given the geographic nature of the American film business, many aspiring composers consider whether they should move to Los Angeles to further their career—to the place where every waiter and waitress introduces themselves with the words "Hi, I am an actor," in the hope of better locating themselves in the industry. Certainly, Los Angeles is not for everyone—not even for the established film composers such as Carter Burwell, who confesses:

I can't stand the climate in Southern California. The fact that there is no weather is not for me. [...] I am an East Coaster. I am a New Yorker. Now I live outside of New York, but I like dramatic weather. It's inspiring to me as a composer. I also like to live in a place where people don't talk about the industry all the time. Los Angeles is an industry town. It's a great place to work and to record. You make movies there because you always have talented crews around. But I just don't want to live in a place where that's what everyone talks about.

In a field that is as crowded as writing music for media, a move to Los Angeles can certainly increase one's chances of scoring a gig, as opposed to say a musician quietly working away in a basement in Kazakhstan. In fact, the vast majority of established composers recommend a move to Hollywood wholeheartedly. Says Matthew Margeson:

It certainly makes it easier for young composers to move to L.A., even though a lot of things like shooting and post production and visual effects and sound editing are happening all over the world. Both on independent and $200 million films, there is a constant communication with L.A.. It is the hub, even though the physical work may not be being done there. That's where all the information filters to and from.

Edwin Wendler agrees:

I would say that it is in general beneficial to be physically present in L.A.. There are some very successful composers who do not live here, who live in London or New York, but they are the exception. I would recommend to anybody who wants to be in any project of significance to move to L.A. because these face-to-face meetings are still very important.

Helping Out

The common perception among aspiring composers is that starting out as an assistant to an already established composer is the best entry into the business. Beginning as an assistant can provide aspiring composers with valuable insights into the everyday routine of a busy composer, inviting the recently graduated students to compare what they have learned with the actual practice of the film music world. Moreover, working as an assistant can see aspiring composers writing small pieces of music for a film, while helping out and earning money through doing what they love early on—not that the young film scoring graduates have much of a choice. Richard Bellis contemplates it thus: "It's one of those things that you have to try and find work. The gamut of people who employ assistants or interns is as wide as in any other business. Some are abusive, some will elevate you and give you cue sheet credit and will eventually suggest you for a series that they can no longer handle. It runs the gamut."

Generally, the field experience an assistant earns by being close to a composer can be substantial. As John Ottman says: "I think anything that you do that's involved within the world of film is helpful. You learn by doing and by being in the environment. You can only learn so much by schooling. Exposure is better than no exposure. I was lucky. I just started composing and didn't have to do that. The more you are exposed to the real world the better."

The job description of the assistant can be vague, encompassing everything from brewing coffee to sorting out a mess of cabling to handling the appointments and the schedule, to writing small pieces of music. Which tasks assistants eventually end up doing depends on the composers they are working for, their schedules and demands. These requirements and duties can be quite onerous, as the following job advertisement on Facebook exemplifies in listing the qualifications a potential assistant should have:

> Deep knowledge of Pro Tools, Sibelius, Vienna Ensemble Pro and Kontakt are a MUST. Formatting, copying, printing and taping scores and parts for recording sessions. Preparing Pro Tools sessions for recording sessions. Conforming cues to new/locked picture with MIDI and/or audio. Building/creating original Kontakt instruments using recorded material. Updating template/troubleshooting tech issues. Finessing mock-ups/music production. Making cue sheets. Possibly some additional orchestration. Possibly some additional music writing. Some light errands (must have own car). Attention to detail is key, so please follow these instructions carefully. Please send: Your resume, including a hyperlink to your IMDb page. Keep it short—experience, credits, school. Do not apply unless you have a degree in music and a solid understanding of orchestration. Film scoring grads (USC, Berklee, UCLA, Columbia, etc.) are preferred. A list of programs/applications (with version numbers) you own and are set up to use at home. What is your primary DAW? Sample libraries can be provided if needed so no need for a list of those. A quick description of your home set up—your computer (must be Mac), how many GB of ram, etc. Computer may be provided by me, but this info is important. A zip file of PDFs of one single cue that you orchestrated—scores and parts, separated. Two cues you have written (mp3s)—one orchestral (would be great to hear your mock-up skills here!) where I can hear your knowledge of harmony/voice-leading, etc.; and one synth/electronic style piece to show off your production skills.

For all this skill, knowledge and technology the assistant was required to have the composer was willing to pay $15 an hour.

As demanding as the working requirements for assistants are, this is not reflected in the salary—as the budgets for film scores have dropped, so has the remuneration paid to assistants. Such positions are traditionally either paid per hour, as salaried employees—or not paid at all. Admits one former assistant in Los Angeles in a Facebook post:

Most of us [work] for less than $15/h for quite a while. That's the reality of being an assistant in L.A. where the number of young composers exceeds the amount of job openings every year—whoever wants to work here needs to come to terms with that, because if one person doesn't take the job, there are several hundred standing in line for it. [...] Fairness isn't always part of the game and I sure would have liked to not live at the edge of poverty for years.

When the money is scarce paid assistants are a luxury few composers can afford. Therefore, more and more composers in the industry rely on interns, well aware that they won't run into any problems filling any position since enough creative minds are desperate to garner experience in the field. Even an established composer and Oscar winner such as Mychael Danna admits to relying on interns from time to time, choosing the applicants from a vast pool that never drains:

I have tried not to have interns. The value of everything we are doing is so low and there are so many people out there and so much competition. I get e-mails every week where people say, "I will work for you for free!" I resisted it for a long time. In this last spade of work where we had a lot of things going on at once it was very busy and the projects were all low-budget. This all happened in the same six months. I couldn't afford to hire somebody else but we had an intern from Berklee. [...] It's one of the few times, maybe the only time I have ever done it, because I don't feel good about it. I feel guilty about exploiting somebody like that.

The intern was incredible and I wanted to hire her, so I am hoping that I have a project coming up, that things will get busy enough and that they will have a big enough budget that I can pay her instead of bringing her in for free. She was here for five or six weeks. I am probably the only guy in town to say that. Everybody else in town has interns all the time. It's the state of things. The value of everything has dropped so low that the people are willing to work for free. It makes me shudder to think this, but I am pretty sure I could charge people to work for me. It's just ... deeply horrible—but it's probably true.

Even with a small to nonexistent payment, the advantages conferred by working as an assistant or intern continue to prove attractive. Shadowing an established composer can prepare young graduates for working on projects on their own, as London-based Charlotte Raven, Guy Farley's assistant, describes:

Sitting in, watching them write to picture in their studios teaches you every-thing you would need to know, from how to score emotion in certain film cues, to learning how to move the smallest of MIDI files across a page; all valuable lessons when starting out. From shadowing, I managed to learn everything I would need to know within a composers' writing, studio environ-ment, from the use of programs and gear, to understanding how to write to picture, although I will be forever learning and trying to better myself on this skill.

Assistants, depending on the composer they are working for, can benefit from experiences few other people are allowed to share—such as attending the recording sessions and supervising the necessary preparations. Raven continues:

Another amazing experience gained would be the days spent at session in recording studios, an experience as a young aspiring composer that is like no other; the dream. Here, all that is learned and applied in the comfort and privacy of the studio walls is brought to the magnificent foreground of a recording studio, heard with real instruments in real time; a recording for a real film. As a young composer, these opportunities would never be seen in such an early stage of their own career.

The tips and tricks assistants can acquire just by attending a recording session alone can prove invaluable for their later career. If the composer they are working for is gracious enough to grant them this insight, the helping hands can gain experience in managing and running the entire recording process, from microphone placement to the tweaking of the final mix. While all this is certainly helpful, no assistant should rely on their position, nor rely on the fact that they are working for an established composer, to secure their own first gigs. Assistants or interns are very much in the shadow of their employer—that's what one gets paid for (or doesn't). Composers can hardly do more than point in the right direction through giving advice, if they are so inclined—many composers are too busy with their own to-do-list to have time to focus on the requests of their assistants.

Quite a few assistants have been fortunate enough to step out of the shadow of their (former) employers and embark on a successful career themselves. One of the more prominent examples is the celebrated composer Nico Muhly, who keeps himself busy writing for film, television and theater. It was Rachel Portman who turned to Muhly when the latter was working for Philip Glass, to create the demos of her music for Jonathan Demme's remake of *The Manchurian Candidate*. They were among the first demos Portman made and they introduced Muhly to the film community further.

More recently, Sven Faulconer, after working as an assistant for James Newton Howard for years, providing additional music for *Nightcrawler*, *Concussion* and other projects, was able to prove himself by writing the music for the Netflix show *A Series of Unfortunate Events* and the Mel Gibson movie *Blood Father*. Joanne Higginbottom worked for Tyler Bates as assistant and music programmer on high profile gigs such as *Guardians of the Galaxy* before venturing out on her own and writing the music for the series *Samurai Jack* and, with Bates, the Emilio Estevez' film *The Public*.

Rob Simonsen has become one of the most sought-after composers in the industry, providing music for productions such as *Foxcatcher*, *The Age of Adaline* and *The Front Runner*. But Simonsen didn't simply leave education and embark on a solo career. Instead, he met Mychael Danna, which not only led to him working as Danna's assistant, and eventually his own high-profile film scoring assignments, but also to a lasting friendship. Remembers Simonsen,

> My first film score was premiering at Seattle International Film Festival in 2003. Mychael was a guest speaker. I saw him in the program for the festival and thought, "That would be interesting to go hear him speak." I went there and they played beautiful clips from *The Ice Storm* which Mychael had scored. I loved everything that he had to say and was very excited to hear him talk. So I gave him a CD of mine. The programmer for the festival, that helped to bring him there, was also a great fan of the score that I had done for the film.

Simonsen ended up having dinner with Mychael Danna and fellow composer Hummie Mann. Simonsen and Danna quickly sensed a strong bond between them—but nothing might have happened afterwards, had fate not played its hand:

> That night my friends and I were walking into a party where we knew no one and Mychael was walking into a party by himself because he was there for a night or two only. We were walking in at the same time and we said, "Hey, how is it going?" One of my best friends, who was also a producer on my film, had just gotten back from two months in India. Mychael has spent a lot of time in India, his wife is Indian, he loves Indian culture and it's very much part of his music. It was a great time and we fell into hanging out.

A year later, Simonsen decided to get himself a mentor who would guide him through the process of developing, writing and recording a film score. At that time, Simonsen was still living in Oregon and called up Mychael Danna in Toronto, who was just about to move to Los Angeles. As it happened, both moved to the big city at the same time, and so it was natural that they started working together.

These examples, though, should not be taken to suggest that a smooth ride is guaranteed for every composer who starts to work as an assistant.

Few Doors

The fact that composition technology is now available to anyone with a computer has increased the competition in the field exponentially. Suddenly, aspiring composers are everywhere, always ready to promote their work on social media or other channels. Since producers and directors don't necessarily have the musical background and knowledge to distinguish between elaborate compositions and an elaborate sound-production (as Nan Schwartz and Jeff Rona mentioned earlier, directors are not generally looking for the next Beethoven, but rather for someone who can deliver the appropriate product on time), this has opened doors for a wide range of emerging musicians to take their shot at writing music for a media project.

The good news is that with films, TV, streaming services, apps and video games there are more products made than ever before which need composers to supply the necessary musical accompaniment. Ergo, more composers are needed. However, since the competition has also greatly increased, the bad news is that it has become much harder for composers to get a gig to score. New services such as Netflix have quickly become aware of the competition among composers, and used the situation to their advantage by trying to offer the composers on some of their productions a direct license (which means no royalties are paid to the composer). In a situation such as this composers may consider they have little choice but to accept such a deal in order to gain credits on their resume, yet still see the dangers to their own creative community in taking part in a race to a financial bottom.

But then how to score a gig? In some ways the issue hasn't changed much since the invention of the wheel—connections being the primary route to success. Herein lies the actual problem of the increase in competition. According to John Ottman:

[Technology] has devalued film music as well. It used to be when a film composer arrived at a meeting, the angels sang and the sea parted. It was like, "My God, the film composer is walking in, he is going to save our movie and create this amazing thing." Now a lot of producers in town have sons and daughters whose friend has Garage Band and they are like, "My neighbor's kid can do this, so what's the big deal?"

A professional field that has been similarly affected is photography. Everyone with a smartphone automatically has not only a camera available but sophisticated editing programs which can transform snapshots into images that users might perceive as works of art. One young photographer wrote: "Every respect for my job has been lost since everybody has a camera in their phone. The market is flooded with amateur photographers who [...] take photographs for a few bucks.... I was lucky enough to find a regular job at all" (earning little more than $600 monthly).[2]

The problem primarily is that the sheer volume of people who use music-making equipment and try to sell their work has resulted in a devaluation of the craft, as Jeff Rona explains in citing simple economics: "The value of something is based mostly on its scarcity and demand. The more people want something and the less there is of it the more expensive it is. That's the nature of economics. With more and more people who have the interest in being a film composer, who have a laptop and a couple of samples, they take away from the scarcity."

Unfortunately, the end of this scarcity is inevitable in a world where everybody can suddenly do everything to some degree, and where everybody knows somebody who has some creative ability. It has definitely made it harder for classically trained and talented artists to make their voice heard, for often it is not the most talented artist who will get heard, but the one with the loudest voice. Richard Bellis warns about this development. He suggests that if everyone, through an inexpensive technology, has the resources to compose and distribute music easily, then common aesthetic value systems will fragment, thus reducing the impact of music beyond small cliques of devotees.

Since no one can stop the development of technology (and since few want to) it is difficult to propose a possible solution to increased competition and resultant devaluation of creativity in a field where the actual quality or complexity of the musical composition itself isn't of primary importance. It would be naive to think that by suggesting rules and a behavioral code every person would follow such guidelines so as to try to raise appreciation for film music as an artistic process. Bellis tries anyway:

> I pledge to: not use Autotune—if I can't sing it in tune, I will hire someone who can. Not quantize—if I can't play it in correctly I will hire someone who can. Make singers sing every chorus and verse until they get it right. These things I pledge in the hope of returning professionalism to the music industry. The question is whether copying and pasting is creating. Maybe. Maybe not. Certainly the ability to perform (playing or singing) is subject to varying degrees of proficiency.
>
> Applauding proficiency is our musical legacy. Encouraging non-proficiency because technology has made it unnecessary is not a creative step forward. Singing in tune, playing in time are, at least to me, skills worth honing even if we have the technology with which to compensate for a degree of incompetence in those areas. When anyone can sound as if they are a performer who has studied and practiced for years merely because of technological enhancement, it belittles those who have put in the effort and the time to become proficient and dehumanizes the performance of the music. AutoTune as an effect is one thing. As a deception it's another.

Very Little Money

"Because of technology we think we can do it ourselves," continues Richard Bellis, "so we bought into it, largely because there were so many of us and because there was so little money that we said, 'All right, it's $5,000, I will do it all.'" Indeed, the budgets for music and therefore the fees for composers who are not on the A-list have, in the twenty years since *Titanic* was released, gone down as steadily as the ill-fated titular ship. The widespread availability of composing technology has resulted in producers and directors saying "Everybody can do it," and the resulting devaluation of the craft of cinematic music-making.

The future looks grim for serious musicians trying to make a viable income in film and television music. The fact that music can be recorded with synthesizers and/or samples—something which has become particularly prevalent in television—so that it is no longer necessary to employ highly skilled, trained composers and a large orchestra to supply the right musical atmosphere, means that there is far less money available to be earned. This situation had already been foreseen by film music agent Seth Kaplan in 2008 when he noted the increasing competitiveness among film composers:

> A composer who has done his first or second studio movie and who is making $250,000–$500,000 on a picture is seeing all of these composers who were at a higher income level coming down and taking those films because there are fewer films available in the higher bracket. People in the upper strata don't have enough upper-strata movies to keep them busy, and that puts pressure on and limits the opportunities for up-and-coming composers.[3]

Deregulation also plays a significant role, as Richard Bellis explains: "The budget for a film or movie for television in the late '70s, early '80s, was $3 million and the music budget was $50–60,000. When deregulation happened and the networks didn't any longer have to hire a third party to produce the movie, the budgets went to a million dollars and the music budgets went to $14,000 dollars. That was pretty significant."

According to film music agent George Christopoulos there are currently 3,500 working film composers in the United States alone, with an estimated 15,000 new graduates from film music courses every year—this doesn't even include the self-taught composers who venture into film music. If one composer gets lucky and can land a gig working on an independent film, he or she might receive a package deal of $10,000. To write the required perhaps 40 minutes of music, the composer might need to work approximately 200 hours. Add spotting sessions, orchestration and mixing supervision, and this could easily increase to around 270 hours of work, which equates to $37 an hour. It would only be understandable if the composer decides not to record any live instruments—$10,000 is not a lot of money for 270 hours work for someone who is likely to have an irregular income.

But still there will be composers lining up for the job. As Jeff Rona says: "You can fire a composer and hire another composer. There are composers who will work for free. There are composers who would kill their grandmothers to get a chance at their first big job. I understand all that. Yes, there is more competition and that drives the cost down." Rona's statements are supported by advertisements from directors and producers on Craigslist looking for aspiring composers willing to work for free:

Producer looking for a skilled, non-generic, film composer to head the musical composition for a short film. Looking for someone with their own sound,
who can arrange using orchestral instruments. Skilled in composition. We'll
provide the master. This is an unpaid position at the momoent [sic]. We'll give
you music composition credits as well as on IMDb. It is about 10–12 minutes
of music for a short dramatic film.[4]

Even more controversial are aspiring composers looking to gain experience by offering their services for free. For instance:

Film Composer Seeking Short Films, Web Series (Free): I am a composer
looking for experience scoring short films, student films, or a web series. I
graduated from USC's Thornton School of Music with a Studio/Jazz Guitar
degree, and am going to study Composition for Screen at University of Edinburgh in the fall. I am looking for a project or two to work on before I leave,
to gain experience.[5]

Composers willing to work for little money or for free will have no problems finding a project to work on. After all, technology has not only enabled
everybody to produce their own music, but also to produce their own films—
and even amateur films need music. But because they are amateur films and
therefore are unlikely to have any substantial financial backing, they need
the music to be as cheap as possible. And so it happened that composers are
advertising to work for free and filmmakers are advertising for composers
without any financial reward, hoping that the catchword "credit" is enough
in a saturated market.

Filmmakers have become very aware of young composers' willingness
to work for free, or even to pay to work on a film, as this advertisement—
which was posted at the "Young Entertainment Professionals (YEP)—
Nashville Network" platform on Facebook—shows:

Want your song in a movie? I am working with a company that is editing 2
movies from the same executive producer who has his movie *The Letters* on
Netflix right now. Both movies need music added. [...] The movie producer is
asking for the right to use the song 1st, and asking for $5,000 as well. This
money will be used for marketing the movie, buying posters, ads, etc, to make
the movie a higher success. What you will get for $5,000 is a chance to grow
your fan base, the movie *The Letters* has already reached millions of viewers
on Netflix, and became a success. This movie will as well get pitched to Netflix, Amazon Prime, and Hulu. It has the chance to reach millions as well. The
company editing the movie has agreed to film a performance music video for
each artist, and add the b-roll from the movie in the music video for the artist
has something to promote as well to get the movie more attention.

Some filmmakers are no longer just eyeing composers to contribute music,
but also to become investors in the films they work on.

The offers and requests on Craigslist and similar websites are endless, with at least two such job descriptions posted daily for the Los Angeles area alone. It must be highlighted that even composers offering to work for free (or who don't have the budget to record with a live orchestra or ensemble) often actually pay to provide their own services, not only in the indirect way of the value of the working-time that they expend, but more directly by providing free use of their own technical gear: sample libraries require frequent updates, as do software programs and physical hardware such as keyboards and recording equipment. This doesn't come cheap, as Bellis illustrates:

> You go to USC and take a one year music course, it's very close to $50,000 for one year. Then you buy $30,000 worth of gear. Then you start looking for films for $5,000 all in. What people do is they get their masters or their doctorate in film scoring and they go out this graduation door and go right back in the other door as teachers without spending any time in the field. [...]
>
> Everybody is equal. We have a lot of people who are now becoming equal through the technology. That's why skill sets will be the things that separate us and set us apart. Film scoring only used to appeal to music nerds. Now it appeals to technology nerds and music nerds. Everybody likes to play with music. It's the old saying, "Everybody knows their job and music." But I don't think this explosive interest in film music was merely the result of technology. I think it was *Star Wars* and *Jaws*. It was the participation in music on a grand scale that hadn't been seen for a while.
>
> The reason people go to film music concerts is not that the music is necessarily great but because they remember the film. [...] It's the memory of the film, the memory of the entire experience. That and music technology lead to the large community that we have now.
>
> Since the beginning of commerce, people who wanted to get into a new field used the same marketing strategy. "I'll do it for less in order to get experience, to make contacts and to get credits." Young film composers are using this exact strategy. This marketing method when used by a few aspiring individuals is likely to have little or no effect but, when used by a large community of emerging composers, it can and will significantly alter the economic and working conditions of the entire profession.

John Ottman agrees: "The value has really gone down. Because of all the composers writing on their home programs, they are not necessarily great at what they do. So they get a gig and then the bar just keeps dropping lower and lower."

We Used to Be Stronger

It is not only the increased competition that makes composers in the media easily exploitable. It is also the fact that composers in film and television in the United States no longer have the backing of a union as they once did. The history of the film composer's union and its subsequent demise is particularly interesting, though the absence of a union for composers working in the media shouldn't be surprising. As Noam Chomsky has said: "Unions are bitterly hated by private power. That's always been true. The United States is a business-run society, much more so than comparable ones. Correspondingly, it has a very brutal labor history, much worse than in other societies. There have been constant efforts to try to destroy unions."[6]

The film industry is, of course, a private power and the CEOs of the individual studios can certainly very well do without the problems, including extra costs, that unions cause them. However, in the case of the union for film composers, it wasn't the studios that disbanded it but the composers themselves. While composers have to do without the protection and benefits that unions offer, such as a retirement and health plan, they are a minority among the groups working in the film industry—set dressers and cinematographers, for example, are still unionized and therefore employees instead of independent contractors, much the same way that film composers used to be before their union was dissolved. How did this situation come about?

In 1945, the Screen Composers Association (SCA) was formed, an offshoot of the American Society of Music Arrangers. The group, with members such as Max Steiner, Alfred Newman, Franz Waxman and Alex North, among many others, was set up to bargain with the studios on behalf of composers and arrangers. One of the SCA's earliest achievements was significant: they forced the performing rights society ASCAP to accept film composers as members, a change which significantly increased their royalty payments. It took another eight years for the first American composers guild to be formed, though, and in 1953, the Composers Guild of America was created after more than 150 composers voted for its inception. Their reason was that they were the only group in the entertainment fields that didn't enjoy such support. Two years later, the guild added lyricists and was re-branded accordingly as the Composers and Lyricists Guild of America (CLGA).

The National Labor Relations Board (NLRB), a commission to certify unions that had been formed in the 1930s, recognized the group as a bargaining agent in negotiating with studios. After tough negotiations the CLGA and the studios agreed on a payment for film scoring on a per-minute basis in 1960. The guild was then added to the industry's health, welfare and pension plans. The members of the guild also came to a basic agreement that specified minimum wages and working conditions. However, these conditions didn't last long. In 1970 the CLGA made the Oscar-winning composer Elmer Bernstein their president, and Bernstein and the negotiating committee soon agreed to a decision that would prove fatal for the union.

Previously, although the union had increased the power of composers and lyricists when dealing with the studios, it also resulted in a situation in which their artistic creations were the property of the studios, since any member of any union was an employee instead of an independent contractor. Ironically, it was exactly this disadvantage that had led the studios to allowing their composers to form a union in the first place: they were very well aware that with a union for composers and lyricists, there could be no argument as to who owned the music they composed—it was the studios. In order to change this situation the CLGA proposed to the Association of Motion Picture and Television Producers (AMPTP) that composers and lyricists should own the publishing rights to their own music.

Their proposal fell on deaf ears. Even a strike of the CLGA members in 1971 couldn't change matters. As a result, in 1972 the members proceeded with a lawsuit against the studios, networks and producers, arguing that they didn't exploit the composer's works in other markets and therefore didn't act as proper publishers. Seventy-one composers filed a $300-million class-action lawsuit against Universal, 20th Century–Fox, Warner Bros., MGM, Paramount and other studios. Elmer Bernstein was one of the plaintiffs. The plaintiff's complained that

> the producers, acting appropriately enough in concert, refused to contract for their services except on certain standard terms, which reserved to the producers the copyright and other ownership rights in the words and music composed on their behalf. This was asserted to constitute a conspiracy in restraint of trade, as well as an attempt to monopolize the sheet music publishing industry.[7]

Composers gave many statements in court, trying to win their case by stating that they were more like independent contractors than employees, since they no longer worked on a studio lot, on a piano owned by the studio. The advantage of being an independent contractor is that they are allowed to retain ownership of their creations—the disadvantages are everything else: a lack of right to collective bargaining, no paid vacation, and no retirement, pension or health plans. It was only the beginning of an arduous legal battle between the CLGA and the studios, which refused to budge.

In 1974, a federal district court judge dismissed the suit, before the New York Court of Appeals directed that the case go to trial. However, the suit never progressed further because the studios used their legal departments to delay judicial proceedings as much as possible, aware of the fact that the composers, as plaintiffs, would need to pay the legal costs out of their own pockets. After paying close to a quarter of a million dollars, the plaintiffs relented, and in 1979 agreed to a settlement, seven years after the filing of the lawsuit. As part of the settlement, some limited rights were granted to composers and lyricists who had worked for the studios before 1973.

Judge Charles L. Brieant of the U.S. District Court approved of the settlement, finding it adequate and reasonable. The composers and lyricists didn't. However, they had few options. One they pursued (or at least tried to pursue) was to negotiate a new contract with the AMPTP after both parties had agreed to the settlement. Unsurprisingly, the studios, represented by AMPTP, refused to even discuss the matter.

With the CLGA relenting and their funds having run dry, their composers and lyricists were now independent contractors instead of employees, and were therefore unable to secure health, welfare and pension benefits. Another important factor that played into the hands of the studios and made them agree to a settlement was the Copyright Act of 1976, which determined the creation of music to be work for hire. In the case of film composers, work-for-hire agreements create a pseudo employee status for someone who is actually an independent contractor. That means "ownership," which would normally be the right of the composer as independent contractor, is assigned to the employer in the same way as if the work was created by an employee. At the same time the creator of the work (the composer) is not entitled to the benefits of a traditional employee—i.e., collective bargaining, healthcare insurance and a retirement package. Richard Bellis explains:

> My guess is that with the addition of music as a work-for-hire in the 1976 Copyright Act, the studio lawyers realized that they didn't need to make composers employees [unionized composers] in order to own the copyrights to the music. All future scores [in the U.S.] would be treated as works made for hire, giving the studio automatic ownership. Then, without unionized composers, they would not have to allow collective bargaining, nor would they need to provide other traditional benefits afforded union employees. So the studios decided to settle the lawsuit and disregard the composer union, effectively breaking the union. That's basically what happened. It cost the composers a lot of money. A lot of the A-list composers had business managers who said, "Wait a minute, we can't keep giving $10,000 here and $10,000 there for legal fees. We have got to cut our losses and get out of this." As they started to drop out it made a settlement possible with the studios. It was a little bit of money that went to a few people. That was the end of the union.

The CLGA was finally disbanded in 1982.

That doesn't mean that composers and lyricists haven't actively tried again to form a union. In 1984, the newly formed Society of Composers and Lyricists (SCL) went before the NLRB to gain status as a union. Aware of the troubled history of unionized composers and lyricists, the NLRB decided that the creators were indeed independent contractors and not employees. After an unsuccessful appeal in 1985, composers and lyricists had to accept the fact that they couldn't get the SCL recognized as an employee organization. The main complaint of composers and lyricists concerning not having a union is that there are several other fields of work that enjoy the backing of a union which share more similarities with composers than differences.

Writers working for the film industry, much like composers, don't work on the studio lot on typewriters provided by the studios anymore either. Fortunately for them, the Writer's Guild hasn't come under the same scrutiny as the CLGA, which is why the Writer's Guild has been most careful to voice public support for their musical colleagues. Correspondingly, it also means that composers have been careful to push their unionization. Edwin Wendler remarks:

> The reason that composers have not been pushing it may be fear. They know we are not the only ones who are independent contractors. All the other professions may be negatively affected. Composers don't want to be responsible for that. They don't want to say, "Thanks to us, all these other peoples have lost their rights to unionize." That's not a great thing to wear as a badge. That's one of the reasons why composers have been hesitant to push that point in court.

After its unsuccessful plea to be recognized as a union, the SCL looked into unionization again in the early '90s with the (careful) support of the Writer's Guild, but were turned down again by the NLRB. There were two options left: in 2010, Bruce Broughton, as member of the AMC organizing committee which represented composers for film and television, looked into the possibility of forgoing the NLRB by joining forces with the Teamsters. This was after his colleague Richard Bellis, as president of the SCL, had tried to unite with the International Alliance of Theatrical Stage Employees (IATSE) in the '90s.

As it turned out, IATSE was indeed interested in taking composers and lyricists under their wing. It was the SCL which rowed back after the initial negotiations—for good reasons, says Bellis:

> In Hollywood the build-up of emerging composers was starting to happen. If we had formed a union it became pretty obvious that this large community of aspirings would have tried to find any way they could to have an advantage in the workplace, and would undercut the union by taking jobs that were non-union. Every person who is trying to break into a field has the same approach, which is in order to gain experience, make contacts and get credits they will work for less. A competitive advantage when there is a union is to work non-union, regardless of who it is: "I don't work for less than X and Y because I belong to the union." "I will!" You create an environment of non-union employees. You inadvertently establish a non-union marketplace.

Joining the Teamsters posed a similar problem for the AMC in the early 2010s. Their plan to form a union failed (again), despite the prominent backing of powerful composers such as Hans Zimmer. According to Mychael Danna:

There were meetings and there was interest and then it fell apart. If this had happened during the '90s, where we had a position of power, it might have happened, but then the greed might have taken over at that point. Composers are just the wrong personality type to be unionized. We used to have a union but once it went away the terrible combination of greed and competition has just taken over. I don't see any hope there. I would be very much in favor of it and I went to some of those meetings, but I don't see it happening. If Hans Zimmer wants it to happen and it doesn't happen then it's not going to happen.

Richard Bellis summarizes the problem they had to face: in order to demonstrate their power, the Teamsters go on strike when and if necessary. The Teamsters' demand, therefore, was for the composers to go on strike as well. Only with the composers agreeing to a strike at the same time as the Teamsters would they be able to form a powerful union that could actually change their working conditions for the better. The composers were reluctant, as Bellis remembers: the teamsters "got the impression that composers were not willing to go out on strike when they needed it. I think they were right. [...] The teamsters were initially very interested in the composers joining them. But their culture is one of standing together. Our culture is one of individuals none of whom is prepared to turn down work for any reason ... even or especially a union strike."

As it stands, composers and lyricists are still in the unfortunate position of working for hire. While independent contractors have ownership of their works and employees can enjoy collective bargaining, a healthcare and retirement plan, work-for-hire puts the composers in the worst possible situation: while working as independent contractors they are stripped of the ownership of their works, can't collectively bargain and have no health or retirement plans. Richard Bellis suggests the following: "We should be allowed the benefits of either the independent contractor—(ownership of our work)—or the benefits of the employee (collective bargaining and employee fringes)." Currently many of the people working in the film business are working under work-for-hire laws but at the same time enjoy union status. "We don't," continues Bellis.

Would it create a non-union work environment? Not nearly as much as it would have in the '90s because more and more people are finding that the way into the business is through an established composer. Theoretically, the established composers would see the benefit of being a member of the union. This composer would suggest strongly to those assisting them that they also become a member of the union. This would strengthen their own position and the union's position by encouraging their people that this is the best way to work. It would still be a good thing. Is it doable? I am very skeptical.

The situation continues to be a cause of great concern among many creative minds working in the United States, only adding to the discomfort they may already experience in other areas. Mychael Danna says: "Certainly [the lack of a union] might be a fundamental reason why this devaluation has happened. It's a race to the bottom. I don't see the bottom yet. It's still going down. With a union that wouldn't be the case, but I just can't imagine that could come out of nowhere. People have tried many times."

Summary

Nothing lasts, and yet nothing passes, either. And nothing passes
just because nothing lasts.—Philip Roth, *The Human Stain*

A media composer's job is now more challenging than ever before. Film
music has been exposed to the same changes as other more industrial fields:
ever-evolving technology and outsourcing, for example, geared to minimize
costs and allow more participation by those who might be less qualified.
Before they even write the first note composers have to contend with temp
tracks, put under the film by the editor in accordance with the director and
the producers. Composers then either have to copy colleagues or themselves,
making it increasingly difficult to come up with their own concepts, especially
if the temp tracks are compiled from widely different sources and approaches.
In this environment it becomes the ultimate challenge for an emerging composer to develop their own style.

Technology has simplified many aspects of the movie-making process
in a positive way. For example, composers can now save time by using patches
and copying-and-pasting musical sequences in digital notation programs.
However, in some respects it has also disadvantaged composers and the creative industries in which they work. Updating gear at regular intervals and
delivering carefully crafted demos and mock-ups consumes a lot of time that
could be spent composing. Moreover, the final recording then needs to sound
like the demo, to which orchestrators are forced to stick as closely as possible.

Technology is now available to anyone and everyone who can afford it.
Democratization is always reason for celebration, but, since everybody can
now produce music on their computers, it has resulted in increased competition in the industry. This has, in turn, led to a decrease in budgets. Instead
of producers guaranteeing composers a fee and setting a finite budget to cover
all other musical expenditure, they subject composers to package deals. These
require composers to become their own accountants, taking their fee out of

the overall music budget. Thus expenditure on musicians and the like can only increase if composers reduce their own fee.

Companies such as Cutting Edge have become players in the market by way of further outsourcing. Instead of having a studio finance a film score recording, a third party gives money to the production in return for the rights to the music. This means the composer no longer negotiates the budget with the studio, but with said third party—generally with their appointed representative, the music supervisor. This is resulting in the ever-increasing significance of the music supervisor's role.

Digital editing presents another hurdle. It has many perks for editors but few for composers, who have to continually restructure their music cues. Continued re-cutting makes it difficult to commit to certain score elements such as long sustained melodies since they are hard for editors to cut around and equally difficult for composers to re-conceive when a new cut demands it.

Further unpleasant surprises can occur during the final mix. If composers and sound designers didn't have a chance to work together during the composing process, conflicts between the two elements can occur easily. Moreover, sound design has become more elaborate than ever, thanks to digital technology, and now takes up more sonic space than it did in the '70s or '80s.

Much to the chagrin of musicians, some composers have to record their works by striping, which means recording parts of the orchestra separately. This is done in order to give mixers, editors, directors and producers more control over the music in the final mix. For musicians this is an arduous process. For composers it can be equally dissatisfying since it precludes the entire ensemble of musicians from interacting in holistic way with each other.

Challenges continue after the recording sessions. If a movie is judged disastrous in test screenings, quick changes will be needed. At the least some elements of the music will have to be changed; at worst the entire score will have to be replaced, if so decided by the financiers. This happens quite frequently. The number of rejected scores has skyrocketed. For more information on rejected scores, Gergely Hubai's 2012 book *Torn Music* is a recommended read.

The pressure on composer's backs has been further increased by the team mentality enforced by Hans Zimmer and his facility Remote Control. This offers combined services that no single craftsman in the field can provide. It is therefore of little surprise that composers complain about physical and mental issues that plague them, such as insomnia and anxiety. It is not easy to satisfy directors and a multitude of producers and financiers while coming up with original music for a new production.

As Elmer Bernstein eloquently put it, as society changes, so does the film industry, and with it, naturally, film music and the working conditions for its composers. It has always been a process of progress and setbacks. The new studio system, which followed the independent era of the '90s, has a clear pecking order in which the status of composers is lower than that of their counterparts in the Hollywood studio era and in the New Hollywood.

The system will change and is, in fact, already changing. Netflix and similar streaming services have influenced cinema and film productions. So have political changes in the past few years, especially in the United States. Political and societal changes will influence how we consume art and what kind of art we consume. Will the result be more freedom for composers? Or even less? Everything is evolving. And so it goes.

Chapter Notes

See the Bibliography for full citations to books

Introduction

1. Thomas, *Film Score*, p. 43.
2. Schelle, *The Score*, p. 60.

The Sound of Change

1. Schelle, *The Score*, p. 60.
2. Thomas, *Film Score*, p. 33.
3. Thomas, *Music*, p. 192.
4. Karlin, *Listening*, p. 75.
5. Thomas, *Music*, p. 200.
6. www.theguardian.com/music/2016/
   aug/23/quincy-jones-jazz-sinatra-
   michael-jackson-proms-interview
7. *The Courier Journal and Times*. March
   18, 1973. Louisville, KY: Gannett.
8. Biskind, *Easy Riders*, p. 260.
9. Biskind, *Easy Riders*, p. 381.
10. Schelle, *The Score*, p. 222.
11. Biskind, *Down*, p. 443.
12. Biskind, *Easy Riders*, p. 345.
13. Karlin, *Listening*, p. 73.
14. Schelle, *The Score*, p. 178.
15. Thomas, *Music*, p. 141.

Sir, You Are Standing on My Toes, Sir

1. Thomas, *Film Score*, p. 43.
2. Karlin, *Listening*, p. 181.
3. Karlin, *Listening*, p. 181.
4. Karlin, *Listening*, p. 182.
5. Karlin, *Listening*, p. 175.
6. Thomas, *Film Score*, p. 168.
7. Karlin, *Listening*, p. 177.

8. Biskind, *Easy Riders*, p. 377f.
9. www.hollywoodreporter.com/heat-
   vision/why-danny-elfman-wants-make-
   just-1-a-score-1013290
10. www.nytimes.com/2011/01/31/business/
    media/31score.html
11. www.aboutus.aberdeen-asset.com/en/
    aboutus/expertise
12. www.telegraph.co.uk/finance/com-
    ment/richardfletcher/3778064/Bramdea
    n-makes-a-right-old-Horlicks-of-its-
    mad-mad-Madoff-punt.html
13. www.variety.com/1998/more/news/ice-
    capital-offers-pic-coin-1117471135/
14. www.conductww.com/people/
15. www.conductww.com/about/
16. www.bit.ly/2g9TiWA
17. www.mjic.com/management/
18. www.bit.ly/2xF5VPN
19. https://variety.com/2013/music/news/
    cutting-edge-wood-creek-buy-varese-
    sarabande-1118064253/

Lieutenant Gadget

1. www.youtube.com/watch?v=utTVuhY
   blM
2. Schelle, *The Score*, p. 264.
3. Davis, *Complete*, p. 285.
4. Karlin, *Listening*, p. 185.

Something Familiar, Something Similar

1. Hubai, *Torn Music*, p. 423.
2. www.people.com/archive/as-it-
   ponders-the-color-purples-sound-track-
   hollywood-hums-ive-heard-that-song-
   before-vol-25-no-13/

3. www.nationaljazzarchive.co.uk/stories ?id=83
4. www.filmmusicsociety.org/news_ events/features/2016/122016.html
5. Schelle, *The Score*, p. 159.
6. *Cinema Musica*, No. 35, Jan. 2014. p. 29. Translated by Stephan Eicke.
7. *Cinema Musica*, No. 38, Apr. 2014. p. 15. Translated by Stephan Eicke.
8. Glass, *Words*, pp. 328ff.
9. Morricone and Miceli, *Composing*, p. 57.
10. Thomas, *Film Score*, p. 95.

Turn Down the Sound, I Can't Hear the Music

1. Karlin, *Listening*, p. 47f.
2. Schelle, *The Score*, p. 23.
3. Schelle, *The Score*, p. 230.
4. Schelle, *The Score*, p. 203.
5. Schelle, *The Score*, p. 24.

Let's Do It Together!

1. www.youtube.com/watch?v=tK-_ODY cizo
2. Schelle, *The Score*, p. 190.
3. Previn, *No Minor Chords*, p. 89.
4. Karlin, *Listening*, p. 35.
5. www.mvdaily.com/articles/2009/01/ lawrence.htm
6. Previn, *No Minor Chords*, p. 16.
7. Karlin, *Listening*, p. 36f.
8. Thomas, *Film Score*, p. 110.
9. Karlin, *Listening*, p. 195.
10. Schelle, *The Score*, p. 194.
11. Schelle, *The Score*, p. 341.
12. Schelle, *The Score*, p. 261.
13. Karlin, *Listening*, p. 26.
14. Previn, *No Minor Chords*, p. 95.
15. Davis, *Complete*, p. 270.
16. Schelle, *The Score*, p. 364f.
17. Schelle, *The Score*, p. 364.
18. www.filmmusicmag.com/?p=278
19. www.courtlistener.com/docket/41445 57/daniel-p-kolton-v-universal-studios/
20. Thomas, *Film Score*, p. 207.
21. hwww.colonnesonore.net/contenuti- speciali/interviste/428-intervista-a- paolo-e-gianni-dellorso.html
22. www.arild-rafalzik.de/CDs04.htm

The Hans Method

1. www.vi-control.net/community/ threads/working-at-remote-control. 33535/page-3

2. www.soundonsound.com/sos/oct02/ articles/hanszimmer.asp
3. www.vi-control.net/community/ threads/working-at-remote-control. 33535/page-3
4. www.vi-control.net/community/ threads/working-at-remote- control.33535/page-3
5. Wißmann, *Deutsche Musik*. Berlin, D: Berlin Verlag, 2015. e-Book.
6. www.walker.cinemusic.net/interview. html
7. Schelle, *The Score*, p. 365.
8. www.soundonsound.com/sos/oct02/ articles/hanszimmer.asp
9. www.soundonsound.com/sos/oct02/ articles/hanszimmer.asp
10. https://variety.com/2003/biz/markets- festivals/music-ends-as-rifkin-sues- zimmer-10-mil-1117896642/
11. *Cinema Musica*, No. 24, Feb. 2011, pp. 44ff.
12. *Cinema Musica*, No. 34, Apr. 2013, pp. 18ff.
13. www.vi-control.net/community/ threads/hans-zimmer-sound.24544/
14. *Cinema Musica*, No. 41, Jan. 2016, pp. 10ff.
15. www.vi-control.net/community/ threads/working-at-remote-control. 33535/page-3
16. www.hanszimmerwantsyou.com/
17. www.studiodaily.com/2013/12/hans- zimmer-goes-in-with-extreme-music- on-bleeding-fingers/
18. www.hanszimmerwantsyou.com/sound cloud-contest-terms-and-conditions.pdf
19. www.indi.com/genius/showusyour musicalgenius
20. www.14thstreetmusic.com/about-us/
21. www.spitfireaudio.com/shop/ranges/ signature-range/hz01-london-ensembles/
22. www.steinberg.net/en/artists/commu- nity_stories/hans_zimmer.html
23. www.vi-control.net/community/ threads/hans-zimmer-sound.24544/
24. https://www.adweek.com/brand-mar- keting/range-rover-hired-hans-zimmer- to-compose-a-stirring-score-for-l-a-s-m ost-scenic-drive/
25. www.theguardian.com/business/2006/ mar/10/greaterlondonauthority. olympics2012
26. www.hans-zimmer.com/index.php? rub=news&anneemois=201309
27. www.masterclass.com/classes/hans- zimmer-teaches-film-scoring

28. https://variety.com/2014/music/awards/hans-zimmer-talks-about-collaborations-with-pharrell-1201369189/
29. www.bbc.co.uk/mediacentre/worldwide/2017/radioheadcollaboration
30. www.lat.ms/2oGr6lb
31. *Los Angeles Magazine*, March 1997, p. 81.
32. www.vi-control.net/community/threads/working-at-remote-control.33535/page-3

Instead of a Fireman

1. www.bluntinstrument.org.uk/elfman/archive/KeyboardMag90.htm
2. www.zeit.de/campus/2018–01/fotografin-ausbildung-gehalt-einkommen-gehaltsprotokoll Translated by Stephan Eicke.
3. www.hollywoodreporter.com/news/inside-music-composer-agents-117508
4. www.losangeles.craigslist.org/lgb/tlg/6133715805.html
5. www.losangeles.craigslist.org/lac/crs/6133614336.html
6. Chomsky, Noam. *Power Systems*, p. 40.
7. www.law.justia.com/cases/federal/appellate-courts/F2/517/976/156273/

Bibliography

Biskind, Peter. *Down and Dirty Pictures.* London: Bloomsbury Publishing, 2005.
Biskind, Peter. *Easy Riders, Raging Bulls.* London: Bloomsbury Publishing, 1998.
Davis, Richard. *Complete Guide to Film Scoring.* Boston: Berklee Press, 1999.
Glass, Philip. *Words Without Music: A Memoir.* London: Faber & Faber, 2015.
Hubai, Gergely. *Torn Music: Rejected Film Scores—A Selected History.* Beverly Hills, CA: Silman-James Press, 2012.
Karlin, Fred. *Listening to the Movies: The Film Lover's Guide to Film Music.* New York: Schirmer Books, 1994.
Morricone, Ennio, and Sergio Miceli. *Composing for Cinema: The Theory and Praxis of Music in Film.* Lanham, MD: Scarecrow Press, 2013.
Previn, André. *No Minor Chords: My Days in Hollywood.* London: Transworld Publishers Ltd., 1992.
Schelle, Michael. *The Score.* Los Angeles: Silman-James Press, 1999.
Thomas, Tony. *Film Score. The View from the Podium.* New York: A.S. Barnes, 1979.
Thomas, Tony. *Music for the Movies.* New York: A.S. Barnes, 1973.

Author Interviews

Alexander, Darrell. Phone, October 13, 2017.
Badalamenti, Angelo. Phone, August 17, 2012.
Badelt, Klaus. Skype, January 10, 2017.
Balfe, Lorne. Phone, February 14, 2017; February 24, 2017.
Bellis, Richard. In person, October 11, 2016; October 19, 2017.
Beltrami, Marco. Skype, August 4, 2017.
Beresford, Bruce. Phone, September 25, 2011.
Blake, Howard. In person, April 4, 2012; April 19, 2013.
Broughton, Bruce. Skype, October 10, 2016.
Burwell, Carter. Phone, August 7, 2017.
Danna, Mychael. Skype, September 20, 2017.
Fenton, George. In person, February 24, 2017.
Gold, Murray. In person, May 26, 2015.
Guo, Tina. In person, December 8, 2012.
Jackman, Henry. Skype, February 2, 2017.
Korzeniowski, Abel. Skype, July 20, 2017.
Kraemer, Joe. Skype, November 29, 2016.
Lynch, David. In person, October 10, 2010.

Margeson, Matthew. In person, October 8, 2016.
McCann, Gerard. In person, February 30, 2017; May 17, 2017.
Messina, Matteo. Phone, August 28, 2017.
Moross, Philip. In person, August 23, 2017. Phone, September 14, 2017.
Murch, Walter. In person, March 15, 2017.
Navarrete, Javier. Phone, January 24, 2013.
Nielsen, Tim. In person, July 4, 2014.
Örvarsson, Atli. Skype, September 25, 2013.
Ottman, John. Skype, October 15, 2016.
Portman, Rachel. In person, September 27, 2017.
Raine, Nic. Skype, September 22, 2017.
Raven, Charlotte. Email, February 6, 2018.
Rona, Jeff. Skype, April 18, 2017.
Schurmann, Gerard. Skype, August 13, 2011.
Schwartz, Nan. Phone, April 27, 2017.
Shire, David. In person, October 10, 2013.
Silvestri, Alan. Phone, January 27, 2017.
Simonsen, Rob. Skype, April 29, 2017.
Suett, Daniel. Email, June 24, 2016.
Thom, Randy. Email, March 12, 2017.
Wendler, Edwin. Skype, November 17, 2016.
Yershon, Gary. In person, June 23, 2015.
Young, Christopher. In person, July 11, 2016.

Index

Aberdeen Asset Management 42
Adagio 99
Adams, Amy 96
Addison, John 150
advertising 11, 40, 48, 171, 194
Age of Adaline 189
Agnes of God 95
AIR Studios 30
Albinoni, Tomaso 99
alcoholism 5
Alexander, Darrell 41, 43–5, 47, 49
Alexander's Ragtime Band 137
Alien 100
Alien: Covenant 100
Alive 132
Also sprach Zarathustra 81
Altered States 98
Altman, Robert 112
Always Look on the Bright Side of Life 175
Alwyn, William 149
Amazing Spider-Man 2 172–4
Amazon Prime 194
American Beauty 12, 88, 91, 93
American Horror Story 92
Anchor Bay 149
Angels and Demons 159, 170–1
Antheil, Georges 7, 82
anti-monopoly ruling 8
Apes Past Prologue 148
Apocalypse Now 3, 10, 108
Argentina 9
Argent's Keyboards 154
Armageddon 13
Arrival 17, 20, 96–7
Artist 97
As Good as It Gets 175
ASCAP 38, 158, 196
Asphalt Jungle 143
Association of Motion Picture and Television
    Producers 197
At Long Last Love 10
Atlantic (magazine) 171
Attenborough, David 23, 167, 174
AutoTune 192

avant-garde 9, 17, 105
Avatar 29, 106
Avengers 13, 111

B-pictures 12, 27, 135–7
Baby Elephant Walk 10
Bach, Johann Sebastian 144
Bad and the Beautiful 1
Badalamenti, Angelo 79–81, 103
Badelt, Klaus 27–8, 56, 84–5, 89, 103, 110,
    159–60, 180, 183
Badham, John 4–5
Balfe, Lorne 43, 62, 68, 70, 123, 126, 157, 164,
    166, 168, 176
Ballet Mécanique 7
Baron, Bebbe 6
Baron, Louis 6
Barry, John 95, 104, 114, 116
Bartek, Steve 184
Bartók, Béla 7, 10
Bassman, George 5
Bates, Tyler 94, 189
Batman 18, 184
Batman & Robin 94
Batman Forever 94
Battle 159
Bay, Michael 13, 20, 155
Beach Boys 98
Beatles 9
Beethoven, Ludwig van 144, 191
Behind the Lines 32
Belle 47, 49
Bellis, Richard 56, 82, 102–3, 123, 184, 186,
    192–3, 195, 198–200
Beltrami, Marco 2, 31–2, 36–7, 39, 41, 43, 183,
    185
Benny and Joon 86, 138
Benzedrine 137
Beresford, Bruce 155–6
Berklee 181, 187–8
Berlioz, Hector 156
Bernstein, Carl 23
Bernstein, Elmer 1, 5, 7, 9, 16, 62, 196–7, 211
Bevan, Tim 155

Beyond Rangoon 157
Billboard Electronic Album Chart 174
Biskind, Peter 13
Black Death 43
Black Rain 156–7, 173
Blair Witch Project 111
Blake, Howard 10, 99–100, 143, 154–5
Bleeding Fingers 165–7, 174–5
blockbuster 11–4, 17, 29, 34, 39, 66, 82, 98,
    106, 131, 135, 159, 169, 173, 180
Blood Father 189
Blue Max 81
Blue Planet II 174
Blue Velvet 79
Blumenthal, Darren 43
BMG 44
BMI 38
Bogdanovich, Peter 10, 28
Boss Baby 157
Bource, Ludovic 97
Boy in the Striped Pyjamas 179
Bramdean Asset Management 42
Bresson, Henri-Cartier 84
Brexit 127
Brieant, Charles L. 198
Brion, Jon 66
Britten, Benjamin 149
Brokeback Mountain 17
Broughton, Bruce 95, 119, 136, 138–40, 143–4,
    199
Bruckheimer, Jerry 159
Buggles 173
Burton, Tim 20, 184
Burwell, Carter 29–31, 34, 36, 41, 43, 185
Buttolph, David 137

Cable Guy 73
California 8–9, 23, 43, 128, 175, 186
Capaldi, Peter 22
Captain America 13
Carnegie Hall 80
Carol 43
Casio 52
Castelnuovo-Tedesco, Mario 65
Cats & Dogs 83
Cave, Nick 92
Cayman Islands 43
Chang, Gary 89
Chaplin, Charlie 8, 137
Chicken Run 176
Children of the Night 12
Chomsky, Noam 196
Christopher Robin 66
Christopoulos, George 193
Cinderella Man 92
Citizen Kane 7, 155
City of Prague Philharmonic 38
Clausen, Alf 146, 167–8
Clayton, Jack 95
Clearscore Music Limited 43
Cleopatra (film) 28

Cleopatra (series) 149
click track 73–5
Clooney, George 175
Clouzot, Georges 111
Coachella 175
Cobain, Kurt 15
Cobweb 6, 10
Cocoon 143
Coen, Joel 41
Colbert, Stephen 175
Colombier, Michel 150
Color Purple 95
Columbia 181, 187
Composers Guild of America 196
Con Air 159
Conan the Barbarian 148
Concussion 189
Conduct 43
Conn, Didi 3
Conspirators 89
Contagion 100
Conti, Bill 95
Conversation 3–5, 108–9
Cool Music Ltd. 42
Coppola, Francis Ford 10, 28, 109
copyright 26, 43–4, 48, 94–5, 149, 151, 197–8
Corigliano, John 98
Corman, Roger 9
Cosma, Vladimir 150
Craigslist 193–4
Creative Arts Agency 11
Crossbones 23, 25
Cruise, Tom 30, 157
CSI 88
Cubase 52, 54, 171
Cutting Edge 41–9
Czechoslovakia 76

Damon, Matt 131
Dances with Wolves 13
Dancing with the Stars 167
Danna, Mychael 1, 2, 32, 42–3, 45, 48–9, 93,
    163, 181, 188, 190, 199, 201
Dark Spanish Symphony 80
Debney, John 83
de Laurentiis, Dino 96, 143
Delerue, Georges 9, 95, 156
Dell'Orso, Edda 150
Dell'Orso, Giacomo 150–1
Dell'Orso, Gianni 150–1
del Toro, Guillermo 105
Demme, Jonathan 189
demo 35, 51, 54, 59–60, 64–5, 68–72, 78, 170,
    177, 181, 189, 200, 202
depression 4–5
Despicable Me 2 173–4
Desplat, Alexandre 43, 64, 66, 99, 178
Destiny's Door 166
Devil's Knot 42, 45
digital editing 51–2, 69, 81–7
Digital Performer 54

Distorted Reality 54
Djawadi, Ramin 159
Doctor Dolittle 28
Doctor Strange 17
Doctor Who 22
Doctor Zhivago 135
Dog's Purpose 29, 86
Dolan, Xavier 104
Dooley, Jim 135, 145, 159–60
Downes, Geoff 154
Doyle, Patrick 162
DreamWorks 175–6
Drive 100
Drive, He Said 4
Driving Miss Daisy 156
Drop Zone 27, 157, 159
dubbing 117–9, 125, 128–9
Duellists 99–100
Dunkirk 157

Easy Rider 20
Eddie the Eagle 160
Edgerton, June 27
Egoyan, Atom 42, 45
Einziger, Mike 172
Eisler, Hanns 8
El Mariachi 19
electronic music 4–6, 11–12, 14, 17, 30, 53, 62,
   71, 154–5, 174
Elfman, Danny 39, 184–5
Elgar, Edward 157
Ellington, Duke 97
Ellis, Don 10
Ellis, Warren 92
Emanuel, Russell 166, 174
England 72, 133, 149–50, 154, 157
Enigma Variations 157
Eskenazi, Bonnie 158
Estevez, Emilio 189
Everest 120
Exorcist 108
Expendables 38
Extreme Music 165–6

Facebook 112, 131, 187, 194
Fame (series) 146
Fantastic Four 13
Far from Heaven 1
Farley, Guy 179, 188
Father Murphy 146
Faulconer, Šven 189
Fellowship of the Ring 107, 113, 128
Fenton, George 67, 71, 109, 116, 167
Fidenco, Nico 150
Fielding, Jerry 9, 143
Final Destination 148
final mix 70, 84–5, 106–8, 115–29
Final Portrait 179
Fincher, David 5, 20
Finest Hours 34
First Grader 43

Fitzpatrick, James 38
5AM Music Limited 43
Five Easy Pieces 108
Flash Gordon 143
Focus Features 30
Forbidden Planet 6
Foreman, Carl 8
Forever Amber 1
Fortune 4
Fortunella 96
47 Ronin 105–6
Foster, Ben 22
4AM Music Limited 43
14th Street Music 168
Foxcatcher 189
French Connection 10, 108
Freud 10
Frida 13
Friedhofer, Hugo 5, 7, 65, 137
Friedkin, William 10
Front Runner 189
Fusco, Giovanni 150

Garage Band 62, 170, 191
Garfunkel, Art 175
Genius 168
Gerrard, Lisa 175
Gershenson, Joseph 136
Gershwin, George 133
ghostwriting 131–52
Giacchino, Griffith 148
Giacchino, Michael 17, 148, 179
Giacchino, Mick 148
Giacometti 179
Gibson, Mel 189
Gladiator 27, 159, 175
Glass, Philip 101, 189
Glazer, Jonathan 92
Glennie-Smith, Nick 157
Godfather 96
Gold, Murray 22–3, 93
Golden Age 6, 9–11, 17, 20, 109, 140
Golden Globe 17
Goldenthal, Elliot 13, 94
Goldfinger 114–5
Goldsmith, Carrie 9
Goldsmith, Harvey 171–2
Goldsmith, Jerry 4, 9–10, 16–7, 81, 99–100
Goldstein, Bill 146
Gone with the Wind 136–7
Good German 89, 100
Google Play 89
Goslar 78
Graduate 20
Grand Budapest Hotel 178
Grand Meaulnes 150
Great Depression 9
Great Escape 176
Green, John 26
Gregson-Williams, Harry 176
Gregson-Williams, Rupert 146

Grusin, Dave 5
Guardian 171
Guardians of the Galaxy 189
guide track 115–7
Guillermin, John 81
Guo, Tina 172

Halten, Christian 153
Haneke, Michael 111
Hans Zimmer Music Studio 170
Hans Zimmer Wants You 165, 168
Hansel and Gretel: Witch Hunters 159
Hanson, Howard 100, 157
Happy 173–4
Haring, Keith 42
Harry Potter 88
Harvey, Richard 157, 172
Hateful Eight 17
Hawks, Howard 28
HBO 13, 29
health 32
Heffes, Alex 43
Heindorf, Ray 27
Hellraiser 116, 130
Hell's Angels 90
Hemingway & Gellhorn 105
Henson, Christian 43, 55
Hercules (series) 148–9
Herrmann, Bernard 7, 10, 16–7, 97, 111, 143
Herzog, Werner 40, 110
Higginbottom, Joanne 189
High Noon 8
Hindenburg 4
Hitchcock, Alfred 97
Holdridge, Lee 146
Holiday 159
Holmes, David 89
Holst, Gustav 95
L'Homme de Buick 150
Honeyman, Ian 159
Horlick, Nicola 42
Horn, Trevor 154
Horner, James 16, 99, 143
Howard, Ron 172
Hubai, Gergely 211
Hulu 194
Hungary 76
Hunger 155
Huston, John 10, 143

ICE Capital 42–3
Ice Storm 190
Iglesias, Alberto 100
IMDb 139, 187, 194
In the Bedroom 92
Inception 172, 174
Independent Era 6, 11, 13, 204
Inferno 157
Inland Empire 78
International Alliance of Theatrical Stage
    Employees 199

Interstellar 17
Invincible 40
iPod 120
Ireland 24
Iron Man 13
Ironclad 43
Isham, Mark 115
Island 175
It Goes As It Goes 4
iTunes 89
Ives, Charles 4, 7
Ives, Ralph 114

Jack of All Trades 149
Jack Reacher 14
Jack Ryan: Shadow Recruit 162
Jackman, Henry 92, 115, 120, 122, 127–8
Jackson, Peter 107–8, 128
Jagger, Mick 99
Jarre, Maurice 16, 99, 134–5
Jason X 170
Jaws 11, 16, 20, 88, 195
jazz 5–6, 9–10, 17, 97, 143, 150, 154, 182
JFK 89
Jóhannsson, Jóhann 96
John Carter 148
Johnny English 175
Jones, Quincy 9, 95
Jones, Trevor 83–4
Junkie XL 166, 174, 177
Jurassic Park 89
Jurassic World 148

K2 157
Kaleidoscope 154
Kaplan, Seth 193
Karban, Sturges J. 43
Kaun, Bernhard 133
Kazan, Elia 9
Keyboard Magazine 184
Kidman, Nicole 175
King Kong (2005) 66
King's Speech 43
Kingsman: The Golden Circle 160
Klebe, Jasha 175
Knick 100
Kofsky, Steven 165
Kolton, Daniel 148–9
Kong: Skull Island 122
Kontakt 54, 187
Korngold, Erich Wolfgang 7, 16, 20, 26, 122
Korzeniowski, Abel 33, 35, 40
Kraemer, Joe 14–6, 19–20, 30, 37, 54, 87–8, 90
Kraft, Richard 18
Kramer, Stanley 8
Kundun 101
Kung Fu Panda 175
Kung Fu Panda 3 175

Lady from Shanghai 82
Laine, Frankie 8

Lambert, Constant 149
Land Rover Presents: Scoring the Drive with Hans Zimmer 171
Lang, Lang 175
Lang, Fritz 111
Last Detail 108
Last Samurai 27, 159
Late Show 175
Lavagnino, Angela Franceso 150
Lawrence of Arabia 134–5
League of Their Own 156–7
Legend 99
Lego 120, 123
LEGO Batman Movie 123
Legrand, Michel 9, 150
Leibovitz, Annie 172
Leigh, Mike 17, 178–9
Leone, Sergio 101
Letters 194
Levi, Mica 17, 92
Licht, Daniel 12, 115
Life Story 22–3
Light Between Oceans 66
Lion King (1994) 157, 172
Lion King (2019) 168
Liszt, Franz 82, 133
Little Children 92
Little House on the Prairie 146
Little Prince 157
LoDuca, Joseph 148–9
Logic 52, 54, 58, 145, 168
Lohner, Henning 153, 159, 165
London 22–3, 30, 36, 42, 48, 50, 75–6, 122, 151, 154–6, 178–79
Lone Ranger 157, 172
Lord of the Rings 106
Los Angeles 12, 23, 48, 75–6, 120, 166–9, 178, 185–8
Los Angeles Times 175
Lost Horizon 133
Love 157
Love, Actually 90
Lucas, George 10–1, 107, 109, 114
Lynch, David 78–81, 103
Lyricists Guild of America 196–9

M 111
M., Lebo 172
Macedonia 76
Mad Max: Fury Road 88, 174
Madoff, Bernie 42
Madonna 33
Magne, Michel 150
Magnum Photography 84
Majewski, Hans-Martin 151
Maleficent 106
Malick, Terrence 99, 155
Maltby, Richard 4
Man for All Seasons 175
Man of Steel 13
Manchester by the Sea 99

Manchurian Candidate 189
Mancina, Mark 155
Mancini, Henry 7, 10, 17, 27, 136
Manfredini, Harry 170
Mann, Thomas 8
Margeson, Matthew 18, 28, 36, 83, 91, 103, 132, 135, 140, 143, 145–7, 160, 186
Marianelli, Dario 120
Marijuana International Corporation 43
Martinez, Cliff 100
Marx, Groucho 8
master rights 40–1, 44, 46, 48
MasterClass 172
mastering 34, 39–40
May, Billy 143
McCann, Gerard 46, 55, 59–60, 68–71, 74–5, 85, 87, 92, 111–2
McCarthy, Joseph 8–9
McKee Smith, James 159
McNeely, Joel 58, 142–3
McQuarrie, Christopher 30
McRitchie, Greig 143
Media Ventures 153–4, 157–9, 162–3, 165
Medium Cool 108
Messiaen, Olivier 10
Messina, Mateo 24–5
Metro-Goldwyn-Mayer 26–7, 76, 146, 197
MGM *see* Metro-Goldwyn-Mayer
Microsoft Excel 36
MIDI 52–4, 65, 71, 185, 187–8
Milius, John 11
Miller, George 174
Miramax 12, 28, 90
Mirren, Helen 172
Mirrors 105
Mission: Impossible 10
Mission: Impossible—Rogue Nation 14, 30
Mission: Impossible 2 175
Mr. Turner 17, 178
mixing 34, 46, 60, 84, 101, 107, 123, 125, 161, 193
mock-up 24, 46, 51–2, 55–6, 61–73
Mockridge, Cyril 137
Modern Times 137
Monkey King 132
Monroe, Michael 171
More 174
Morgan, John 27
Morley, Angela 65, 95–6
Moroder, Giorgio 11
Moross, Philip 42–9
Morricone, Ennio 17, 99, 101, 150
Morrissey 174
Morte di un Amico 150
Mother Wore Tights 137
Moviola 82, 87
Mozart, Wolfgang Amadeus 99
Muhly, Nico 189
Mulholland Drive 79
Mummy Returns 72
Murch, Aggie 50

Murch, Walter 4, 29, 50–2, 87, 108–9, 111, 114–5
Museum Masters Intl. 42
music editing 25, 27, 46, 60–1, 68, 71, 75, 81, 83, 85–9, 112, 121, 126–7
music preparation 34–6, 185
music programming 25, 132, 139, 154, 189
music publishing 38–46, 197
Musketeers 22
My Suicide 97
Myers, Stanley 154–6, 172

Napster 89
Nascimbene, Mario 150–1
National Geographic 168
National Labor Relations Board 196
Navarrete, Javier 105–13
NBC 23–4
Neely, Blake 159
Neo-Realism 9
Neon Demon 17
Netflix 189, 191, 194, 204
Nevermind 15
New Daughter 105
New Haven 3
New Hollywood 4–10, 16, 28, 108–10, 114, 128, 204
New Jersey 3, 79–80
New Studio System 6, 13, 204
New World 99
New York City 3, 23, 48, 100, 186
New York Court of Appeals 197
Newman, Alfred 26–7, 137
Newman, Thomas 12, 14, 91, 93
Newton Howard, James 18–9, 66, 123, 141, 189
Nichols, Mike 155
Nicholson, Jack 4
Niehaus, Lennie 143
Nielsen, Tim 106–8, 113, 118, 121, 128
Nightcrawler 189
Nirvana 15
No Country for Old Men 41
No Minor Chords 134
Nocturnal Animals 33
Nolan, Christopher 18, 155, 157
Non-Stop 43, 147
North, Alex 6, 9, 196
Noto, Alva 17
Nott, Julian 176
Notting Hill 84
Nouvelle Vague 9
November Man 43

Ocean Bloom 174
Octopus Investments 42–3
Olivier, Laurence 152
On the Nature of Daylight 96–7
Once Upon a Time in the West 101, 150
One from the Heart 10
Only God Forgives 100
orchestration 132–4

Örvarsson, Atli 57, 98, 159, 164, 177
Oscar 4, 13, 17, 93, 95–8, 105, 137, 150, 156, 165
Ottman, John 13, 18, 41, 43–5, 65, 73, 83, 88–90, 122, 132, 140, 145, 147, 182, 187, 191, 195
Our Mother's House 95
Out of Africa 13, 95
Outlaw Josey Wales 143
Oxygen 149

Pacific Heights 156
package deal 11, 33–8, 183, 193, 202
Palmer, Christopher 143
Pan's Labyrinth 105
Paper Moon 108
Paramount 30, 197
Paranormal Activity 111
Park, Nick 176
Parkinson's Disease 167
Parks, Walter 23
Peacemaker 175
Peckinpah, Sam 5, 9
Pemberton, Daniel 15
Penderecki, Krzystof 57
People Magazine 95
Pereira, Heitor 173
performing rights organization *see* PRO
Petit, Jean-Claude 150
Photoshop 119
Picasso, Pablo 42
Pinder, Dan 163
Pirates of the Caribbean 27, 56–7, 110, 159
plagiarism 86–8, 94–6, 151
Planet Earth 167
Planet Earth II 167, 175
Planet of the Apes (1968) 10
Planets 95
PLAY 54
Player 112
Playing by Heart 104
Pledge 159
Plus Vieux Métier du Monde 150
Poledouris, Basil 148
Poledouris, Zoe 148
pop music 5, 8, 11–4, 58, 71, 162, 173, 180–2
Pop, Iggy 157
Pope, Conrad 65, 157
Portman, Rachel 29, 47–8, 86, 138, 189
Powell, John 156, 163, 176–7
Previn, André 133–4, 143
Prince of Egypt 159, 175
PRO (performing rights organization) 38, 196
Prometheus 100
ProTools 52–4, 83, 165
PRS 47
Public 189
Puttnam, David 99

Queen 144

Rabin, Trevor 159
Rack Module Kit 170
Radcliffe, Sarah 155
Radio Flyer 156
Radiohead 174
Rafalzik, Arild 151
Rain Man 14, 155–7, 173
Raine, Nic 176–7
Raksin, David 1, 25, 65, 137
Raven, Charlotte 179, 188–9
Rawsthorne, Alan 149
RCI Global 165, 175
Reeves, Keanu 105, 154
Remember Us 94
Remote Control 2, 27, 135, 153, 158–66, 169–77
Renaissance Man 156
Renaissance Pictures 149
Renner, Jeremy 96
Resonant Music 43
Return to Oz 4–5
Returns a King 94
Reuters 158
Revenant 17
Revolutionary Road 92
Reznor, Trent 16
Richard III 152
Richter, Max 96
Ride the High Country 5
Rifkin, Jay 157–8
Right Stuff 95–6
Ring 2 163–5
Rise of the Planet of the Apes 162
Road to El Dorado 175
Rock (film) 13
rock music 9–11, 14–17, 171–2
Rocket, Lauren 174
Rocky 4
Roeg, Nicolas 155
Rona, Jeff 56, 58, 63, 100, 170, 182–3, 190–1, 193
Rose, David 146
Rosenman, Leonard 6, 10
Ross, Atticus 105
Rossini, Gioachino 157
Rota, Nino 96
Rounders 131
Royal Academy of Dramatic Arts 179
Royal Albert Hall 22
Royal College of Music 179
royalties 38–44, 81, 143, 147–51, 164–66, 183, 191
Rózsa, Miklós 6, 17, 26, 143
Rubinstein, Micah D. 184
Rush, Geoffrey 168

Sable Ensembles 55
Sakamoto, Ryuichi 17
Salter, Hans J. 135
Salton Sea 92
sample library 54–6, 66–7, 170

Samurai Jack 189
Sanders, Buck 185
Sandloff, Peter 151
Santaolalla, Gustavo 17
Scene d'Amour 97
Scharf, Walter 137
Schifrin, Lalo 9–10, 30, 146
Schlegel, Stefan 150
Schönberg, Arnold 6–8
Schurmann, Gerard 133–4, 149, 151
Schwartz, Nan 59, 61, 64–5, 67, 75–6, 124, 126, 182, 190
score coordinator 25
Scorsese, Martin 101
Scott, Ridley 99–100, 155
Scott, Tony 155
Screen Composers Association 196
Season of the Witch 159
Selznick, David 136–7
Series of Unfortunate Events 189
Sex, Lies and Videotape 19
Shea, Jacob 166, 175
Shire, David 3–5, 10, 109
Shore, Howard 66, 107, 141
Short Circuit 4
Show Us Your Musical Genius! 168
Shrek 175
Sibelius 187
Sicario 17, 46
Silver, Joel 45
Silverado 95
Silvestri, Alan 16, 31, 53, 67, 72, 117, 159
Simonsen, Rob 55, 58–9, 62, 66, 74, 189–90
Simpsons 167
Simpsons Movie 168
Single Man 33
Single Shot 57
Sisters 10
Sitting Target 154
Skinner, Frank 135
Skywalker Sound 128
Smells Like Teen Spirit 15
Smetana, Bedrich 99
Smiths 174
Snow Girl and the Dark Crystal 106
Snowman 99
Soderbergh, Steven 20, 89, 100
Sommers, Stephen 72
Son of Frankenstein 135
Sony/ATV 165
Sopranos 79
Sorcerer 10
Sorkin, Aaron 172
Sound Cloud 180
sound design 106–19, 126–8
Sound on Sound 154, 157–8
Speed 154
Spencer, Herbert 26, 76
Spider-Man 13
Spielberg, Steven 10, 16, 19–20, 95, 175
Spies, Werner 79

Spitfire Audio 55, 169, 171
Spotify 110
Spring Breakers 100
Stalingrad 80
Star Wars 10–1, 13, 16, 20, 88, 154, 195
Star Wars: Rogue One 148
Starr Score Holdings, LLC 43
Statham, Jason 42
Steelyard Blues 4
Steinberg 169–71
Steiner, Max 5, 7, 16, 20, 26–7, 136–7, 196
Stella 75
stemming 46–7, 75, 119, 122, 124–6
Stinson, Bill 134
Stockhausen, Karlheinz 99
Stofle, Emily 78
Stone, Oliver 89
Stothart, Herbert 7, 134, 137
Strauss, Richard 4, 6
Stravinsky, Igor 182
Straw Dogs 143
streamers 73–5
streaming 191, 204
Streetcar Named Desire 6
Streitenfeld, Marc 100
striping 107, 119–26
studio orchestras 7–9
Styles, Eric 83
Suett, Daniel 167
Sunset Boulevard 82
Superman 16
Syco Systems 154
Symphony Fantastique 156
Synclavier 52
synthesizer 12, 52, 138–9, 154–5, 173, 193

Taking of Pelham 1-2-3 4, 10
Tangerine Dream 11, 99
Taymor, Julie 13
Tchaikovsy, Peter 95, 144
Tears of the Sun 172
technology 50–73
temp tracks 14, 78–104
Ten Commandments 1
Terminal Velocity 142–3
test screenings 13–4, 90–1
Their Finest 47, 49
Thin Red Line 159
Thom, Randy 110, 113, 115, 121, 127–8
Thomas, Tony 20
3AM Music Limited 43
300 94
THX 1138 114
Tillman, Martin 165
Tiomkin, Dimitri 8, 10, 102, 133
Titanic 192
Titus 94
Tom à la ferme 104
Tom Jones 150
Too Many Notes 159
Torn Music 203

Towelhead 92
Toys 156
Transformers 111, 175
Tree of Life 99
True Romance 157
Tucci, Stanley 179
20th Century-Fox 18, 27, 100, 137, 197
Tyler, Brian 38, 146
typecasting 91, 141

UK *see* United Kingdom
Under the Skin 17, 92
unions 33–5, 76, 109, 196–201
United Kingdom 23, 127, 154
U.S. District Court 197–8
U.S. Supreme Court 8–9, 20
Universal 27, 44, 136, 149, 197
University of California–Los Angeles (UCLA) 187
University of Edinburgh 194
University of Southern California (USC) 144, 181, 184, 187, 194–5
University of Utrecht (HKU) 100
Up in Arms 27
Urban Legend 131
Used People 138
Usual Suspects 89

Vangelis 11
Van Outen, Denise 42
Varèse, Edgard 7
Varèse Sarabande 43, 44, 49
Vertigo 97
Video Killed the Radio Star 173
Vienna Ensemble Pro 187
Vienna Strings 55
Vietnam War 8, 32
Vikings 151
Villeneuve, Denis 96
Violenza Segreta 150
Violin Concerto (Tchaikovsky) 95

Wages of Fear 111
Walker, Bart 13
Walker, Joe 96
Walker, Shirley 14, 65, 146–8, 156, 184
Wall Street Journal 11
Wallace & Gromit: The Curse of the Were-Rabbit 176
Wallfisch, Benjamin 157
Walton, William 149, 152
War Horse 106
War of the Planet of the Apes 148
WarGames 4
Warhol, Andy 42
Warner Bros. 26–7, 94, 197
Water for Elephants 66
Waxman, Franz 7, 82, 196
W.E. 33
Weinstein, Bob 12
Weinstein, Harvey 12–3, 33, 131

Weissmuller, Johnny 8
Welles, Orson 7, 82
Wembley 22
Wendler, Edwin 16, 20, 34, 38–40, 70, 76, 88, 122, 136, 147, 186, 199
WhatsApp 112
Wherry, Mark 170
White Fang 156
White Oleander 92
White Ribbon 111
White Squall 99
Wild at Heart 80
Wild Bunch 143
Wilden, Gert 151
Wilder, Billy 81
William Tell 157
Williams, John 4, 11, 16–7, 20, 89, 100
Williams, Pharrell 173–4
Williams, Robbie 175
Woman in Black 43
Wood Creek Capital Management 42–3
Woodward, Bob 23
World War II 8

Wrath of the Titans 105
Writer's Guild 199
Wurman, Alex 157

X-Men 2 18
X-Men: Apocalypse 83, 122
X-Men: Days of Future Past 18
X-Men: First Class 92–3
Xena: Warrior Princess 148–9

Yared, Gabriel 61, 74, 104, 125, 181, 183
Yershon, Gary 17, 178–9
Yorke, Thom 174
Young, Christopher 104, 116, 130–2, 184
YouTube 110

Zack, Andrew 164
Zanelli, Geoff 66, 157, 159
Zemeckis, Robert 16, 20
Zimmer, Hans 2, 14–5, 18, 27, 40, 56, 135, 146, 153–77
Zinneman, Fred 8
Zodiac 3–5